CHILD OBSERVATION

A GUIDE FOR STUDENTS OF EARLY CHILDHOOD

IOANNA PALAIOLOGOU

4TH EDITION

Learning Matters
An imprint of SAGE Publications Ltd
1 Oliver's Yard
55 City Road
London EC1Y 1SP

SAGE Publications Inc.
2455 Teller Road
Thousand Oaks, California 91320

SAGE Publications India Pvt Ltd
B 1/I 1 Mohan Cooperative Industrial Area
Mathura Road
New Delhi 110 044

SAGE Publications Asia-Pacific Pte Ltd
3 Church Street
#10-04 Samsung Hub
Singapore 049483

Editor: Amy Thornton
Senior project editor: Chris Marke
Project management: Deer Park Productions, Tavistock, Devon
Marketing manager: Dilhara Attygalle
Cover design: Wendy Scott
Typeset by: C&M Digitals (P) Ltd, Chennai, India
Printed in the UK

First published in 2008 by Learning Matters Ltd
Second edition published in 2012
Third edition published in 2016

This book was previously available (first edition) as *Childhood Observation* written by Ioanna Palaiologou, with Gill Goodliff and Lyn Trodd as series editors. The second edition was called *Child Observation for the Early Years*. The third edition was called *Child Observation: A Guide for Students of Early Childhood*. This new edition has been fully revised.

Library of Congress Control Number: 2019944360

British Library Cataloguing in Publication data

A catalogue record for this book is available from the British Library

ISBN 978-1-5264-6067-7
ISBN 978-1-5264-4999-3 (pbk)

At SAGE we take sustainability seriously. Most of our products are printed in the UK using responsibly sourced papers and boards. When we print overseas we ensure sustainable papers are used as measured by the PREPS grading system. We undertake an annual audit to monitor our sustainability.

CONTENTS

ACKNOWLEDGEMENTS

In this fourth edition of the book I would like to express my gratitude to all the children, parents, practitioners and early childhood settings for offering me a warm welcome to carry out the observations that I have used as examples in the book.

A special thank you to my nephews and their parents (Demos, Haralambos, George and Harry) who have given me permission to use their photographs to elaborate examples throughout the book.

I also want to express my gratitude to my colleagues and very good friends who provided me with a wealth of observations from their practice to enrich the examples provided in the book:

Nyree Nicholson

Aderonke Folorunsho

Angie Hutchinson

Last, but not least, a thank you to all the users of the book who have provided me with valuable, critical and constructive feedback to improve it. I hope you will find the fourth edition as useful as the previous ones.

Every effort has been made to trace the copyright holders and to obtain their permission for the use of copyright material. The publisher and author will gladly receive any information enabling them to rectify any error or omission in subsequent editions.

THE AUTHOR

Dr Ioanna Palaiologou (CPsychol AFBPsS) has worked as a university academic in education and early childhood education in the UK for the last 20 years. She is a Chartered Psychologist of the British Psychological Society with a specialism on child development, learning theories and assessment and was appointed as Associate Fellow of BPS in 2015. Since 2015, she has been working as a child psychologist and as an Academic Associate of the Department of Learning and Leadership in UCL Institute of Education.

She writes extensively in the field of early childhood education and among her most popular books is the *Early Years Foundation Stage: Theory and Practice*, published by Sage.

She has been awarded best published paper in 2017 by the European Early Childhood Education Research for her paper: Children Under Five and Digital Technologies: Implication for Early Years Pedagogy, in the *European Early Childhood Research Journal*, vol. 24 (1), pp. 5–24.

DEDICATION

To my boys: Demos, Haralambos, George and Harry for the happiness they have offered me and continue to offer me all these years.

PREFACE

The field of early childhood is concerned with the study of the child mainly from philosophical, sociological, anthropological, psychological, historical, political and educational perspectives. In all of these fields observation has become an important tool. Nowadays observation is central to early childhood education as it provides a systematic way of understanding children's development, learning, interests and experiences. Observation allows us to understand children and provides a reflection of how they behave.

However, although observation is a valuable tool for early childhood, it cannot be seen only as a tool as we need to consider other factors that are involved to shape our understanding of what is learned. Our views about children, pedagogy and practice are shaped by factors such as the policy, the constructions of childhood each society holds, economic and cultural contexts that subsequently form our thinking on what a child is and the most appropriate practices for them. Thus Martin (2019) urges us to consider *lens* and *filters* when we study observation, suggesting that *nothing we see or hear can be perceived without the lens of the past experience. So what we see, or rather how we interpret what we see, is determined by what we already know* (p.47). She explains that:

> *Lenses: in the observation sense, an abstract viewpoint that shapes what is observed and how it is understood. Some lenses are chosen by educators deliberately, while others are an integral part of how individual educators are and what they believe [. . .]*
>
> *Filter: in the observational sense, a guided viewpoint that may help reshape an observation [...] typically a filter may help reshape an observation and might be applied with or without a lens. A filter might involve adding some information or involve being aware of something that changes the way that you see something.*
>
> (p.47)

For example, if we believe that children should be engaged with messy or risky play then we are more likely, for instance, to interpret an observation when a child is climbing a tree as the child trying to challenge his/her physical skills. On the other hand, if we think that such play is of high risk then the same observation might be interpreted as the child not following the rules and trying to climb a tree.

Observation skills can be learned through study and practice, but the lenses and filters that we use to interpret them are shaped by our beliefs. Thus this book aims to help you locate observation in the context they take place and reflect on the policy context (Chapter 1), the ideological context of early childhood pedagogy (Chapter 2) and how these might impact on you practising observation.

Chapters 3, 4, 5 and 6 intend to support you to become a skilled observer by explaining the different techniques that are most commonly used. Chapter 7 will support your ability to use *refined professional lenses and filters to observe and interpret [. . .] as [you] will learn to clean [your] lenses and filters* (Martin, 2019, p.47) when analysing and interpreting observation.

In the twenty-first century, with the increase use of digital media, paper-based observation and documentation is now blended to create multimodal recordings and documentation. Thus in this fourth edition a new Chapter 8 has been added to discuss observation and documentation in the multimodality era. This chapter explains the variety of media available and aims to assist you in developing interpretive strategies to understand multimodal observations and documentation.

Chapter 9 addresses the observation process in relation to the documentation of your findings as an integral part of ethical procedures and considerations. Although the choice of observation, analysis and documentation is regulated by legislations in many countries, the chapter argues for the creation of an ethical protocol within each early childhood education context.

Once you have developed your skills and built a theoretical understanding of the observations after studying these chapters, the book aims to link observation with the context in which they are happening and its purposes. Chapter 10 explores key issues when observing for child development and offers practical examples.

Chapter 11 addresses the differences between pedagogy and curriculum. Through practical examples, it shows that an effective curriculum for early childhood places an emphasis on observations.

Chapter 12 aims to help you understand how observations can be used as research tool and what the similarities and differences are between using observation for research and practice.

Finally, the concluding chapter discusses the role of adults and draws conclusions as to the importance of observation skills.

In this edition of the book there is an intention to widen the focus and look at observation in early childhood education and its relevance to the curriculum. The intention is, no matter what curriculum you are working with, the observation skills you need should develop to help you to become a responsible, accountable and skilled practitioner, able to fulfil your role and curriculum requirements whether they are standardised and statutory requirements or non-standardised and less formal. Observation skills are required in your career path to develop your practice, assessment and evaluation and to enable you to respond to any situation that occurs in your context.

Moreover, in the context of the changes in the early years sector and its workforce across not only the UK but in many nations, as well as the demands of the twenty-first century, systematic observations and assessments play an important role within the portfolio of skills. Thus this book discusses the role of observation as a tool for practitioners, with links to current policies and initiatives nationally and internationally. The skill of observation is very important to all people working with children and this is reflected in national and international curricula. The observation process is not isolated from the rest of your practice, or from the educational programme, and should be integral to it, helping you develop your practice and your understanding of it. This book thus aims to help further your understanding of observation and your ability to make full use of it in your workplace.

To navigate you when studying this book below are the key definitions used:

- *Observation* refers to the systematic methods (formal, such as recorded in a written or visual way or informal, such as watching and then make notes) using particular ways to look at and record children's behaviours that always have clear intention(s).

- *Early childhood education* is used collectively for 'early years practice' and 'early childhood education and care' and is used to describe the field of study that is concerned with children below the compulsory school age.
- *Early childhood education setting* refers to all formal (such as nurseries) or informal contexts (such as playgroups or childminders) that host children from birth to children below the compulsory school age.
- *Practitioner* is used to describe the people who work within early childhood education settings (e.g. nurseries, day care, childminders, early childhood education settings). In the UK as well as internationally there are several terms depending on the qualifications of the people working in the field, such as the early years workforce, professionals and teachers. Thus the term 'practitioner' is used collectively to describe the staff working with children in early childhood education below the compulsory school age. When international examples are discussed, however, then the term that each curriculum is using to describe its staff in the sector will be used.
- *Curriculum* is used collectively to describe any educational programme that is implemented with children below the compulsory school age. As will be seen throughout this book some educational programmes are called 'frameworks' and there is the assumption that these are not curricula. In the literature there are 120 definitions of the term 'curriculum' (Marsh, 2004). This book's intention is not to address the complexity of discussing the difficulties around the definitions of a curriculum, but instead the term is used to refer to a programme that is designed to provide a frame of reference (i.e. government requirements, ideology or philosophy of the social context) that is conveyed through the actions that take place with children. This might involve instructions, guidance, teaching, learning, the design of activities or projects and determines the aims and objectives oriented by the characteristics of the particular group for whom they are implemented: in this case children below the compulsory school age.

INTRODUCTION: THE ROLE OF OBSERVATION

Chapter objectives

Through reading this introductory chapter, you will understand:

- the origins of observation;
- the nature of observations within early childhood education and its related practices;
- the role of observation in early childhood education;
- the reasons for observing in early childhood education.

Observation is the most valid tool to gather in-depth information for the children and their practice. It offers early childhood educators valuable lenses to understand children and reflect on the learning environment and curriculum.

Introduction: why observations?

While working within a curriculum practitioners have a responsibility to understand its aims and purposes and to ensure that their actions are meeting them. In many curricula, as is the case in the UK context, the assessment of children is central. For example, as will be shown in Chapter 1, in the Early Years Foundation Stage in England, the assessment is a formal and statutory requirement whereas the Scottish and Northern Ireland curricula do not have formalised assessment but are a part of the curriculum requirements. The practitioners in these contexts have a duty of being accountable for progress, as well as for children meeting the goals and learning outcomes of the curriculum they are working with and for providing high-quality environments for the young children in their care. Assessment and evaluation are central processes in the practitioner's daily work life. The debate around assessment should not be whether to assess or evaluate, therefore, but how we should do this in a child-centred way and not in an adult- or outcomes-driven way. Observation provides the appropriate tool for assessment and evaluation. Practitioners making use of observation can collect relevant, valuable and useful information to inform their assessments and evaluations so they can meet the curriculum-based assessment requirements as well as fulfil their role of accountability towards children and their families.

Whether working in a curriculum-based assessment that is standardised and statutory (such as the EYFS and the Foundation Phase in England and Wales (see Chapter 1) or non-standardised (such as the Curriculum for Excellence and the Learning to Learn in other parts of the UK – see Chapter 1) assessments and evaluations should be child- and activity-centred, meaning that the focus should be on the child and the activities within the curriculum, with observation providing a valuable, reliable and valid tool. As will be explored elsewhere in the book, observation provides practitioners with individualised information based upon children's strengths, interests and emerging skills. Consequently, among other skills there is a need to develop and master an in-depth understanding of observation when working with young children, meaning that the utilisation of observation skills is at the heart of the practitioner's role and practice.

It is important to state here that as a practitioner, no matter what curriculum you work within, it is essential to develop observation skills as they offer flexibility to adapt to changes in curriculum and make you diverse in working with any changes that might happen in the future. Essential skills for an observer practitioner include:

- depth and breadth of understanding of the purpose of the observation process;
- depth and breadth of understanding of observation techniques that you want to employ depending on the context and situation;
- the ability to construct and evaluate evidence-based feedback for each child that will inform the curriculum requirement assessments within your curriculum;
- reflexivity and responsiveness to each situation in your context;
- continuous professional development.

In order to develop effective observation skills, it is important to understand firstly the origins of observation and its purposes. Thus the following sections offer firstly a brief overview of the history of observation in early childhood education and look at why it is important to integrate observation in the daily routine of your setting.

The integration of observation in early childhood education

Observation in education, and in particular early childhood education, has a long history. As will be discussed in Chapter 2, observation of children was used heavily in psychology and especially in the psychoanalytical field. Melanie Klein, a contemporary of Freud, started with the belief that children can be analysed (especially very young children whose language has not yet fully developed) and sought ways and methods to analyse them. She showed play to be an important behaviour which could be observed, but rather than only observing children during play, she experimented with a number of toys and materials. Klein was a pioneer in the way she observed children and analysed them. Her approaches and techniques were based on her beliefs that clinical observation from a very young age has significant importance for understanding children's behaviours. In fact, one can say that Klein was one of the first to use observation as a way of applying scientific methods.

Klein's view that children could be observed went against the prevailing attitude of her era in that children were to be seen and not heard. Klein moved to London in 1926 where there was already interest in analysing children through observation. Mina Searl, Mary Chadwick, Susan Isaacs and Ella Freeman Sharpe were also working towards developing techniques for child analysis through observation. Susan Isaacs was influenced by Klein and established the first experimental school based on psychoanalytical views. Isaacs (1933) brought psychoanalytical ideas of observation to the educational setting in England to develop a pedagogy for children that was connected with emotional development and encouraged play as a way by which children could express, discover and master the world.

In the international arena of education outside the field of psychology, educators similarly started to use observations in a systematic way from the early nineteenth century. One of the pioneers, Friedrich Froebel in Germany, embraced systematic observations in his kindergarten. His belief was that teachers should be able to observe children as a way of enabling them to gain in-depth understanding of how children learn so they can build upon their interests and the importance of play in their lives. As will be discussed in Chapter 2, he emphasised the role of play in the lives and education of young children and promoted the idea that they learn skills such as problem-solving, understanding the world around them and being creative through how they interact with objects. He considered that teachers have an obligation to observe children's actions, are equally learners of the children they had in their classrooms and needed to observe them as the only way of gaining the whole picture of how children develop and learn (Froebel, 1826/1902).

Another influential educationalist, Pestalozzi, took up French philosopher Rousseau's ideas and tried to investigate how children developed based on systematic observations rather than just anecdotal stories. His early experiments in education became known as the 'Pestalozzi Method' and he implemented this in his school at Yverdon (established in 1805). At a time when children were viewed as 'objects' that needed training to be able to enter the adult world and were seen as passive learners, Pestalozzi argued that children should be educated through activities, able to pursue their own interests and given opportunities to make their own conclusions. In his book *How Gertrude Teaches Her Children* (1894), Pestalozzi modelled in his education the 'reflective practitioner'. He valued observation as a tool for reflection and, using psychological tools, observed children's experiences and actions as a way of trying to make sense of them and understand children's development.

In Italy, Montessori (1912) introduced the Montessori Method: a systematic, scientific way of observing children in order to develop early childhood practice, focusing on physical needs, especially movement and play. She designed child-friendly material such as small chairs, tables and activities to help children develop their senses, literacy skills and numeracy strategies.

While across Europe educationalists such as Pestalozzi, Froebel, Montessori and Isaacs were seeking ways of using systematic observation as a way of improving the education of young children, in the United States a psychologist Stanley Hall (1844–1924) initiated the child study movement. Being influenced by evolutionary theory (Darwin), developmental psychologists and education in Germany, in 1882 he introduced a course for child study, promoting the idea that child study is the core element for pedagogy. In that sense observation is key for teachers as he argued that for teachers to provide a meaningful education they should gain an in-depth understanding of children. Using direct systematic observations of children, teachers are able to find out about their interests and thinking. Hall invited parents as well in this approach and was interested in their views. For example, he sent out hundreds of questionnaires to collect observations of children through parents. The Child Study movement influenced other Western countries such as Germany and the UK and brought systematic, scientific approaches to early childhood education. The Child Study movement aimed to bridge methods of experimental psychology such as systematic observation and ideals of child education to establish a pedagogy based on scientific evidence.

Other educationalists such as John Dewey (who embraced ideals of social justice, equality and democracy in education and emphasised the social interactions of young children), Arthur Jersild (who encouraged teachers to observe and have conversations with children no matter how young they are to understand them and their interests) and Margaret McMillan (who viewed child study as a key element for training of teachers) started integrating observations as a daily practice in the (class)room. Observation was offering teachers scientific ways to reflect on and gain an understanding of how children interact with the environment around them and to learn more about how children use play.

In the twenty-first century early childhood education has embraced the use of observation as a valuable tool to understand children, but at the same time has been developing skills among teachers to think about what they observe and to integrate those reflections in practice that supports children's learning. Observation in early childhood education is now not only about watching for children's actions and interactions during play, such as in Froebel's version of play, or examining children's stages of development like in Hall's child study, but is also about discovering the ways children make attempts to understand the world, experience materials and attempt to communicate. As Malaguzzi – the founder of Reggio Emilia, one of the most influential approaches of the twenty-first century to early childhood education – suggests, observation is seen as a way of capturing and understanding children's ideas that emanate from activities and the ways in which children *become even more curious, interested, and confident as they contemplate the meaning of what they have achieved* (Malaguzzi, 1998, p.70) and also a way to hear the *hundred languages [. . .] hundred hands, [. . .] hundred thoughts, [. . .] hundred ways of thinking, of playing, of speaking* (Malaguzzi, 1996).

Observation as an educational tool is now a dominant aspect of many curricula in the world and should aim to bridge teaching that is dominated by specific goals, the plasticity of children's development, learning, play, assessment and evaluation of this process. In the following section we examine some curriculum approaches and the role of observation within them.

Observation, curriculum and assessment

Throughout this book the role of observation and its importance will be explored and examples of different curriculum approaches will be offered. Discussed in more detail in Chapter 11, observations play an important role in early childhood curriculum and practice. No matter in which part of the world you are working, observation is an important tool for you as it helps you to build understanding about children and build relationships with them by getting to know them better by understanding their competences, emotions and abilities in varied situations. Observing children in a formal situation, such as working with a formal government-imposed curriculum or framework, or in an informal curriculum such as directed by the specific setting, supports you to inform this curriculum and your practice.

As Dewey (1938, p.68) cautions us, however, *Observation alone is not enough. We have to understand the significance of what we see, hear and touch. This significance consists of the consequences that will result when what is seen is acted upon.* This advice should be enacted in the form of assessment. Assessment should go beyond the simplistic approach of reporting what children can or cannot do and in order to be effective and meaningful is about making sense of what observations are communicating to us through analysis and documentation (for more on this, see Chapters 7 and 8).

Assessment in education includes two types:

- formative assessment – which is the process of observing children in their daily routine and attempting to understand those observations and what information they are offering us;
- summative assessment – which is more official in terms that include a collection of observations to offer a summary of children's development and learning.

Formoshino and Formoshino (2016, p.98) extend our views on assessment and suggest that *assessment and evaluation should acknowledge the complexity of children's experiences and of the educational act* and promote the idea of respecting these complexities rather than compartmentalising assessment to be only on children's development. They argue for a holistic assessment by describing the following characteristics for evaluation which should:

- *seek to understand learning and contribute to further learning;*
- *be participatory, holistic, ecological and inclusive;*
- *encompass integrated learning in all areas;*
- *be oriented towards contexts, processes and outcomes;*
- *be a participatory process, involving the contribution of practitioners, the children and the families;*
- *be an ecological process open to various contexts;*
- *be a process which focuses on what the learner knows in order to enlarge and enrich it;*
- *recognise that the inclusive dimension is of paramount importance.*

(p.99)

In this sense observation should aim beyond an evidence-based assessment and be considered as a tool to build a rich, holistic and evaluative portrait of each child by seeking information not only from their activities, work (such as artwork, constructions, photos, etc.) and social interactions, but also from parents/carers and the children's environment, as will be explored later in Chapter 3.

CASE STUDY 1

Statutory assessment: the case from the English curriculum

This case study from the Early Years Foundation Stage (EYFS) in England shows how observation can support you with the statutory requirements for a standardised curriculum. Emphasis on the EYFS is placed more on summative assessment.

Observation and assessment in EYFS in England

One of the main principles outlined within the EYFS (DfE, 2017) states that observations, assessment and planning are all central elements of practice within the setting. It emphasises that observation of children should prioritise a child's development and learning. At the same time, it stresses the importance of observation in terms of planning activities. The role of observation is a subject of ongoing discussion as the basis for planning practice that enhances children's development and learning.

Since 1990 the Rumbold Report emphasised the importance of assessment in context:

We believe there is a need for guidance for educators on the achievement of more consistent and coherent approaches to observing, assessing, recording and reporting children's progress in pre-schools provision [. . .] such guidance is to inform and to improve on what is offered to the under fives and the early stages of the post five provision.

(DfES, 1990, p.17)

Ten years later, one of the key principles identified within the Curriculum Guidance for the Foundation Stage was that practitioners must be able to observe and respond appropriately to children, informed by a knowledge of how children develop and learn (QCA, 2000, p.11).

Today there are expectations for the early childhood workforce to be able to observe, record and assess young children. The EYFS (DfE, 2017) identifies four main principles:

- *an emphasis on the individual child as a learner (unique child);*
- *a recognition of the interpersonal relationships and the loving environment that all children need in order to develop (positive relationships);*
- *an appreciation of the learning environment as a vehicle for all children's development and learning (enabling environments);*
- *a recognition that each child develops and learns at different rates and ways.*

Central to the EYFS is the assessment of children with a focus on ongoing assessment and day-to-day observations. It is stated:

Assessment plays an important part in helping parents, carers and practitioners to recognise children's progress, understand their needs, and plan activities and support. Ongoing assessment (also known as formative assessment) is an integral part of the learning and development process. It involves practitioners observing children to understand their level of achievement, interests and learning styles, and to then shape learning experiences for each child reflecting those observations. In their interactions with children, practitioners should respond to their own day-to-day observations about children's progress and observations that parents and carers share.

(DfE, 2017, p.13)

EYFS currently has two key formal procedures for children's assessment which are summative at the point they will be taken:

1. *Progress check at age two: where practitioners are expected to provide a short written summary of the child's progress in the prime areas (communication and language, physical development, personal, social and emotional development). This progress check must identify the child's strengths, and any areas where the child's progress is less than expected.*
2. *Assessment at the end of the EYFS – the Early Years Foundation Stage Profile (EYFSP): all children should have this profile completed by the end of the final term of the year in which they will reach 5. The profile aims to provide parents, carers, practitioners and teachers rich information on children's progress and development against levels for their readiness to enter Year 1. The EYFS Profile should be completed based on observations.*

(DfE, 2017, pp.13–15)

Within the EYFS, however, it is the government's intention to introduce a baseline assessment – Reception Baseline Assessment – by 2020 where all children will be assessed within the first six weeks starting their reception year, the year in which they turn five years.

The purpose of the reception baseline assessment is to provide an on-entry assessment of pupil attainment to be used as a starting point from which a cohort-level progress measure to the end of key stage 2 (KS2) can be created.

The reception baseline is not intended to:

- *provide ongoing formative information for practitioners*
- *be used in any way to measure performance in the early years, evaluate preschool settings or hold early years practitioners to account*
- *provide detailed diagnostic information about pupils' areas for development*

(DfE, 2019, p 4)

This baseline assessment will be piloted in schools from September 2019 and is expected to be rolled out nationally in 2020–2. The process has been the subject of criticism by a number of academic researchers (e.g. Roberts-Holmes and Bradbury, 2017) as well as practitioners (see for example

(Continued)

(Continued)

National Children's Bureau): **https://www.ncb.org.uk/news-opinion/news-highlights/facing-baseline-assessment-view-early-years?gclid=EAIaIQobChMIhNSAyZnK4QIVCp3tCh0AWwIiEAAYASAAEgJeq_D_B** as it is not based on observational process but on standardised tests.

Within the EYFS observation and assessment have thus been formalised and make up part of the statutory requirements for young children in England. (To learn more on the EYFS and the statutory assessment requirements, visit: **https://www.gov.uk/early-years-foundation-stage**.)

CASE STUDY 2

Formative assessment

This case study from the Australian curriculum similarly shows that observations are an integral part of the curriculum, but emphasis is placed on formative rather than summary assessment.

Observation and assessment in Australia: an international perspective

Australia has introduced the National Quality Framework for Early Childhood Education and Care (NQF) that aims to ensure high-quality early childhood education and care. It is available in several languages as Australia is a multicultural, multi-ethnic country so the aim was to reach all families that have an interest. The NQF regulates the sector (day care, family day care, pre-school, kindergarten and outside school hours care services) in terms of quality assessment of childcare and early learning services. It provides a:

- *national legislative framework that creates a uniform approach to the regulation and quality assessment of education and childcare services in Australia;*
- *a National Quality Standard that sets a national benchmark for education and care services;*
- *rating and assessment processes that rate services against the National Quality Standard.*

Australia has implemented the Early Years Learning Framework (EYLF) which is the key component of their National Quality Framework for early childhood education and care. Emphasis in the EYLF is on three key terms: belonging, being and becoming. The Council of Australian Government's vision is that: *All children have the best start in life to create a better future for themselves and for the nation* (DEEWR, 2019, p.5). The aim is to provide early childhood education and care where all children become:

- *successful learners;*
- *confident and creative individuals;*
- *active and informed citizens.*

The EYLF defines belonging, being and becoming:

Belonging: Experiencing belonging – knowing where and with whom you belong – is integral to human existence. Children belong first to a family, a cultural group, a neighbourhood and a wider community. Belonging acknowledges children's interdependence with others and the basis of relationships in defining identities. In early childhood, and throughout life, relationships are crucial to a sense of belonging. Belonging is central to being and becoming in that it shapes who children are and who they can become

Being: Childhood is a time to be, to seek and make meaning of the world. Being recognises the significance of the here and now in children's lives. It is about the present and them knowing themselves, building and maintaining relationships with others, engaging with life's joys and complexities, and meeting challenges in everyday life. The early childhood years are not solely preparation for the future but also about the present

Becoming: Children's identities, knowledge, understandings, capacities, skills and relationships change during childhood. They are shaped by many different events and circumstances. Becoming reflects this process of rapid and significant change that occurs in the early years as young children learn and grow. It emphasises learning to participate fully and actively in society.

(p.7)

Similar to the curriculum in England, the EYLF sets out the learning outcomes for children from birth to five, in that children:

- *have a strong sense of identity;*
- *are connected with and contribute to their world;*
- *have a strong sense of well-being;*
- *are confident and involved learners;*
- *are effective communicators.*

The EYLF states: *[a]ssessment for children's learning refers to the process of gathering and analysing information as evidence about what children know, can do and understand. It is part of an ongoing cycle that includes planning, documenting and evaluating children's learning* (p.19). The main focus of the assessment is gathering information through observations to ensure an effective use of time to inform curriculum decisions and enable teachers to share evidence of children's learning with their families and other professionals.

Educators use a variety of strategies to collect, document, organise, synthesise and interpret the information that they gather to assess children's learning. They search for appropriate ways to collect rich and meaningful information that depicts children's learning in context, describes their progress and identifies their strengths, skills and understanding.

(DEEWR, 2019, p.17)

(Continued)

(Continued)

Throughout the EYLF there are strong connections between observation and assessment. The main focus is on the learning outcomes and the ways that observations are recorded and recognised so that they can contribute to the requirements of the National Quality Standards (NQS). Unlike England, the EYLF does not have standard national requirements about children's assessment records or profile, being based on the principle that children's assessment is to inform the curriculum and communicate with parents. Educators have flexibility and decide what to observe and how to construct their assessments for each child. The only requirement for settings is that all educators have a good knowledge and understanding of each child which informs their daily practice.

For more information visit: **https://www.education.gov.au/early-years-learning-framework**

CASE STUDY 3

Observing and assessing children's digital play: suggestions from research

Bird and Edwards (2015) and Edwards and Bird (2017) examined how observations of young children's play can inform the assessment process. They were concerned about how educators can use *formative approaches to assessment when considering children's learning to use technologies through play* (Edwards and Bird 2017, p.160). They argued that as children now use digital technologies in their play, there is limited observation and assessment practices that help us to understand *how children learn to use technologies through play in early childhood education settings. This means that it can be difficult for early childhood educators to know 'what' they are assessing when observing young children's digital play activities in early childhood classrooms* (Edwards and Bird 2017, p.161).

Based on the work of Vygotsky on the influence of culture in children's play (1997) and Hutt's (1966) definitions of play as epistemic, meaning exploratory, and ludic, meaning symbolic, they developed a Digital Play Framework for observing and assessing children (see Table 1) on how they learn to use technologies through play.

Table 1   The Digital Play Framework

Digital technologies-as-tool			
Object of activity	Behaviours (from Hutt et al., 1989)	Indicators	Description
Epistemic play	Exploration	Seemingly random use of the device	Seemingly random footage, images, pressing the iPad, moving or clicking the mouse
		Locating the operating functions of the device	Locating the on/off button (video camera), shutter button (still camera), home button
			(iPad), keyboard (computer) or mouse (computer)

Digital technologies-as-tool			
Object of activity	Behaviours (from Hutt et al., 1989)	Indicators	Description
		Exploring the operating functions of the device	Exploring the on/off button (video camera), shutter button (still camera), home button
			(iPad), keyboard (computer) or mouse (computer)
		Following directions of the device or other people	Following the directions of the device or other people
		Seeking assistance for desired outcome	Asking adults or peers for assistance to use the device
	Problem-solving	Relating actions to the response/function	Pressing the on/off button, relating turning the camera to what is in the viewfinder (video camera), pressing the shutter button, relating turning the camera to what is in the viewfinder, pressing the Home button to change Apps, scrolling through Apps (iPad), relating mouse and keyboard to actions on the screen (computer)
		Trying different actions to solve an issue	Returning to the menu button; asking peers or adults for advice/help
		Intentional use of the operating functions	Selecting record functions to create footage
	Skill acquisition	Intentional and deliberate use of functions for desired outcome	Being able to view taken footage (video camera) or images (still camera), scrolling and tilting (iPad), using mouse to move cursor, click and double click program icons (computer)
		Sharing learned actions with others	Being able to share knowledge of functions of the device with others for the purpose of teaching others (ZPD)
		Intentional and controlled footage of observable people, events and situations or manipulating the App or program for own purpose	Creating and filming deliberate play scenarios

(Continued)

Table 1   (Continued)

Digital technologies-as-tool			
Object of activity	Behaviours (from Hutt et al., 1989)	Indicators	Description
Ludic play	Symbolic	Deliberate use of device for pretend play	Using the device to record already established pretend play or to record re-enacted play (video and still cameras), selecting an App specifically for pretend play (iPad), selecting a program specifically for pretend play (computer)
	Innovation	Creating pretend play deliberately for use of the device	Creating a pretend play to record (video or still cameras), selecting an App specifically for pretend play (iPad), selecting a program specifically for pretend play (computer)

(*Source*: Edwards, S and Bird, J (2017) Observing and assessing young children's digital play in the early years: using the Digital Play Framework, *Journal of Early Childhood Research*, 15(2), pp.158–73).

With an increasing use of digital technologies (see, for example, the work of Dunn and Sweeney, 2018; Marsh et al., 2016; Kurcirkova, 2017) this framework offers help to practitioners to use observation to assess children's learning when using digital technologies for play. It can also become a useful tool for other aspects of children's play and learning (see examples in Chapter 6).

ACTIVITY 1

The role of observation in your context

Reflecting on the above case studies what do you think the role of formative and summative assessment should be in early childhood education?

- How are observations used in the setting you are currently in placement or working in?
- Reflect on the curriculum that you are working with and examine the role of observation in relation to children's assessment. Examine the formative and summative requirements and discuss how you rate these practices as holistic approaches to assessment and evaluation.

The nature of observations

Although there is a wealth of literature about observations, Drummond (1998) suggests that we ought to develop manageable systems for being able to watch children interacting with one another and their environment in order to create comprehensive portraits of children as autonomous individuals.

> *Observing learning, [and] getting close to children's minds and children's feelings, is part of our daily work in striving for quality [. . .] Our careful observations of children's learning can help us make [early childhood] provision better. We can use what we see to identify the strengths and weaknesses, gaps and inconsistencies, in what we provide. We can identify significant moments in a child's learning and we can build on what we see.*
>
> (Drummond, 1998, p.105)

When considering the nature of observations, the main goal should be to help practitioners understand child development and learning and to help them plan their activities and practices. It should also help to create an environment which will allow opportunities for children to make choices and decisions, to use their imagination and creativity for meaningful experiences, to promote interactions and extend conversations, and to encourage the *holistic entity and identity* (Formoshino and Formoshino, 2016, p.101) and become involved in play and learning. However, carrying out observations requires skill and expertise as Nutbrown and Carter (2010, p.210) emphasise: *Watching children as they learn and understanding their learning moments is complex and difficult work and places the highest of demands upon their educators*. When moving away from the simplistic gathering of information that summarises the same information for each child and to have instead observations that reveal patterns of play, development, learning, behaviours and interactions it is important for practitioners to have in-depth knowledge of children, to develop skills such as critical thinking, reflection and careful ongoing attention to children's actions and to continue to develop and apply these skills to gather information to understand the child and also inform planning.

On this basis when the nature of observations is discussed, it is important to understand the term comprehensively. Gillham (2008, p.1) claims that observation *deals not with what people say they do, but what they actually do*. Observation is a systematic method of studying human behaviour or phenomena within a specific context and should always have a precise purpose. It involves key cognitive dimensions: attention, working memory, perception and time as it requires recording and watching over a period of time. Smith (1998, p.6) claims that observation is a *deliberate, active process, carried out with care and forethought, of noting events as they occur*. Observation is a complex activity because the way we see (perception) other people and their behaviours is related to our self-experiences as we all have a *preferred way of viewing ourselves and others* (Gillham, 2008, p.1). Our skills, such as focusing intensively for a period of time (attention) and working memory capacity, are unique to the individual. All these factors make observation a highly skilled method.

Observation as a systematic method of looking at and recording children's behaviours should always have a clear intention. In an attempt to define observations we might argue that it is a valid tool for understanding children's development to help practitioners with their assessment. The term 'observe' literally means 'to look at', to 'watch something closely'. The term describes the systematic and *structured way* (Faragher and MacNaughton, 1998) in which the workforce views children in order to understand them, with the ultimate purpose of assessing their development and informing any future planning. This systematic way of scrutinising enables us to understand in-depth children's development, gain insight into children's daily routines and, therefore, be a useful resource, not only in the training of practitioners, but also as a way of deepening early childhood education practice.

At another level, by observing what children do we understand their development and the way in which they behave and react within certain situations and contexts. This reflection informs not only our practice but is also an important channel of communication for the children's families.

ACTIVITY 2

What should we observe?

With reference to the curriculum within which you work try to answer the following questions:

1. What place do observations have in your setting? What is the focus of your observation?
2. How do they inform your practice?
3. How could you use observations to help you learn more about children?
4. How can you communicate the observations with the children's families?

If possible, try to pose the same questions to a more experienced practitioner in your setting and then compare your answers with theirs.

Observations for a reason

Observations are the *foundation of education in the early years* (Hurst, 1991, p.70). The main reason why observations are subsequently emphasised by many curricula around the world is that they can offer us important information about children, their abilities and their interests that are not available elsewhere. Furthermore, closely watching children via systematic techniques can give the observers and practitioners an in-depth look. This can enhance our understanding of children and their actions. Observations focus on a child's natural behaviour in a given setting, which is the key process for assessing their development. Looking at children closely helps observers to recognise stages of development and to take responsibility for progress.

Through the systematic collection of information about children, practitioners are able to gather a number of incidents and evidence which can offer an accurate picture about behaviours and development. This evidence, gathered through observations, is a very important tool in the hands of practitioners. Young children have a limited repertoire of language and behaviours and when practitioners are asked to explain and to try to provide a supportive learning environment it is necessary to be able to understand the children involved first and foremost. Young children, through their play and through their interaction with others, make meaningful suggestions about their thoughts and feelings. Thus, via observations, you can collect accurate and pertinent data about these children. Accordingly, the most accurate way for practitioners to study children is through these observations.

Systematic observations also help practitioners to understand the reasons behind children's behaviour in certain situations. Benjamin (1994, p.14) emphasises their importance thus: *Observations play an important role in assessment, either by replacing or by supplementing standardised evaluation instruments.*

Consequently, observers can recognise stages of child development, relate these to the theoretical stages of normal development and then subsequently take responsibility for helping a child's progress. In this sense observations not only help practice, but also provide a reliable context to make links with theory to demonstrate what has been learned about children.

Observations allow practitioners the opportunity to implement theory in their daily practice. It is by no means presumptuous to say that observations facilitate practitioners' reflective thinking and thus empower them to evaluate their practice in an attempt to develop effectively. Thus there is a dual purpose to observations: to help practitioners understand children, but also to help progress within their own practice through reflection.

Observations focus on what a child *can* do (and not on what a child *cannot* do) as a basis for forward planning. It is important to highlight what a child is capable of in order to plan activities. An observation's main focus is on what can be achieved and it is in the nature of observations to focus on a child's natural behaviour within the setting. The information collected can be a valid starting point for assessing a child's development.

Observations offer an in-depth look at a child not available in other ways. Discussion with the parents can offer an insight about their children within the family environment, which is a very helpful tool. However, there is a necessity for practitioners to try and investigate children's behaviour within the context of the classroom.

A body of literature (Clark and Moss, 2001; Clark et al., 2005; Rinaldi, 2006) is promoting observation as a way of listening to children and giving voices to them. Luff (2007, p.189) stresses that *observing and documenting learning can be a way of valuing and listening to children.* Elfer (2005) adds that within current legislation, such as the requirements raised by the Children's Act (HM Government, 2004) and the United Nations Convention on Children's Rights (1989a), observations can provide an effective context for listening to children's attempts to communicate and for practitioners to take into consideration a child's distinctive voice. Thus observations can become a suitable path for opening up communication with children.

Evidence through observation helps us to consider children's voices and their needs and experiences in order to create pedagogical activities that will comply with their interests. This can create learning environments for children that are not only safe, enjoyable and applicable, but also exciting. However, one should be very careful about how to use observations as a way of listening or offering voices to children as there are occasions when the privacy of conversations with other children is violated. There are questions regarding whether we have the right to photograph and record children's activities and where we draw the line when something is private among children. Pascal and Bertram (2013) offer us a valuable reality check in active listening to children voices:

- to be attentive;
- active listening (the use of body language, gestures that indicate that you are attentive);

- provide feedback (do not assume that what you have listened to is what children have said and hasten to judgement. Be reflective and ask questions such as: What I am hearing is . . .; What do you mean?);
- defer judgement (respect the child and what the child says rather than pre-empt what is said with your own view or judgement);
- be candid, open and honest in your response.

It can also be added that to ensure children's voices are heard we do need to remember one key element is silence. It is not possible to hear children if there are not moments of silence and pause. As practitioners sometimes we are concerned with talking to children, explaining and engaging in language interactions and forgetting to pause which allows space for children to express themselves. Our physical interactions with children and our body language can also become an obstacle that will prevent children from expressing themselves. As adults we have a physical superiority over children so it is important to 'silence' this superiority by considering how we physically position our body when we try to communicate with them. Do we sit among the children? Do we sit separately from them when we talk to them? Do we stand? Do we go to their eye level when we talk to them? Adults' physical positioning in a (class)room can intimidate children, especially infants and toddlers, who rely so much on physical contact with adults (see Chapter 9 for ethical implications when we observe young children).

It is in the nature of observations to provide opportunities for collaboration. In an era when most policies are moving from a mono-professional culture to multi-professional collaboration in early childhood education there needs to be a recognition that working with young children involves a team of people such as health visitors, social workers, paediatricians and educational psychologists. The multi-professional workforce should seek ways of communicating and sharing information about their understanding of children to address early any issues in a child's development and learning and create effective interventions and appropriate quality practices. The basis of multi-disciplinary work can be provided by evidence collected via observations so different professionals can develop a common understanding and language about the needs of children. Observations can provide possibilities for pulling together the team around the child and offer strategies so that the captured information can be communicated efficiently to enrich communication and collaboration.

ACTIVITY 3

Sharing Observations

1. Consider your setting and try to think of any occasions where observations became a suitable source for listening to children and what action you subsequently took.
2. Can you recall any opportunities where you used information from observations to work in a multi-professional way?

Here observations should be viewed as part of the daily routine of the classroom and not as a separate tool. Observation is *not* a tool where children with a problem are studied in an attempt to resolve dilemmas. These are instances when there is a specific problem with a child. Observations ought to be implemented as part of *everyday* practice. Observations should focus on children's development and learning and an interpretation of observations as a reflection on daily practice which *is unobtrusively woven into classroom activity and inter-action* (Pratt, 1994, p.102). Education should be determined not by how much we observe a child, but what we observe so we can achieve an in-depth knowledge about the child.

CASE STUDY 4

Te Whāriki and observations

An example of how observations have been integrated or 'woven' into the everyday life of the classroom comes from New Zealand. The curriculum was introduced by the Ministry of Education in 1996 and was revised in 2017 to meet the demands and changes of the twentieth-first century, aiming to create a multicultural learning environment. Underpinning Te Whāriki is the vision that children are *competent and confident learners and communicators, healthy in mind, body and spirit, secure in their sense of belonging and in the knowledge that they make a valued contribution to society* (Ministry of Education, New Zealand Te Tāhuhu o te Mātauranga 2017, p. 2)

Te Whāriki is underpinned by four principles and five strands:

Principles	Strands
Empowerment	Well-being
Holistic development	Belonging
Family and community	Contribution
Relationships	Communication
	Exploration

Consequently, observations look at the behaviours that are central to children. These behaviours are important for the development of children as effective learners. Carr (2001) stresses the importance of children obtaining these behaviours and suggests a focus on the curriculum principles and strands for assessment.

Table 2   Five behaviours and five strands of the curriculum

Strands of the curriculum	The behaviour we look at
Belonging	Taking an interest
Well-being	Being involved
Exploration	Persisting with difficulty, challenges and uncertainty
Communication	Expressing a point of view or feeling
Contribution	Taking responsibility

(Continued)

(Continued)

In Carr's work observation is central to the curriculum. It is integrated into the daily practice of the class – *woven within the curriculum*. It is important to see that observation has a definite purpose and that this purpose is oriented by curriculum learning objectives and outcomes.

Carr (1998, p.15) claims that observations are central in creating

learning communities [. . .] where children [can]:

- *take an interest in an activity;*
- *become involved in it over a sustained period of time;*
- *persist when they meet difficulty, challenges or uncertainty;*
- *express their ideas or feelings in a range of ways;*
- *take responsibility to change the way things are, to teach others and to listen to another point of view.*

According to Carr, these processes are linear and appear in sequence; thus she characterises them as *learning stories* (see Chapter 6 for examples). The main interest/focus of these learning stories is the merging of dispositions and the accompanying people, places and phenomena that make the emergence more likely to show how practitioners can strengthen these dispositions. The importance of these learning stories is that they provide guidelines for the adults' planning of activities which can also provide families with an insight into their children's day, giving the parents a view of learning that is valued and encouraged.

So we can see in the curriculum the use of observation is twofold: firstly, to help improve practitioners' practice, pedagogy and activities; and, secondly, as a valid tool to communicate with the children's families. In addition, the children themselves participate in writing these stories. Therefore observations in the Te Whāriki classroom are part of daily life and routine and are used not only in certain circumstances, but as part of the curriculum as a whole to be able to monitor a child's progress.

ACTIVITY 4

Observe for the curriculum requirements

Carry out an audit of these types of observations that take place daily in your setting.

How can these observations be integrated within the implementation of your curriculum requirements?

Why observe children?

As noted above, observations formalise the link between theory and practice so we are able to demonstrate what they have learned about children across all areas.

THEORY FOCUS

- There is a need for a systematic way of making observations within the learning environment.
- Observations are the structured way of studying children.
- Observations inform pedagogy and curriculum structure.
- Observations underpin the everyday activities of the classroom.
- Observations can become the tool for multi-professional collaboration.

Observations help us to:

- collect and gather evidence that can offer an accurate picture of children, their learning and development;
- understand the reasons behind children's behaviour in certain situations;
- recognise stages in child development;
- inform planning and assessment;
- provide opportunities for collaboration with parents and other services;
- find out about children as individuals;
- monitor progress;
- inform curriculum planning;
- enable staff to evaluate their practice;
- provide a focus for discussion and improvement.

Thus far we have discussed the origins and the key purposes of observation. In this section we will briefly discuss what observations should aim towards. To begin with, observations as a methodological tool in the hands of a practitioner address a child's development. All aspects of development are under scrutiny where children are involved. Emotional, social, physical, cognitive and moral awareness are all crucial aspects of a child's progress and are all interlinked. We might study and observe them separately, but they all come together in order to offer us a complete portrait of individual development and progress.

All children go through observable sequences of behaviour at their own pace and this sequence of development can be traced by the practitioner from the perspective of an observer. The main issue is that practitioners should know what to look and listen for in each instance and reflect this in their planning. For example, in the following observation, after observing the child in relation to his physical development, the practitioner is not making judgements in relation to the child but uses the observation in the 'Ways Forward Box' (as shown in Table 3) to inform future planning.

Table 3 Ways Forward Box

Child's name: Kieron

Adult observer: KP

Area of provision: Physical development

Age in months: 29 months

Time/duration: 10 mins

What happens/happened:

The KP has set out a tub of popoids – this is the first time the children have seen these popoids.

Kieron sees the popoids being put out and climbs up to the table to explore. He carefully selects different sections of the popoids and sets them out in front of him. The KP watches from a distance and does not intervene, waiting to see what Kieron will do with the popoids. He examines one of the ends and explores it using his fingers. He looks up at the KP and holds out the popoid.

P – Shall I show you what the popoids can do Kieron?

K – More

The KP demonstrates how the two pieces of popoid fit together. The popoids are rarely played with and so are very stiff. Kieron copies the KP and joins various pieces together, but when he picks up his model the pieces fall off as he does not have enough dexterity to push the pieces together and snap them into place. Kieron tries again. This time when they fall apart Kieron gives up.

Personal Social Emotional Development	Physical Development	Communication Language	Literacy	Mathematics	Understanding the World	Expressive Arts Development
	M&H Develop grasp and release, refined pinches, eye-hand coordination, and in-hand manipulation (translation and translation with stabilisation)			SSM Shows interest in shape by sustained construction activity or by talking about shapes or arrangements. 30–50 months		UEMM – Uses various construction materials. 30–50 months

Playing and Exploring	Active Learning	Creating and Thinking Critically
Finding out and exploring	*Being involved and concentrating*	*Choosing ways to do things*

Ways forward:

Kieron was very interested in the construction but lacked the dexterity in his hands to force the pieces of popoids to fit together. Plan more activities that can improve dexterity and strength by squeezing and palpitating the dough, threading beads and lacing cards.

ACTIVITY 5

Why observe children

Read the following case study and try to identify which areas of development Sue needs encouragement in.

- Use your curriculum learning areas or outcomes as your guideline in order to complete the activity.
- Consider the ways forward for Sue.
- Consider how you can help Sue and her parents.

Sue's story

Sue is a two-year-old girl, the only child in her family, and she joined the setting three weeks ago. She is a lively and active child, but she cries a lot every day and the practitioners cannot calm her. She appears to be in distress, sad and stressed when her mother leaves her in the morning. She does not interact with other children and only wants to be in the company of the adults. She does not want to share any toys when she plays and during the activities she sits quietly and does not talk to other children. She appears not to interact with other children and has not made any friends.

Limitations of observations

Throughout this book the value of observation in early childhood education will be emphasised. However, you need to be aware of the limitations, in the same way as any method or tool. One of the main limitations of observation is that capturing what actually happens or a certain behaviour or activity divorces it from its history. Using only observation as a method to collect evidence of children's development, behaviours or learning, or to inform your planning, does not answer the key question of how the behaviour occurred, how the learning occurred or how the activities developed.

A key element in the development and behaviour of each child is his/her personal history and the culture in which that child has been brought up, any changes in the family structure (if any), the dynamics of the child's direct and indirect environment and the impact this may have had on the their behaviour. We are all part of a community and its ecology (beliefs, customs, values, services and policies) and, as such, these aspects may not become apparent by visual observation alone. Such evidence on its own decontextualises the behaviour.

Thus it is important to use methods or techniques other than observation to gain a broader picture. This is an important limitation to consider and finding other ways of answering the question should also be found. Team meetings, parental involvement and child involvement are essential elements to minimise this limitation. These can offer information you are seeking, unavailable in the observation. In the analysis and documentation processes, it is important to consider the origins of what has been observed, cross-referencing with evidence from other sources. Gillham (2008, p.100) concludes that: *Observations cannot tell the whole story; and even when extended over time, it can only incorporate a narrow section of evolution of a group, a culture or an individual.* Thus there is always a need for complementary methods.

SUMMARY

This introduction has investigated the nature of observation within early childhood education. In the light of most government policies these observations hold an important and essential role to gather evidence for a child's assessment in terms of development and learning. The workforce is asked to use observation as a systematic way of assessing children within curricular practices for an evidence-based assessment of children.

Observation is a valid tool to understand children's development and learning and inform practice. It has a key role in practice as it helps us to find out about children, monitor their progress, inform curriculum planning, enable staff to evaluate the provisions they make, provide a focus for discussion and improvement and better understand practice. It has been emphasised that observations should be 'woven' into daily practice and not seen as an external aspect of our work. In the next chapter, the aim is to locate observation in the policy context with particular emphasis on curriculum and assessment.

Further Reading

For more general information on observation in early childhood education:

Brodie, K (2013) *Observations, Assessment and Planning in the Early Years – Bringing It All Together*. Maidenhead: Open University Press.
Papatheodorou, T, Luff, P and Gill, J (2011) *Child Observation for Learning and Research*. Essex: Pearson Education.
Smidt, S (2015) *Observing Young Children: The Role of Observation and Assessment in Early Childhood Settings* (2nd edn). London: Routledge.

Based on the Canadian context this book is a comprehensive guide on observations with a number of exemplary practices for learners:

Martin, S (2019) *Take a Look: Observation and Portfolio Assessment in Early Childhood* (7th edn). Canada: Pearson.

Websites

To learn more about the Early Years Foundation Stage in England visit: **https://www.gov.uk/early-years-foundation-stage**

To learn more about Te Whāriki visit: **https://www.education.govt.nz/early-childhood/teaching-and-learning/te-whariki/**

CHAPTER 1

OBSERVATION IN THE POLICY CONTEXT

Chapter objectives

In reading this chapter, you will:

- consider the changes to the policy context of early childhood education;
- have an overview of influential curricula;
- develop an understanding of curricula and assessment requirements in the UK;
- consider provision for children from birth to five years;
- explore the role of observation and the impact of policy within early childhood education.

Policy impacts on the daily practice of practitioners as it can determine the curriculum, assessment and expectations from each child in the setting. Practitioners need to demonstrate how these polices are met in their own setting and understand how observation can be affected as a consequence of the policy.

Introduction

The interest at policy level nationally and internationally is increasingly on the use of standardised tests and assessments. For example, the international organisation for promoting economic growth, the Organisation for Economic Co-operation and Development

(OCED), has established standardised tests to assess the educational progress of 15-year-old children with the results being compared among its member countries. The Programme for International Students Assessment (PISA) is used by many countries to rate a country's progress in relation to their education system. In 2015 the OECD announced the introduction of a standardised assessment programme for five-year-old children, the International Early Learning and Child Well Being Study (IELS). The IELS was piloted in England, Estonia and the United States at the end of 2017 with over 1,000 children, their parents and teachers taking part. It is stated that: *The study takes a holistic approach and includes multiple domains of early learning: emergent cognitive skills such as literacy and numeracy, social and emotional skills such as empathy and trust, and skills that draw from both cognitive and non-cognitive capacities, such as self-regulation* (OECD, 2018: Findings from the IELS 2017 Field Trial). The programme used direct assessments, collecting information from five-year-old children, where children completed tasks on tablets. The assessment takes about 15 minutes per domain with only two domains assessed per day. The OECD (2018) has now announced that the assessment instrument will be finalised in 2018, with the aim to be used by countries to inform policy and practices by 2020. This international standardised assessment of young children has received a number of criticisms (e.g. Moss and Urban, 2017; Pence, 2017) which argue against standardised assessment tests and urge *the international early childhood community [to] be supportive of a meaningful, contextualised learning initiative, conducted in respectful and participatory ways* (Urban, 2018, p.97).

However, educational policies are increasingly seeking for a more standardised approach to assessment as is the case in England currently with the introduction of the Baseline Assessment (as discussed in the Introduction). Yet research evidence shows that assessments should not be based on tests, but should embrace a wide array of formats such as observations, portfolios, parents and practitioner views in the process of development and learning in a given individual child, taking into account a child's home culture or any other spaces that a child moves in daily. Thus this chapter aims to discuss the policy landscape

ACTIVITY 1.1

The role of policy, why is it important?

Fitzgerald and Kay (2016, p.1) argue that policy-makers impact on the way practitioners are working with children:

> *Policies are not just conjured up out of thin air. People who make policies have reasons for what they do. We may not agree with them, but they are reasons, not mere whims. We need to understand those reasons in order to implement more effectively those policies that appear to be useful and to challenge more effectively those that do not. We want to argue against the sense of helplessness. Practitioners can do more than just cope, particularly when policies are not seen as appropriate or effective.*

Reflecting on the above quote, consider the value of understanding policy. Discuss the role of policy in your context and how it is impacting in your work.

of early childhood education which has left the field with a variety of terms, ideologies and practices examining the role of educational policy with a focus on curriculum and assessment and the role of observations. Knowing the policy context in which you work with young children will help you understand the value of observation and determine its uses.

Policy context and early childhood education

Historically, early childhood education policy and quality in many countries has been influenced by distinctive strands of thinking, ideology and practice. The OECD (2001 and 2006) in two reports argues that:

ECEC [Early Childhood Education and Care] policy and the quality of services are deeply influenced by underlying assumptions about childhood and education: what does childhood mean in this society? How should young children be reared and educated? What are the purposes of education and care, of early childhood institutions? What are the functions of early childhood staff?

(OECD, 2001, p.63)

In a recent examination of 30 countries' educational policy on ECEC it was found that although there is progress made among many countries in improving quality, systems are still divided between education and care and the professionalisation of staff varies depending on the ages of the group of children (Oberhumer and Schreyer, 2018; full report on all countries can be found at: **http://www.seepro.eu/English/Country_Reports.htm**).

Policy reforms have left ambiguity and competing discourses regarding the nature and role of ECEC. For example, from one perspective, the idea as to whether provision should focus on care or education that is based on children's needs still dominates discussions of its nature that are reflected in the role societies promote. On the other hand, the age boundaries of early childhood education are still debatable. For some, early childhood education is concerned with the period between birth and five years (e.g. the UK) while for others it is between birth and six years (Austria, Greece, Italy, Sweden). Moreover, even the terminology has been diverse: the terms 'early childhood education and care' or 'early years' or 'pre-school education' have been used to describe areas that are hosting children from birth to five or six that we refer to variously as 'nursery', 'child care', 'day care', 'pre-school', 'kindergarten' and 'early years setting', each of which follows different programmes that have their own philosophy, mission and approaches to practice (see the Theory Box on p.28, Table 1.1) that presents some of the most influential approaches that have shaped curricula and educational policies around the world).

This diversity is also mirrored in the people who are responsible for working with young children – normally referred to as 'early years teachers', 'early childhood teachers', 'early years practitioners', 'early childhood practitioners', 'pre-school teachers'. Questions have been raised as to what extent they are perceived as professionals or whether it is just an occupation. In the UK, for example, people who worked with young children were considered part of the social care sector and under the responsibility of health and social care (Chalke, 2013). Earlier, Cohen et al. (2004), in a cross cultural-national study which examined reforms for young children in three countries (England, Scotland and Sweden), concluded that the relationship between education and care is problematic and linked with society's understanding of childhood. For many years in many western countries (i.e. England, Scotland, Greece, Sweden) early childhood was the responsibility of welfare services and it a relatively recent phenomenon that it has become the responsibility of education. Consequently, the people who were working in the sector were received with scepticism by the rest of the established educational world as part of the education community (Brock, 2012; Taggart, 2011). Moyles (2001, p.81) addresses this from earlier on:

> [I]t seems impossible to work effectively with very young children without the deep and sound commitment signified by the use of words like 'passionate'. Yet this very symbolisation gives a particular emotional slant to the work of early childhood practitioners which can work [. . .] against them in everyday roles and practices, bringing into question what constitutes professionalism and what being a 'teacher' means.

At the policy level, and considering the long history of different provision in the field, it has taken a long time to actually merge the terms 'education' and 'care for children'. In many western countries the introduction of curricula for ECEC emerged in the 1990s. For example, in the US, although the National Association for the Education of Young Children (NAEYC) – initially the National Association for Nursery Education (NANE) prior to the change of name to NAEYC in 1964 – has existed since the mid-1920s, it took until 1995 to develop a set of recommendations for early childhood education and educators (that were revised again in 2006).

Another example comes from public pre-school in Sweden that has had a long tradition of regulation and working towards professionalisation. As early as the 1960s the government organised committees to examine content and working methods in the pre-school class for six-year-olds (OECD, 2010, p.23). Professionals working in day care and the pre-school class were expected to have similar training and work on similar content for children of all ages. The educational function of both day care and the pre-school was recognised, as well as the key notions of interaction, communication and dialogue. It was in 1996 that the Ministry of Education and Science took over responsibility for day care from the Ministry of Social and Family Affairs where day care and the pre-school class merged under one term to become known as 'pre-school'. Pre-school has now become the foundation stage of the school system and of lifelong learning (Lpfö, 2010). The aim of pre-school integrated childhood education and care (known as EDUCARE) places emphasis on being the first step in the child's lifelong learning, a perspective which is obvious in the first national curriculum for one to five-year-old children (Swedish Ministry of Education and Science, 1998).

In the UK, the introduction of the Plowden Report in 1967 merged care and education and suggested that part-time nursery provision has a dual purpose: education and welfare. However, the actual acceleration of progress in the sector came in 1989 with the United Nations Convention on the Rights of the Child (UNCRC). The UNCRC, adopted by the United Nations General Assembly in 1989, brought about changes in terms of policy-making and its implementation for children. The UNCRC is an agreement between the United Nations and individual countries that have chosen to ratify the Convention. Central to this is the recognition that all children have the right of and access to education, which should be free, and the UN nations involved are responsible for providing this. It also recognises diversity among children and the issue of equal opportunities, no matter the socio-economic, political or racial group to which each child belongs. Countries which have ratified the UNCRC have made a commitment to deliver these rights and to incorporate them into their policies for children. The Convention has had a great impact on services and policies for children at a national and international level.

ACTIVITY 1.2

Children's rights and the role of the curriculum

Take some time to study an international curriculum of your interest and the position of the country under investigation in relation to children's rights. How does this compare to your own experiences in the curriculum you are working with?

These web pages will guide you official reports:

- Organisation for Economic Co-operation and Development (OECD): **www.oecd.org/ education/school/earlychildhoodeducationandcare.htm**
- UNICEF and children's rights: **http://unicef.org.uk/UNICEFs-Work/UN-Convention/**

To sum up, although there are improvements in policy for ECEC provision in many countries across the world today, the divide between education and care still underpins many policies. There is a variety of qualifications among practitioners, with staff either lacking relevant professional qualifications or these being of a lower level compared to other areas of education, while provision for children under three still remains underdeveloped. To conclude, the diverse policies in many systems has left the field with a wide range of quality of experience offered to children and their families.

ACTIVITY 1.3

Comparing curricula: what is the role of observation?

- After studying the different curricular approaches in the Theory Box set out in Table 1.1 can you identify any similarities and differences with the curriculum you are working with?
- What is the role of observation in each of these approaches?

(Continued)

Table 1.1 Theory Box 1: Influential approaches to early childhood education

Types of early childhood education and care	Key philosophical ideas	Environment	Role of staff
Froebel	Established the first early childhood education setting for children from 3–4 years old: 'kindergarten'.	Emphasis on the 'gifts and occupations'.	Teachers should guide children through the gifts and provide opportunities for children to participate in occupations.
	Emphasis on human creativity and play as the main drive for learning.	These are toys made specifically for children to promote certain senses. Froebel's occupations included artefacts such as pencils, wood, sand, clay, straw and sticks so that children are given opportunities to construct. They also included a collection of stories and songs designed to facilitate children's sensory and physical development.	Valued women in education.
	Play, games, stories and activities were central to his kindergartens.		Observation central to the everyday life.
	Development is unfolding, so the role of the kindergartens is to provide children with opportunities that encourage self-activity and self-actualisation.		
	Developed 'gifts and occupations' (materials made for children) so that children through playing with these would move from simple to more complex meanings.	Emphasis on the outdoor environment as an essential part of a child's school life.	
Montessori	All children are born with abilities that they can use for their learning and development.	Based on the idea that children should be given opportunities to move to higher levels of cooperation, peace and harmony – planes of development. Children are given materials to explore their senses which will lead them to self-awareness.	Teachers in a Montessori approach should serve as guides to children rather than instructing them towards specific tasks.
	Emphasis on the learning environment to promote children's ability for self-discovery and learning.		

Types of early childhood education and care	Key philosophical ideas	Environment	Role of staff
	Children's sensory awareness is important – learning starts with ways that help children to explore their environment through their senses.	Based on the idea that children absorb knowledge effortlessly from their environment, emphasis is placed on the right materials that will help children develop self-regulation and independent learning.	Teachers are responsible for creating an environment where the appropriate tools are included so children have opportunities to explore their environment by using their senses. Teachers should observe and provide guidance to children based on their observations.
Waldford Education (founded by Rudolf Steiner)	Introduced the term 'anthroposophy', meaning the wisdom of human being. Emphasis on the whole child through the: *Head*: stimulation of mind and cultivation of creativity; *Heart*: engagement of the heart though senses of caring, responsibility; *Hands*: respect for arts, humanity and nature.	Waldford classrooms are designed in ways that are aesthetically pleasing and harmonious. Children's physical and sensory experiences are valued so the indoor and outdoor environments offer experiences for children to explore physical and sensory skills.	Teachers should encourage children daily with creative play and exploration. As children at a young age are discovering and learning though imitation, teachers should be role models. Teachers provide subjects such as maths, reading, science through a process of exploration and constructive and creative play.
Head Start	A programme developed in the US in 1965 targeting low-income and deprived areas.	Emphasis on small class size where there is a close adult–child ratio where children can feel secure and supported. Emphasis on parental involvement.	Teachers and school environment to promote high-quality standards for the children.

(Continued)

Table 1.1 (Continued)

Types of early childhood education and care	Key philosophical ideas	Environment	Role of staff
	Aimed at helping deprived children in their development, offering them a head start for the future.	Emphasis on child initiated/directed activities.	Teachers should create a curriculum where the focus should be on the physical, mental, emotional and social development of a child.
		Respect for diversity and social relationships.	Teachers should be culturally sensitive and respect children's diversity.
		Focus on health, cognitive, emotional, social and physical development activities which should be oriented around developmentally appropriate targets.	Teachers should offer a balance between child-initiated activities and adult-initiated activities.
Reggio Emilia	Children are viewed as co-constructors of knowledge.	The environment is a valuable resource of learning for children.	Teachers are co-explorers with children. Observations are central in the organisation of activities.
	A community: teachers are committed to the creation of conditions for learning through the synthesis of all the expressive, communicative and cognitive languages: 'hundred languages of children'.	Projects are emerging from children's interests.	Teachers are seen as researchers as they also learn alongside the children.
		The curriculum is not set or pre-described, but emerges through conversations with children, community, families and from children's interests.	The environment is seen as the third teacher as children's interactions with the environment and the experiences they acquire enhance children's learning process.
	Respect for the child as a subject of rights and as a competent, active learner, continuously building and testing theories about herself and the world around her.	There is no formal assessment, but emphasis is placed on observations in order to document children's activities.	Involvement of *atelieristas* – highly trained in the visual arts – to work closely with the children and teachers.
		Emphasis on the aesthetics of the environment (natural materials, small intimate spaces, plants, art displays).	

Types of early childhood education and care	Key philosophical ideas	Environment	Role of staff
Te Whāriki	In 1990 in New Zealand, the two early childhood unions amalgamated to form the Combined Early Childhood Union of Aotearoa ('New Zealand' in Maori language). The mission was to promote diversity, equity, biculturalism, respect and integration of the Maori community, raising the standards for early childhood services and training for staff. Based on this mission, Te Whāriki was the first curriculum in New Zealand for early childhood education that was developed by the participation of family/parent/community. Te Whāriki means a 'woven mat' and is used as a metaphor to describe the inclusion of multiple perspectives, cultures and approaches.	The classroom is designed in a meaningful way that children are exploring through play. Continuity between classroom/home and community is promoted by inviting family members and members of the community to the classroom. Biculturalism and bilingualism are promoted.	Teachers are responsible for: 1. the arrangements of the physical environment and equipment; 2. the scheduling of activities and events; 3. the organisational philosophies, policies and procedures; 4. the inclusion and support of parents and the connections with the community; 5. the ages of the children, group size, and groupings. (Ministry of Education, 1996) In *Quality in Action* (Ministry of Education, 1998, p.6), the Ministry stated that desirable objectives and practices in early childhood education in relation to the curriculum are: 1. To work in partnership with parents/whānau to promote and extend the learning and development of each child who attends or receives the service;

(Continued)

Table 1.1 (Continued)

Types of early childhood education and care	Key philosophical ideas	Environment	Role of staff
	It reflects the holistic development of children and the Maori principle of 'empowering children to learn and grow'. There are five major aims for children – *Mana Atua*/Well-being, *Mana Whenua*/Belonging, *Mana Tangata*/ Contribution, *Mana Reo*/Communication and *Mana Aoturoa*/Exploration – which were developed as equivalent domains of empowerment for children in both cultures.		2. To develop and implement a curriculum that assists all children to be: • competent and confident learners and communicators; • healthy in mind, body and spirit; • secure in their sense of belonging; • secure in the knowledge that they make a valued contribution to society.
The Swedish Curriculum (EDUCARE)	The Swedish curriculum is based on the main principle of a democratic society and outlines five groups of goals: 1. norms and values; 2. development and learning; 3. influence of the child; 4. pre-school and home; 5. cooperation between the pre-school class, the school and the leisure time centre.	'The Swedish pre-school should be characterised by a pedagogical approach where care, nurturing and learning together form a coherent whole' (Swedish Ministry of Education and Science, 1998a, 1998b). Care and education form a unity (EDUCARE) in the Swedish pre-school.	Teachers, through systematic observation, should seek to ensure that children are meeting the goals of the curriculum. Teachers ensure that they regularly and systematically document, follow up and analyse each child's learning and development.

Types of early childhood education and care	Key philosophical ideas	Environment	Role of staff
	'An important task of the pre-school is to establish and help children acquire the values on which our society is based. The inviolability of human life, individual freedom and integrity, the equal value of all people, equality between the genders as well as solidarity with the weak and vulnerable are all values that the school shall actively promote in its work with children' (Swedish Ministry of Education and Science, 1998a).	The environment is based on play, creativity and joyful learning, and uses the interest of children in learning and mastering new experiences, knowledge and skills.	
Experiential Education – Effective learning through well-being and involvement	Introduced in May 1976 by 12 Flemish pre-school teachers, assisted by two educational consultants. Concerned with what constitutes quality in early childhood education (and based on close, moment-by-moment description of what it means to a young child to live and take part in the educational setting). Experiential Education is focused on the search for indicators of quality.	Emphasis on interactions between teacher and children. The 'Adult Style Observation Schedule' (ASOS) is used to evaluate: 1. stimulation; 2. sensitivity; 3. giving autonomy. (Laevers et al., 1997). Based on systematic observation activities and materials to promote children's involvement, to encourage children to communicate, confronting them with thought-provoking questions and giving them information that can capture their mind.	10 Action Points for Teachers: 1. Rearrange the classroom in appealing corners or areas. 2. Check the content of the corners and replace unattractive materials with more appealing ones. 3. Introduce new and unconventional materials and activities. 4. Observe children, discover their interests and find activities that meet these orientations.

(Continued)

Table 1.1 (Continued)

Types of early childhood education and care	Key philosophical ideas	Environment	Role of staff
	Involvement and well-being are key in this conception of curriculum. Based on the concept of 'deep-level learning', the 'Leuven Involvement Scale' (LIS) has been developed.	Emphasis on children's needs such as the need for security, affection, attention, affirmation, clarity and emotional support. Emphasis on respecting children's sense of initiative by acknowledging their interests, giving them room for experimentation, letting them decide upon the way an activity is performed.	5. Support ongoing activities through stimulating impulses and enriching interventions. 6. Widen the possibilities for free initiative and support them with sound rules and agreements. 7. Explore the relation with each of the children and between children and try to improve it. 8. Introduce activities that help children to explore the world of behaviour, feelings and values. 9. Identify children with emotional problems and work out sustaining interventions. 10. Identify children with developmental needs and work out interventions that engender involvement within the problem area. (Laevers and Moons, 1997)
High Scope	Developed in the 1960s by David Weikart and his team in Ypsilanti, Michigan (USA) with the aim of helping children from disadvantaged areas to be successful in school and society.	Classrooms and outdoor environment are organised in a way that is meaningful to children.	Teachers are seen as active learners themselves.

Types of early childhood education and care	Key philosophical ideas	Environment	Role of staff
	Based on longitudinal research that followed children from early childhood through adulthood, this programme promotes the idea that a high quality of education offers a better life with higher education and employment.	Areas in the classroom and outdoors are based on children's interests. Children have access to all materials and are allowed to use them responsibly. Materials, activities and interactions are designed through careful and rigorous observations.	Teachers are modelling behaviours to encourage children to pursue their interests. Teachers are careful observers and use observations in a systematic way in order to gain an understanding of children's interests and develop the Child Observation Record (COR).
	Children are viewed as active learners who construct knowledge that helps them to make sense of the world around them. Children through a 'plan-do-review' approach plan their own learning outcomes, carry out their own targets and reflect upon them.		Teachers promote positive relationships and through rigorous observation plan and organise the classroom environment.
Bank Street School for Children	Introduced by Lucy Sprague Mitchell in the US it has its origins in Progressive Pedagogy influenced by John Dewey (see Chapter 2). Emphasis is placed on social justice, equality, safety, respect for diversity. The main mission of this approach was to educate immigrant children that were exploited in unfair labour. Rejected rote learning and memorisation and encouraged children to be active learners.	Based on the idea of children as social beings, emphasis is placed on communication and collaboration by experimentation with materials. Children are encouraged to organise their own classroom with materials that interest and attract them. Promotion of small group interactions. Children choose topics to be explored in depth.	Teachers are facilitators of learning. Teachers offer hands-on experiences and activities to children based on children's interests. Teachers concerned with the development of a sense of community and promote the idea of social responsibility, encouraging children to share and learn from each other's skills.

The UK context

In the UK (England, Scotland, Wales and Northern Ireland) the policy for ECEC provision covers children from the ages of birth to five years. The provision is a mixture of private, volunteer and independent (PVI) sectors, a compulsory schooling age of five (four years in Northern Ireland) and state-funded provision for three to five-year-olds. As mentioned earlier the UK ratified the UNCRC on 19 April 1990 and the Convention came into force on 15 January 1992. Later in the UK the New Labour policy (1997–2010) focused on minimising poverty and eliminating social disadvantage by supporting families and young children and by increasing the quality of care and education. Miller and Hevey (2012), reviewing the policy, concluded that the government aimed to shape early childhood policy under four themes: reducing child poverty, evidence-based policy, supporting parents and parenting, and ensuring maximum support for the most disadvantaged. All the subsequent initiatives and policies introduced by the Labour government in early 2000 aimed to address these four key issues. A high priority in the agenda was to eliminate child poverty and to increase the protection of children. This led to the Green Paper *Every Child Matters* (DfES, 2003) and the subsequent Children Act of 2004.

The Labour government intended to move towards integrated services, whereby a number of professionals from different areas would work together for effective practice with children. On 1 October 2006 the Children's Workforce Development Council (CWDC) became responsible for the implementation of the Every Child Matters (ECM) agenda. Among its duties was to ensure that all children's services were acquiring common skills and knowledge, as the goal is to bring all professionals from different sectors together in order to meet the five outcomes of the ECM.

In 2010, there was a change in the government of the UK, with the coalition government of the Conservative and Liberal Democrat parties coming into power. Due to the prevailing economic climate a number of reductions in public spending including education were introduced. In 2011, the CWDC published *Early Years Workforce – The Way Forward* which set the vision and included key messages and recommendations to the Department for Education (DfE), the Teaching Regulation Agency and other sector leaders who were to support the ECEC workforce in the future. In November 2010, the government announced that it would withdraw funding from the CWDC which, from 1 April 2012, would become part of the Teaching Regulation Agency.

The impact of a range of policies, reforms and initiatives regarding the workforce has led to changes in qualifications and training within the sector. More changes in policy were to come. For example, in 2013 the *More Great Childcare* report was published which announced planned reforms to raise standards in the sector through the introduction of 'new' qualifications such as the Early Years Teachers Status (EYTS) replacing the previous qualification (Early Years Professional Status), the Teacher's Standards (Early Years) and an increase in funding for the two-year-olds that were eligible.

During this period early childhood education saw reviews on the policies, curriculum and qualifications of the people working in the sector. Following the elections in May 2015, the Conservative party formed its government and introduced an Extended Entitlement of around 40 per cent for all two-year-old children, with further revisions of qualifications.

Hevey (2017, p.4) describes the situation:

> *Politically the UK has been undergoing a period of gradual change over the last 30 years with increasing devolution of responsibilities to its four constituent nations. Governance of ECEC services is amongst the devolved matters. This has resulted in increasing divergence between education, social services, policies and systems, including provision and regulation of services for young children and their families. The picture of the ECEC workforce across the UK is confused and confusing. Devolution has resulted in increasing divergence in policies across the four nations, each leading to a different set of problems and anomalies.*

Currently the UK policy context has left early childhood education with patchy provision, with national standards, statutory in some cases as in England with the Early Years Foundation Stage (EYFS) or through guidance of minimum standards for curriculum and qualifications. Due to the diversity of ECEC policy in each nation, currently the core qualifications across the UK require a level 4 EQF/level 3 ISCED for practitioners to work in early childhood education and each nation has developed its own curricular frameworks as will be shown below. In terms of curriculum in the four countries of the UK, the overall picture is illustrated in Table 1.2 and each is discussed in further detail below.

Table 1.2   The curriculum: national picture in the UK

Country	Curriculum	Assessment
England	Early Years Foundation Stage (birth to 5 years)	Statutory:
		Progress check at age two
		Reception Baseline Assessment (currently at piloting stage – to be introduced as statutory in 2020)
		EYFS Profile (EYPS at the age of five)
Wales	Foundation Phase 3–7 years	Statutory: Baseline Assessment
		Foundation Stage Profile (3 years up to the end of Phase in Year 2)
Scotland	Pre-birth to 3: Positive Outcomes for Scotland's Children and Families	Non-statutory requirements
	Curriculum for Excellence (for children 3–5)	
Northern Ireland	Learning to Learn Framework (0–6 years)	Non-statutory requirements

The curriculum in the UK

Before the role of observation in early childhood education curricula is discussed providing examples from international perspectives, it is important to examine the four countries within the UK and their curricular approaches so that an understanding of how observations fit in the curriculum are developed while the observation methods are discussed. As will be stressed elsewhere in the book, observation is a valuable tool and an essential part of any curriculum in early childhood education. In the UK context, the first attempt to regulate and raise standards and quality came with the introduction of the *Nursery Education: Desirable Outcomes for Children's Learning on Entering Compulsory Education* (SCAA, 1996) that set out six goals related to learning areas. This was soon replaced by the *Curriculum Guidance for the Foundation Stage* (QCA/DfEE, 2000), where it was recognised that in early childhood play is central for children's learning and promoted the idea of a children-centred approach. Following political devolution in the late 1990s to the four countries of the UK, England, Northern Ireland, Scotland and Wales all have a different educational policy and curricula. However, one of the key elements that underpins the curriculum in all four countries is the importance and necessity of observation as a tool to understand children at two levels: first, to be able to assess children's progress and development; and second, for practitioners to be able to provide experiences that will promote children's learning and development after gathering information though observation.

England: Early Years Foundation Stage

In England since 2008 all settings hosting children from birth to five have had to implement the Early Years Foundation Stage (EYFS) (DfE, 2017). Although much of the critique that EYFS is evolving around children's *school readiness* and assessment focusing on measuring children by promoting a set of knowledge and skills that children should acquire as the *right foundation for good future progress through school and life* (p.5), the role of observation remains valuable.

The EYFS's vision is to provide:

> • *quality and consistency in all early years settings, so that every child makes good progress and no child gets left behind*
> • *a secure foundation through learning and development opportunities which are planned around the needs and interests of each individual child and are assessed and reviewed regularly*
> • *partnership working between practitioners and with parents and/or carers*
> • *equality of opportunity and anti-discriminatory practice, ensuring that every child is included and supported.*
>
> (p.5)

It places value on practitioners' skills to be able to reflect on the diverse ways children learn, but equally to be able to reflect on their own practice. It describes three key characteristics of effective teaching and learning:

> • *playing and exploring – children investigate and experience things, and 'have a go';*
> • *active learning – children concentrate and keep on trying if they encounter difficulties, and enjoy achievements; and*

> • *creating and thinking critically – children have and develop their own ideas, make links between ideas, and develop strategies for doing things.*
>
> (p.10)

As mentioned earlier, there are now statutory requirements for children's assessment at two key points in each child's life (progress check at two years and the EYFS profile) based on the following principles:

> *Ongoing assessment (also known as formative assessment) is an integral part of the learning and development process. It involves practitioners observing children to understand their level of achievement, interests and learning styles, and to then shape learning experiences for each child reflecting those observations. In their interactions with children, practitioners should respond to their own day-to-day observations about children's progress and observations that parents and carers share.*
>
> (p.13)

There are several polemic voices against the overemphasis of the EYFS on formal assessment that currently have increased with the planned introduction of baseline assessment and the ultimate goal of school readiness (e.g. Cowley, 2019; Bradbury, 2019; or see More Than a Score (2019) 'Four-year-olds don't need exams', *Action Network*, available at: **https://actionnetwork.org/petitions/four-year-olds-dont-need-exams**, or see the TACTYC Position Statement at **https://tactyc.org.uk/wp-content/uploads/2014/10/TACTYC-Baseline-position-paper-1.pdf**). One positive aspect, however, is that it promotes the idea that all information about children should be gathered by recording observations. Assessment of children should be based on evidence and within EYFS such evidence is to be collected by observation.

Wales: Foundation Phase Framework for Children's Learning for 3–7 year olds

The Foundation Phase Framework in Wales (Welsh Government, 2015), aims to promote, through play and hands-on experiences, seven statutory areas of learning for three to seven-year-olds:

> • *Personal and Social Development, Well-being and Cultural Diversity;*
> • *Language, Literacy and Communication Skills (revised to include the literacy component of the National Literacy and Numeracy Framework (LNF));*
> • *Mathematical Development (revised to include the numeracy competence from the LNF);*
> • *Welsh Language Development;*
>
> *(Continued)*

(Continued)

- *Knowledge and Understanding of the World;*
- *Physical Development;*
- *Creative Development.*

Personal and Social Development, Well-being and Cultural Diversity are at the heart of the Foundation Phase and should be developed across the curriculum.

(p. 8)

In the revised version of 2015 (Welsh Government, 2015), all these learning areas are described in detail and the outcomes are clearly set out. Wales has placed emphasis on the bilingual aspect within the curriculum as essential for Welsh identity and culture. As this book is being written a new curriculum is being developed which will be in place in January 2020 and used throughout Wales by 2022.

The statutory assessment arrangements for the Foundation Phase and end of Key Stages 2 and 3 document by Education Wales was published in October 2018 where it is stated:

The Foundation Phase Profile ('the profile') has been developed to support assessment of children's learning and development throughout their time in the Foundation Phase, from entry through to the end of the Foundation Phase. Through the use of observations and formative assessments, the profile supports practitioners to provide a developmentally appropriate holistic curriculum for all children. The profile contains detailed skill ladders in four of the Foundation Phase Areas of Learning that support consistent judgements against the associated Foundation Phase outcomes.

From September 2015 teachers are required to use the profile in order to carry out a statutory baseline assessment within the first six weeks of a child entering the Reception year. The profile will further support assessment through to the end of the Foundation Phase (end of Year 2).

(p. 3)

The statutory areas are Personal and Social Development, Well-being and Cultural Diversity, Language, Literacy and Communication Skills, Mathematical Development. All teachers and practitioners are required to create a Compact Profile using a scoring method for the statutory baseline assessment. At the end of the Foundation Phase there is again a statutory assessment in all four areas.

The Foundation Phase Profile should include:

Record Form – The Record Form is an optional element of the Foundation Phase Profile designed to be used by those who do not use software-based systems. The Record Forms provide a consistent structure to detail evidence of children's development.

> Compact Profile Form – The Compact Profile Form produces a snapshot of a child's development on the Foundation Phase Profile at or before the baseline assessment. It allows practitioners to produce a single outcome for each Area of Learning in the profile.
>
> Full Profile Form – The Full Profile Form produces a snapshot of a child's development using all the skill ladders within the Foundation Phase Profile. It allows practitioners to produce a single outcome for each Area of Learning, on a consistent scale aligning with the Compact Profile.
>
> (Welsh Government Foundation Phase Profile Handbook, 2017, p.4)

Key to the profile is practitioners' ability to collect evidence for each child through rigorous observations in order to complete the three stages of the Profile. *Evidence of children's skills within the profile should be sourced across all Areas of Learning. There is no set method of recording observations for the Foundation Phase Profile* (p.8). However, the handbook provides the diagram given in Figure 1.1 to assist practitioners in the assessment process.

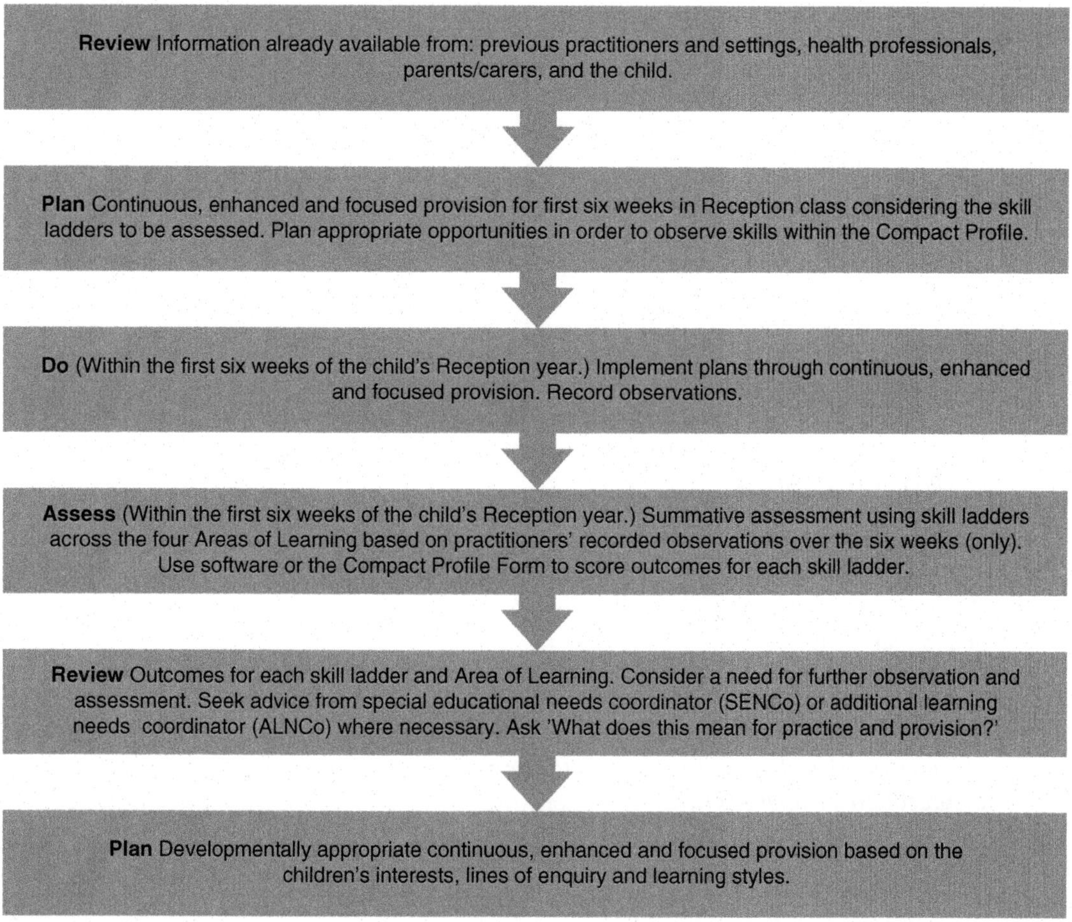

Review Information already available from: previous practitioners and settings, health professionals, parents/carers, and the child.

Plan Continuous, enhanced and focused provision for first six weeks in Reception class considering the skill ladders to be assessed. Plan appropriate opportunities in order to observe skills within the Compact Profile.

Do (Within the first six weeks of the child's Reception year.) Implement plans through continuous, enhanced and focused provision. Record observations.

Assess (Within the first six weeks of the child's Reception year.) Summative assessment using skill ladders across the four Areas of Learning based on practitioners' recorded observations over the six weeks (only). Use software or the Compact Profile Form to score outcomes for each skill ladder.

Review Outcomes for each skill ladder and Area of Learning. Consider a need for further observation and assessment. Seek advice from special educational needs coordinator (SENCo) or additional learning needs coordinator (ALNCo) where necessary. Ask 'What does this mean for practice and provision?'

Plan Developmentally appropriate continuous, enhanced and focused provision based on the children's interests, lines of enquiry and learning styles.

Figure 1.1   Foundation Stage Assessment Process (Welsh Government, 2017, p.7)

The handbook includes a section that emphasises the importance of using observations in a systematic way in order for practitioners to be able to engage in formative and summative assessment of children:

> *Observation plays a key role in the everyday practice in the Foundation Phase. The main purposes of observing children are to determine where they are on the learning continuum in order to progress them, and to identify any difficulties or exceptional ability. Through observing and listening, practitioners are able to gather evidence before and after children have been taught skills and over a period of time. This enables practitioners to assess how much progress the children have made and whether they need further opportunities to consolidate their learning.*
>
> (p. 10)

Scotland: The Curriculum for Excellence

In 2014 Scotland, reflecting on the UNCRC principles, introduced the Children and Young People (Scotland) Act where the term 'early learning and childcare' (ELC) was used as a generic term to include the full range of early childhood education and care that exists in Scotland. According to Education in Scotland, the country aims to increase the hours of ELC for entitled children from 600 to 1,400 by 2020 and at the time of writing this has already started. Key documents are:

- *The Early Years Framework* (2008) sets out a vision for early years services in Scotland to ensure that children get 'the best start in life'.
- *Building the Ambition* (2014) is national practice guidance for all those delivering early learning and childcare to babies, toddlers and young children.
- *Pre-Birth to Three: Positive Outcomes for Scotland's Children and Families* is national guidance to support practitioners and students working with babies and toddlers aged 0–3 and their families.
- *Curriculum for Excellence* (CfE) builds on the solid foundations developed in the critical years pre-birth to three. Within CfE, children are entitled to a broad general education from age three. The early level of CfE for most children spans the period of time from age three until the end of Primary 1. It supports a smooth transition in learning between ELC and primary school.
- *How good is our early learning and childcare?* (2016) provides a suite of quality indicators. These support staff to look inwards, to scrutinise their work and evaluate what is working well for babies, toddlers and young children, and what could be better. The framework is designed to be used to support self-evaluation for self-improvement by practitioners at all levels.

(From **https://education.gov.scot/scottish-education-system/Early%20learning%20 and%20childcare%20(ELC)**)

The vision for early childhood is clearly stated in the Early Years Framework in a way that reflects directly the UNCRC:

> *Children and families are valued and respected at all levels in our society and have the right to have their voices sought, heard and acted upon by all those who support them and who provide services to help them. (Article 12 of UNCRC)*
>
> *Children with disabilities and from minority communities have their individual needs recognised and responded to. (Articles 2 and 23)*
>
> *Children grow up free from poverty in their early years and have their outcomes defined by their ability and potential rather than their family background. (Article 27)*
>
> *Children have good infant nutrition and a healthy diet. (Article 24)*
>
> *Children are not harmed by alcohol, tobacco or drugs during pregnancy.*
>
> *Children have a safe and warm place to stay. (Articles 19 and 20)*
>
> *Every child fulfils their potential as a successful learner, confident individual, effective contributor and responsible citizen. Every child has access to world-class learning and healthcare services that meet their individual needs and which promote resilience and wellbeing. (Articles 24, 28 and 29)*
>
> *Children have safe, stable, stimulating and nurturing relationships with parents that develop resilience and a sense of security and trust in the relationship. Where birth parents are unable to provide those conditions, children are entitled to expect the state to move swiftly to address these needs, including alternative care that fulfils these requirements. (Articles 3, 5, 19 and 20)*
>
> *Children and families are given the support they need to help them build resilience and confidence about dealing with their problems themselves, wherever this is possible, and to have the confidence to approach services for help where this is needed.*
>
> *Young children are protected from harm and have their rights respected. Children have their welfare put at the centre of decisions made by parents and services, including adult and community services. (Articles 3, 4, 12 and 19)*
>
> *Children are entitled to take part in physical activities and to play, including outdoors, and have an opportunity to experience and judge and manage risk. (Article 31)*
>
> (pp.10–11)

The Curriculum for Excellence has two key priorities: firstly it aims to offer all children the best possible *progression in literacy, numeracy and health and well being* and, secondly, to close the attainment gap (Education Scotland Curriculum for Excellence, 2016, p.1). The aims of the curriculum are to develop the knowledge, skills, attributes and capabilities of the four capacities as outlined in Figure 1.2.

successful learners	confident individuals	responsible citizens	effective contributors
attributes	**attributes**	**attributes**	**attributes**
• enthusiasm and motivation for learning • determination to reach high standards of achievement • openness to new thinking and ideas	• self-respect • a sense of physical, mental and emotional well-being • secure values and beliefs • ambition	• respect for others • commitment to participate responsibly in political, economic, social and cultural life	• an enterprising attitude • resilience • self-reliance
capabilities	**capabilities**	**capabilities**	**capabilities**
• use literacy, communication and numeracy skills • use technology for learning • think creatively and independently • learn independently and as part of a group • make reasoned evaluations • link and apply different kinds of learning in new situations.	• relate to others and manage themselves • pursue a healthy and active lifestyle • be self-aware • develop and communicate their own beliefs and view of the world • live as independently as they can • assess risk and make informed decisions • achieve success in different areas of activity.	• develop knowledge and understanding of the world and Scotland's place in it • understand different beliefs and cultures • make informed choices and decisions • evaluate environmental, scientific and technological issues • develop informed, ethical views of complex issues.	• communicate in different ways and in different settings • work in partnership and in teams • take the initiative and lead • apply critical thinking in new contexts • create and develop • solve problems

Figure 1.2

(*Source*: **https://education.gov.scot/scottish-education-system/policy-for-scottish-education/policy-drivers/cfe-%28building-from-the-statement-appendix-incl-btc1-5%29/The%20purpose%20of%20the%20curriculum**)

Although Scotland has introduced standardised assessment for children starting primary education in literacy and numeracy (see **https://standardisedassessment.gov.scot/**), unlike England and Wales which have introduced statutory assessments in early childhood education, the Scottish curriculum has introduced guidance materials to support teachers and practitioners with planning learning, teaching and assessment. It is stated that assessment should be integral to learning and teaching and is an ongoing process. It advises teachers and practitioners to use a range of evidence to plan next steps in learning.

Assessment is used in a way that will achieve the coherence of children's experiences, learning outcomes and teaching practices across the sector. The emphasis is on children's progress and identifying ways forward for the child's learning and progress. Engagement of children with learning and personalisation of intended learning outcomes are key to the assessment process. Consequently, focus is placed on personalised feedback.

The purposes of assessment are to:

- *support learning that develops the knowledge and understanding, skills, attributes and capabilities which contribute to the four capacities;*
- *give assurance to parents, children themselves and others, that children and young people are progressing in their learning and developing in line with expectations;*

> • *provide a summary of what learners have achieved, including through qualifications and awards;*
> • *contribute to planning the next stages of learning and help learners progress to further education, higher education and employment;*
> • *inform future improvements in learning and teaching.*
>
> (Scottish Government, 2015, p.5)

Core to the vision of the Curriculum of Excellence is to gather rigorous information for children that will provide the quality of evidence that offers breadth and depth of children's achievements. As a result, observation is a systematic way of gathering information about children's progress and is essential in the process of assessment in Scotland.

For children under the age of three 'The Birth to Three: Positive Outcomes for Scotland's Children and Families' document, building on research-based evidence, provides guidance of what high-quality care and education should be like for the under threes. The four key principles are:

• Rights of the Child
• Relationships
• Responsive Care
• Respect.

(See **https://education.gov.scot/improvement/learning-resources/Pre-Birth %20to%20Three** for more information.) Within this document it is stated that observation, planning and assessment should be at the heart of early childhood practice which should be child-centred and value the child's voice meaningfully in the process. It is proposed that observations should be meaningful as they are the core to assessment.

Northern Ireland: Learning to Learn Framework

Similar emphasis is placed on the value of observation in the curriculum in Northern Ireland. Although pre-school education is not compulsory, the sector is regulated by the Learning to Learn Framework (DENI, 2013) which now forms part of the Foundation Stage (Walsh, 2016). It is imperative within the Learning to Learn Framework that early childhood education should

> *[embrace] a child-centred and play-based pedagogy, premised on six discrete themes, namely the arts; language development; early mathematical experiences; personal social and emotional development; physical development; and exploration of both the indoor and outdoor worlds. While the guidance recognises that children learn and develop in different ways, it emphasises the need for a programme where children get the opportunity to progress their learning and reach their full potential.*
>
> (Walsh, 2016, p.46)

The vision is to:

- *provide equitable access to high quality early years education and learning services;*
- *support personal, social and emotional development, promote positive learning dispositions and enhance language, cognitive and physical development in young children;*
- *provide a positive and nurturing early learning experience, as well as a foundation for improved educational attainment and life-long learning;*
- *identify and help address barriers to learning, and reduce the risk and impact of social exclusion and the need for later interventions; and*
- *encourage and support parents in their role as first and ongoing educators.*

(pp.17–18)

Embracing the principles of the UNCRC this framework aims to promote children's rights and the guiding principles are:

- *The early years education and learning needs of all children is the key focus of provision – the individual characteristics and needs of each child are recognised and respected and early years education and learning provision helps them develop cognitively, emotionally, physically and socially.*
- *Education and learning begins at birth – the importance of the home learning environment, and children's overall experiences from birth, in improving educational outcomes is recognised and supported through working in partnership with parents and carers as the child's first and ongoing educators.*
- *Children and their families are entitled to high quality, age appropriate early years education and learning services and opportunities – delivered in safe and inclusive environments, led by a skilled workforce, and evaluated against quality standards where the importance of play in its own right, and as a pedagogical tool is recognised.*
- *The rights of children and their families are respected – early childhood is a significant and distinct time in life and as such it should be nurtured, respected, valued and supported in its own right and for the significant foundation it provides for future and lifelong learning.*
- *Equity and inclusion are essential characteristics of quality early years education and learning – all children, regardless of their special educational needs, disabilities, gender, cultural, religious, socio-economic, or linguistic backgrounds are provided with practical, challenging activities in a stimulating environment which helps them achieve their potential.*
- *Collaborative working among the statutory, voluntary, and other relevant sectors and professional bodies will play an important part in securing improved outcomes for young children in their early years – recognising that children are provided with other opportunities to learn and develop outside funded and formal education provision (such as childminding and day care).*

(pp.19–20)

Although the Learning to Learn Framework captures the political vision of early childhood education and care across the sector in Northern Ireland and aims to become an overarching framework that meets the above principles, there are no formal statutory assessment requirements for children.

In the Learning to Learn document the skills that practitioners should develop to raise the standards in are described in detail. Examining the vision of DENI for early childhood education it is evident that in-depth knowledge of children's development and reflection on practice are key priorities for Learning to Learn. Although currently there is *no overall system for collecting, collating and managing information on funded early years education and learning services for children up to compulsory school age* (p.32), this is becoming one of the key priorities by developing a programme of continuous professional development for staff, aiming to promote multi-disciplinary and multi-agency working, together with good communication and information sharing.

Similar to Scotland, assessment is not statutory. The Curricular Guidance for Pre-School Education (2018) offers guidelines for staff in early childhood education in terms of which aspects of development and learning areas they should collect observations.

- *observe children over a period of time and in a variety of contexts;*
- *adopt a flexible approach to observations that allows for the unpredictable reactions of children to the activities offered (this provides some of the most detailed insights into each child as an individual);*
- *record both planned and spontaneous observations;*
- *observe the children's play and use of language so that a holistic and accurate picture emerges of each child's progress across each of the six Areas of Learning;*
- *record this information regularly and systematically, including details on each child's strengths, interests and areas for development;*
- *reflect together on their observations to inform future planning; and*
- *share information with parents/guardians/carers so they have a clear understanding of their child's progress.*

(pp.8-9)

ACTIVITY 1.4

Comparing curricula

With the help of the following web pages examine the assessment requirements in each curricular approach and discuss the following:

1. The role of observation.
2. How observation is used to inform the assessment process.
3. What the learning areas are in each curriculum, and whether you can identify any differences or similarities.

England early childhood provision: **https://www.gov.uk/early-years-foundation-stage**

Wales early childhood provision: **https://gov.wales/foundation-phase-framework**

(Continued)

(Continued)

Scotland early childhood provision: **https://education.gov.scot/scottish-education-system/ policy-for-scottish-education/policy-drivers/cfe-(building-from-the-statement-appendix- incl-btc1-5)/What%20is%20Curriculum%20for%20Excellence**

Northern Ireland early childhood provision: **https://www.education-ni.gov.uk/articles/learning-learn**

SUMMARY

As can be seen from the four curricular approaches in terms of their requirements for assessment and evaluation of children's progress, development and learning as well as for the collection of rigorous evidence to inform practice, the early childhood education practitioner should be skilled in collecting systematic information in order to provide rigorous portraits of children and to evaluate practice. Thus it is increasingly important that practitioners develop skills to observe children in a systematic way.

This chapter has shown how educational policy can impact on your daily routine and the role of observation in early childhood is used for assessment processes. Whether you work with an educational policy framework where there are statutory standardised requirements or more flexible approaches to assessment, as it has been shown in the UK context, in all of these skilful observations are required.

The next chapter will demonstrate how the pedagogy of early childhood has been influenced by socio-constructions of childhood, philosophical ideas, psychology and the role of observation.

Further Reading

For more information on early childhood policy:

Fitzgerald, D and Kay, J (2016) *Understanding Early Years Policy* (4th edn). London: Sage.

To further your understanding on how policy impacts on on the qualifications of early childhood practitioners in England:

Osgood, J, Elwick, A, Robertson, L, Sakr, M and Wilson, D (2017) Early Years Teacher and Early Years Educator: a scoping study of the impact, experiences and associated issues of recent early years qualifications and training in England. Available online at: **http://tactyc.org.uk/research/**

Websites

For an overview of early childhood education and care across thirty countries visit: **http://www. seepro.eu/English/Home.htm**

These are comprehensive reports for thirty countries in Europe which summarise the key issues in terms of workforce profiles and systems in early childhood education and care.

CHAPTER 2

OBSERVATION AND PEDAGOGY

Chapter objectives

Research into the literature on the subject shows that the term 'pedagogy' is a complex one and extends beyond the narrow approaches of teaching and learning. After reading this chapter, you should be able to consider:

- the child in context and how this influences early childhood pedagogy;
- key philosophical ideas and their impact on pedagogy;
- key developmental theories and how they impact on pedagogy;
- the key differences between pedagogy and curriculum and be able to reflect on both in your own context;
- the role of observation in pedagogy.

Introduction: Towards a discussion on pedagogy

This chapter highlights a number of issues that impact on pedagogy in early childhood education. Any discussion about the nature of pedagogy is a complex one for it is a term which is difficult to define and writers have offered a variety of different definitions and explanations about pedagogy, depending on the context, the policy, classroom teaching and practice, teaching styles and learning styles. Alexander (2004a), for example, views pedagogy as an act and discourse of the teaching process while the British Educational

Research Association (BERA) Early Years Special Interest Group concluded that *there is an overemphasis on teaching content, rather than on the process of pedagogy, with particular pressures for performance* (2003, p.13) and stress the centrality of play as a key priority in pedagogy in early childhood.

The term pedagogy is used broadly to describe a

discipline [that] extends to the consideration of the development of health and bodily fitness, social and moral welfare, ethics and aesthetics, as well as to the institutional forms that serve to facilitate society's and the individual's pedagogic aims.

(Marton and Booth, 1997, p.178)

In the twenty-first century, learning environments have changed and they are now concerned not only with teachers, but also with learners. They are also concerned with families, policy reforms and a number of other services such as health, social work and local and national global issues: the ecology of the community (Male and Palaiologou, 2012).

Effective education settings are those which have developed productive and synergistic relationships between learners, families, the team and the community, because the context, the locality and the culture in which learners live are vitally important.

(Male and Palaiologou, 2012, p.112)

In other words, pedagogy no longer occurs in isolation or solely in educational environments: it is part of a wider socio-economic, political, philosophical, psychological and educational dialogue. This view is reflected in the definition provided by UNESCO (2016) in the Documentation of Innovative Pedagogical Approaches and Tools in Early Childhood Care and Education (ECCE) initiative:

Pedagogy is not simply the 'act of teaching' but instead is the 'act of teaching' as informed by the ideas, values and beliefs which sustain and motivate it. Pedagogy is also praxical – in that it aims to produce skills, knowledge structures or ways of thinking which will enable people to participate in, and transform their current and future lives.

(p.6)

Consequently, you need to seek an in-depth understanding of these relationships in order to be able to discuss the pedagogy of early childhood. However, there is a need to acknowledge that this dialogue will never be complete, *stable and finalised as there is no final point of permanent and perfect equilibrium* (Dahlberg and Moss, 2010, p.xix) in any discussion about pedagogy. It is therefore relevant to this chapter to engage with socio-constructions of childhood and philosophical and psychological ideas to gain a broader understanding of those factors which influence pedagogy.

Engaging socio-constructions of childhood in pedagogy

In recent years, research in the field of child development has become increasingly concerned with applying its knowledge base to the educational environment and in creating a pedagogy for children. Now we know much more than ever about the family, the school and the community contexts that foster the development of physically, emotionally and socially healthy, cognitively competent children. More than ever children are actively involved in the decision-making processes and assessments that influence their lives and experiences.

The way societies perceive childhood impacts upon our approaches to and views of children. The early childhood policy services and curricula reflect current perspectives of the child within society and therefore inform our pedagogy, as mentioned above. In examining the social construction of childhood, there are many different readings about children that influence early childhood practice. In an earlier study, Hendrick (1997), examining the social constructions of childhood in Britain since the end of the eighteenth century, suggests nine views of childhood, reflecting the socio-economic, theological, political and historical changes within British society:

- the natural child;
- the romantic child;
- the evangelical child;
- the child as child;
- the schooled child;
- the 'child-study' child;
- children of the nation;
- the psychological child;
- the child of the welfare state.

Mills and Mills (2000), in a review of the literature on perspectives of childhood, suggest that there are several more possible views of childhood:

- *Children as innocent* – representing the theological construct that children are a force for good and that there is a need to protect them.
- *Children as apprentice* – concerning children's need for training in order to achieve adulthood (they are viewed as potential adults).
- *Children as persons in their own right* – mainly a view that emerged from the United Nations Convention on the Rights of the Child (UNCRC, 1989). It is about children as people with rights and responsibilities. Within this view children can be viewed as fully social beings, capable of acting in the social world and of creating and sustaining their own culture (Waksler, 1991, p.23).
- *Children as members of a distinct group* – a similar view to children as persons in their own right (which was first established by the United Nations):

> *The child, for the full and harmonious development of his personality, needs love and understanding. S/he shall, wherever possible, grow up in the care and under the responsibility of his parents and in any case in an atmosphere of affection and moral and material security; a child of tender years shall not, save in exceptional circumstances, be separated from his mother.*
>
> (United Nations, 1959, p.198)

- *Children as vulnerable* – children are more vulnerable to playground bullying, domestic violence, sexual abuse, consumerist advertising, exploitations of childlike innocence and racial harassment.
- *Children as animals* – a view that relates to the biological development of children and which accepts that, as all animals go through biological development before they are fully mature, so the same happens to children.

For those working with young children these constructions of childhood might be seen as philosophical and abstract, but how we view our activities with young children, how we attempt to meet goals with those children and how we seek purposeful and meaningful directions in our practice are formed from our views of childhood and impact on what pedagogy means to our context and subsequently influences the interactions that we have with them.

In the following paragraphs, an overview of the dominant perspectives of childhood is presented to help you reflect on your own views of childhood which might in turn influence your views about pedagogy and practice.

The innocent child

The view of the child as innocent and consequently in need of protection from the evils of society is a view that was derived from Rousseau's philosophical ideas of childhood and was reinforced by theological considerations. Within this idea the child is viewed as being in need of protection and also as representing a force for good. Adults are to take responsibility to ensure that the child is raised outside of the 'evil' influence of society.

Preparing the child for adulthood

This is the view of the child as an apprentice, in which the child is being trained in order to be prepared for adult life and to become a responsible adult. There is an emphasis on training for the child which might include social skills, communication skills and vocational education. This view is reflected in several curricular approaches in the UK, where early childhood education is perceived as a preparation for formal schooling. For example, in the EYFS there is an emphasis on preparing children to be ready for school – placing priority on structured formal activities aiming at the literacy, numeracy and socialisation skills required for effective integration into formal schooling.

The socially active child

This is the view of the child as a social person, capable of creating and sustaining their own culture. An extended view of this is of the child as a member of a distinct group and implies that the child needs a loving and secure environment to develop personally, socially and emotionally. When a child grows up in care, for example, this needs to be in an environment where there are conditions for affection and for moral and material security. This view was illustrated and emphasised, as was shown previously, in the United Nations Declaration of the Rights of the Child 1959 which focused on the harmonious and holistic development of the child alongside the need for an affectionate social environment.

It was not until 1989 that this was fully embraced by the UNCRC, and in June 1994 it was further advanced by the Salamanca Statement of the UNCRC World Conference. The UNCRC lays out rights according to the special needs and situations of children and covers the whole range of economic, civil, political, social and cultural rights, stressing that these rights have to be actively promoted and placing an obligation on governments to do this. It has changed the way children are seen and has moved away from stereotypical views of them as incompetent, powerless and the property of parents and has placed emphasis on children's rights to be consulted, participate and entitled to their views and opinions (voices). Children now are seen as competent to participate in all levels of life and express their opinions.

The developmental child

This is the view of the child from a developmental perspective, where he or she passes through stages, for example the psychological stages in Piagetian theory or psychoanalytical stages. The field of psychology determines the view of the developmental child where, traditionally, education seeks to further its understanding of children. Moreover, early childhood education has been based on developmental views of how children learn. This is a view that is mirrored in curricular approaches as outcomes are related to the development of children such as language, physical development and cognitive development.

The child in need of protection (or the child as potential victim)

The child is viewed as being in need of protection and is vulnerable, reflecting a view of the child as a potential victim. An examination of current policies regarding safeguarding children shows there is an emphasis on protecting them from harm, keeping them safe and promoting their well-being. Thus policies and services are in place in case the child needs protection. This view reflects on issues such as playground bullying, domestic violence, sexual abuse, consumerist advertising, the exploitation of childlike innocence, racial harassment and radicalisation. The vulnerability of children can be seen in times of war or conflict, for example, where they suffer consequences such as losing parents, witnessing or experiencing violence, famine, and lack of safety and security, or are deprived of basic human rights and become refugees, sometimes in hostile countries.

The 'modern' child

This view is dominant in western cultures. Children are seen as socially active citizens with a shift from the non-participant child to one who is a social actor, who enacts agency and is capable of participating in activities involving them. Consequently, listening to children's voices has become an essential aspect of daily life.

This social construct places an emphasis on the 'today' child – children are viewed *as individual human beings and holders of rights who are actively involved in gaining and enjoying their rights [...] so [...] children are placed in the position of 'knower'* (Palaiologou, 2012a, p.1) rather than the child to be, contrasting traditional and mainly developmental views that children can achieve targets when they are developmentally ready.

The digital/multimodal child

In the twenty-first century research has made it evident that children from a very young age are using digital devices and are competent users of technology, develop multimodal literacies and digital play is part of their lives (e.g. Marsh et al., 2016; Edwards and Bird, 2017; Fleer, 2017; Yelland and Gilbert, 2017; Yelland, 2018). Research shows that children from a young age move between digital and non-digital activities engaging *in knowledge exchange and the co-creation of new pedagogies and learning environments, including the development of digital tools and solutions that offer children avenues for digital learning* (Marsh et al. 2017, p. 6) in order to *enhance every young person's digital literacies in meaningful, authentic and consequential ways* (Kumpulainen, 2017, p.13). Although there is evidence to show that children in this current era live in digital landscapes and make use of all available materials, there is still much debate on the role of digital play and to what extent digitalisation has a role in early childhood education and, if so, how pedagogical practices can become multimodal to support the digital/multimodal child.

Summary

As early childhood and care are not isolated from the wider cultural and social context of our views of childhood, pedagogy is influenced by our views. As there is a plethora of views on childhood, it is not the same for everyone and is defined and explained differently in each discipline, culture and society. In that sense how we perceive childhood forms our views on pedagogy. Consequently, policy and curricula are determined by our notions of childhood and reflect these views. Table 2.1 summarises the traditional and emerging views of childhood.

Table 2.1   Summary of dominant views of children

Traditional views	Emerging views
Children are incapable and dependent, powerless	Children are capable, independent, powerful
Children are not able to make decisions or understand fully the work due to immaturity	Children are active citizens, decision-makers, contribute ideas
Children are in a stage of becoming . . .	Children as part of human life, able to contribute to the culture, society
Children are to be seen and not to be heard	Children have the right to voice and can be involved; whatever their age, they have valuable views
Childhood is a phase	Children as 'knowers'

Engaging philosophical ideas in pedagogy

The field of education has been influenced by a number of philosophers and thinkers (see the Theory Focus box in Table 2.2 below). These writers have been influential in questioning the purpose (why?), the nature (what?), the type (how?) and the recipients (for whom?) of education.

THEORY FOCUS

Influential thinkers in education

Table 2.2   Influential thinkers in education

Thinkers in education	Key ideas
Johann Heinrich Pestalozzi (1746–1827)	Pestalozzi promoted the idea of social justice and was one of the first thinkers to emphasise education based on psychological methods of instruction. He placed emphasis on spontaneity and self-activity. He believed that children should not be given ready-made answers but should arrive at answers themselves. He promoted the idea of education for the whole child and developed the 'Pestalozzi method', which is based on balancing three elements – hands, heart and head.
Friedrich Froebel (1782–1852)	Froebel was one of the first thinkers to promote the idea that children's early experiences in life are important in a child's development and education. He introduced the first kindergarten in Germany where self-activity, play and child-initiated experiences were promoted. His philosophy was underpinned by key principles such as respect, emphasis on play and hands-on experiences, creativity, freedom and guidance, outdoors play, respectful communities and valued educators.
John Dewey (1859–1952)	Dewey promoted the idea that education and learning are social and interactive processes. Consequently, schools were viewed as social institutions through which social reform can and should take place. He also promoted the idea of ownership of the curriculum by learners and that all learners are entitled to be part of their own learning. Key terms in Dewey's work are Democracy and Ethics. He strongly emphasised the role of education as one of creating a place in which to learn how to live: *to prepare him [the student] for the future life means to give him command of himself; it means so to train him that he will have the full and ready use of all his capacities* (1897, p.6).
Maria Montessori (1870–1952)	Montessori took the view that all children are competent beings and, with the support of the environment (child-sized environment-microcosm), children can be encouraged to achieve maximal potential. Emphasis on *absorbent mind* and critical periods where, with the support of self-correcting auto-didactic materials, children from a young age can be helped to achieve their potential.
Susan Isaacs (1885–1948)	Heavily influenced by the psychoanalytical school of thought, Isaacs promoted the idea of children's freedom in the classroom – and play as a method of expressing themselves and mastering the world through discovery.

(Continued)

Table 2.2 (Continued)

Thinkers in education	Key ideas
Ludwig Wittgenstein (1889–1951)	Introduced a new way of thinking in philosophy, opposing the traditional philosophical approaches to dialogue. He was interested in language and how humans use language and experience. He used dialogue as a form of investigation and focused on how to pursue a question, how knowledge is learned and how it should be taught.
Carl Rogers (1902–1987)	Rejected the psychoanalytical approaches and placed the self rather than unconscious drives as a key element in personality formation through self-understanding and self-actualisation. He introduced a phenomenological approach which he called client-centred and then person-centred therapy. His ideas about education were derived from his belief that education should be about self-improvement and self-actualisation.
Jerome Seymour Bruner (1915–2016)	Bruner introduced three dominant views: • seeing children as imitative learners: the acquisition of 'know-how' (apprenticeship); • seeing children as learning from didactic exposure: the acquisition of propositional knowledge; • seeing children as thinkers: the development of inter-subjective interchange – pedagogy is to help the child understand better, more powerfully, less one-sided (Bruner, 1996, pp.53–61) He contributed to education the view that children of any age are able to understand complex information if this is done via a spiral curriculum where children discover the information (discovery learning) rather than being taught by the teacher.
Paolo Freire (1921–97)	Viewed education as a form of social inclusion and all his life promoted the idea that it should not reverse the reproduction of the forms of exclusion that are mirrored in society. He viewed the teachers' role as important inside, but also outside the classroom. He promoted the idea of teachers as agents of ethical and political meanings and believed that teachers should show respect for their students and their knowledge.
Jean-François Lyotard (1924–98)	Promoted the idea that the role of education is not to arrive at a unity of agreed knowledge but to celebrate differences, plurality and diversity. He criticised government agendas of *performativity* in education and objected to target/outcome-driven education.

Thinkers in education	Key ideas
Basil Bernstein (1925–2000)	Bernstein did much work on language and social class and introduced the idea of social coding systems in education. He examined the role of social classes in relation to pedagogy and schooling and concluded that working-class children are excluded from formal education as the language used in the curriculum cannot be followed by them.
Gilles Deleuze (1925–95)	Promoted the idea of practice theory and that individuals can only change themselves within practice. He believed that in order to make a difference in education, teaching and learning should be collaborative actions which can lead to change. He introduced the term *assemblage* which is a flexible unit of social organisation and depends on learning.
Michel Foucault (1926–84)	Foucault was concerned with the search for how human beings can develop critical thought to exist as rational beings. He examined the nature of knowledge in relation to education, economy and politics. He contributed to educational thought and provided theoretical and methodological ways to study the field, focusing on the relations of power and knowledge.
Ivan Illich (1926–2002)	Promoted radical humanistic ideals and *consciously secular ideology* as a way of planning and attempting *inventive solutions to social problems* (1970). He viewed education outside formal schooling: *educational function was already emigrating from the schools and [. . .] increasingly, other forms of compulsory learning would be instituted in modern society* (1970, p.70).
Lawrence Kohlberg (1927–1987)	Kohlberg was concerned with moral development and believed it could not be separated from cognitive development. He thought cognitive and moral development developed through levels with each level divided into three stages.
Jürgen Habermas (1929–)	Proposed critical theory as an underpinning ideology for education. He introduced a method of ideology critique with four stages. He claimed that although ideology is theoretical, it directly applies to practice. The methodology suggested by his critical theory is action research. He introduced eight principles for teaching techniques and promoted the idea that teachers should take into account and work with and on the experiences that learners encounter in the pedagogical act.
Pierre Bourdieu (1930–2002)	Promoted the idea of reflexivity in human sciences (epistemic reflexivity) and coined the concept of epistemic individuals. Key concepts in his work are *habitus* (how individuals acquire mental structures which determine their views and behaviours) and social strategies (how individuals engage themselves with beliefs and act upon them).

(Continued)

Table 2.2   (Continued)

Thinkers in education	Key ideas
Jacques Derrida (1930–2004)	He advocated that the role of education is to test questions and education is about experiencing, trying our real ideas and dealing with authentic problems. He showed this process as the only way to improve ideas.
John White (1934–)	Debated the notion of the aim of education and believed in personal responsibility and the autonomy of the learner. He promoted the idea of a curriculum that cultivates learner autonomy.
Henry Giroux (1943–)	Viewed schools as places for cultural production and transformation rather than reproduction of knowledge. He promoted the idea that the role of education is to enable emancipatory citizenship and that pedagogical activity is political activity. In that sense he claimed that pedagogy is about questioning the nature, content and purpose of schooling. As a result, he coined the term *critical pedagogy* and described the principles that underpin it. He viewed educators as transformative intellectuals who raise awareness among their learners and said their teaching and learning activities are political.

Summary

To summarise, philosophical thinking has contributed to the discussion by emphasising that pedagogy and education should:

- be based on rigorous research;
- be characterised by critique on inputs (policy, curriculum, pedagogy) and outputs (learning, outcomes);
- not be about the 'one size fits all' conceptual framing of education (Cole, 2011), but should deal with actions justified by the dynamics of the ecology of the community of learning (Palaiologou, 2011);
- be characterised by the responsible exercise of academic judgement;
- not reinforce a distinction between theory and practice, but should be concerned with the nature of knowledge and how it is acquired;

We [should] conceptualise pedagogy as a branch of professional/practical knowledge which is constructed in situated action in dialogue with theories and beliefs, values and principles. Pedagogy is seen as an 'ambiguous' space, not of one-between-two (theory and practice), but as one-between-three (actions, theories, beliefs) in an interactive, constantly renewed triangulation.

(Formoshino and Pascal, 2015, p.xxi)

Although all these thinkers discussed the issues in general, one can see the applicability in early childhood pedagogy and education. On the one hand, the workforce needs to meet government agendas (such as EYFS) which are based on Principles (official approach), Standards (fixed and limited), Learning and Developmental Goals (developmental approach) and Universal Assessment (as a means of measurement, evaluation, inspection), which has led to reporting 'what to do' rather than actually 'doing'. Practitioners attend extensive training on 'how to do', putting aside the 'known being' which is the essential element in the construction of effective pedagogy. It is argued that while the current policy context in England (the EYFS) in which early childhood education is situated is both exciting and challenging, it remains imperative that practitioners rise to the challenge of critically reflecting on how they are positioned, how they seek to position themselves and to construct effective practitioner identities. In other words, how practitioners will embark upon a search for effective pedagogy is important.

ACTIVITY 2.1

The 'wise' practitioner

Reflecting on the following quote, in your view, who is the 'wise' practitioner in early childhood? What skills do you think a practitioner should have?

> *The wise practitioner is the one who can draw upon and add to a wise set of knowledge, can use that knowledge and professional experience to deliberate about and reflect upon practice, and one who can act wisely within educational situations by relying on a growing and deepening understanding of what it means to teach and be a teacher.*

(Feldman, 1997, p.758)

Engaging psychological theories in pedagogy

The following paragraphs discuss the dominant psychological theories in the field of child development and learning and the role of observation in each theory.

Psychoanalytical theory

The psychoanalytical theory is dominated by the work of two main theorists: Sigmund Freud and Erik Erikson. Both are widely read and influence the way that we think about children today.

Sigmund Freud's theory challenged the view of the child as innocent, provoking a debate about children's experiences and how these subsequently shape children's personalities. The main emphasis in Freud's theory was placed on development being driven by aggressive and sexual instincts (Freud, 1923, 1933). He developed a theory that formulated different stages of psychosexual development. Freud (1964) believed that sex is the most important instinct in human development. In his view the different activities that a baby does – such as sucking the thumb or a child breaking rules – are activities that relate to the child's psychosexual development. Freud did not view sex in childhood from an erotic perspective; instead he believed that when children develop and move through different stages, the focus of the sex instinct is moving in different parts of their bodies. Thus Freud's *stages* are related to parts of the human body.

He suggested that children move through five stages during which three components of personality are developed: the *id*, *ego* and *superego*. When babies are born the *id* is already present and helps the newborn to satisfy basic biological needs. For example, when a baby is hungry, he or she cries for food. The ego is related to consciousness and reflects the child's ability to learn, reason and remember. When a baby is hungry, for example, he or she can remember how to receive food. The final component of personality is the *superego* which starts developing in their third year. The *superego* is related to moral values and is the internalisation of these moral values and received rules (Freud, 1933).

Erik Erikson was a Freudian student who did not agree with Freud's emphasis on the sexual instinct. He modified Freud's theory by also taking into consideration the environment in which that children grow up. Erikson (1963, 1982) introduced the idea of cultural and social influences upon human development and suggested children must cope with *social realities* to develop appropriate patterns of behaviour. He placed an important role on the social environment and suggested eight stages of psychosocial development. He believed (1963) that human beings develop through eight *crises* (or psychosocial stages) during their lives. Each of these stages is related to biological development and to social and cultural interactions at certain times.

Both Freud and Erikson offered us a detailed account of children's personal, social and emotional development. In the field of developmental psychology the psychoanalytical theory was criticised as limited in terms of suitably explaining a child's development and learning comprehensively. Although both theorists had a significant influence on the study of children's development (Tyson and Taylor, 1990), they do not offer us an adequate explanation of *how* and *why* this development takes place (Shaffer and Kipp, 2007).

Psychoanalysis and observation

Observation in psychoanalysis is central and it can safely be said that within this field of psychology the observation of infants was first introduced as a result of the pioneering work of Bick (1964) in the field of observation study, especially infants in family contexts. Bick proposed in 'Notes on Infant Observation in Psycho-analytic Training' (1964) that observations of infants should be integrated into the curriculum for young children as a tool for enabling us to understand their development. Psychoanalysis has introduced precise observation techniques to be used in family contexts. Observers work in the natural environment of the family where they find a space to enable them to experience the interactions between infants and families without participating in any action. Afterwards, observers write the notes in a form of report that conveys their understanding of what has been observed. The field of psychoanalysis has offered us observation techniques in naturalistic environments and these are now widely used in early childhood settings.

Behaviourism

Behaviourism changed ways of thinking in developmental psychology. The behaviouristic school of psychology placed much emphasis on observations. Theorists within the school of behaviourism – such as Watson, Pavlov and Skinner who formed the main ideas of this theory – developed more scientific ways of observing in order to understand development.

The main principles of behaviourism can be summarised by the following:

- human behaviour, especially social behaviour, is acquired rather than inborn;
- emphasis on the role of environmental stimuli;
- a focus on learning. Learning is defined as changes in behaviour which occur as the result of experience and interactions with the environment.

(Glassman, 2000)

This theory offers a detailed account of how human beings learn. It has contributed to furthering our understanding of children's development and learning and has offered a scientific approach to the observation of children.

However, it does not consider the social and cultural context of human beings. One theorist who criticised behaviourism for taking little account of the cognitive and socio-cultural factors that influence human development was Bandura, who proposed social learning theory as an alternative.

Behaviourism and observation

Observation has been central to behaviourism. Behaviourists are concerned with behaviours worthy of study – those which can be observed directly. Thus they have added to observation the elements of measurement and repetition so that, from the same findings, other conclusions can be drawn. They have also offered a quantifying approach to observation. They have contributed to controlled non-participant observation where behaviours are observed, not in naturalistic environments, but in controlled conditions such as laboratory settings. This led behaviourists to suggest that human responses to situations were almost predictable, via trial and error and via the principle of what would be the most profitable, least painful or best for the individual, and thus that, training could shape an individual. This implied the elimination of free will from the individual and the wider socio-cultural environment.

Attachment theory

In early childhood education, one of the most influential ideas in forming relationships with young children is attachment theory.

There are two psychological theories that discuss attachment. The first comes from behaviourism (Dollard and Miller, 1950) which suggests, in line with behaviouristic ideas, that attachment is a learned behaviour. Babies learn to associate the person who feeds them, cleans them and looks after them (mainly the mother or the primary carer) with a feeling of comfort. Thus a bond is developed with the primary carer through classical conditioning. So every time babies see the primary carer, they feel comfortable. A number of behaviours such as crying and smiling bring desirable behaviours, such as breast feeding and social interaction, and through operant conditioning babies learn to repeat these behaviours to get what they want or need.

The second approach comes from the field of ethology. The pioneering work of Bowlby (1958, 1969a, 1969b) and Ainsworth (1973) define attachment as an emotional bond that is established and develops between one person and another, in particular between babies and their mothers or primary carers. Bowlby (1969a, p.194) defines attachment as a *lasting psychological connectedness between human beings*. After researching babies and their relationships with their primary carers, he suggested that the primary carer (usually the mother) provides safety and security to the baby. Babies need that dual relationship in order to survive and develop. Prior work by Lorenz (1935) and Harlow and Zimmermann (1958), based on observations of animal ethology, have demonstrated similar patterns of behaviour with animals. Bowlby extended his work to human beings. He suggested that a child forms one primary attachment (monotropy) and that attachment-person becomes a secure basis for developing and exploring the world. He also believed that the attachment relationship becomes a model for all future relationships.

THEORY FOCUS

John Bowlby's stages in the development of attachment

Table 2.3   John Bowlby's stages in the development of attachment (Bowlby, 1969b)

Approximate age (months)	Stage	Description
0 to 2 and over	Orientation to signals without discrimination of human figure.	The infant shows orientation to social stimuli – grasping, reaching, smiling and babbling. The baby will cease to cry when picked up or when seeing a face. These behaviours increase when the baby is in proximity to a companion, although the baby cannot distinguish one person from another.
1 to 6 and over	Orientation to signals directed towards one or more discriminated human figures (mainly human faces).	Similar orientation behaviours as in the first stage appear, but they are markedly directed to the primary caregiver. Evidence of discrimination begins at one month for auditory and at two and a half months for visual stimuli.
6 to 30 and over	Maintenance of proximity to discriminated human figure by means of locomotion as well as signals.	The repertoire of responses to people increases to include following a departed mother, greeting her on return and using her as a base for exploration. Strangers are treated with caution and may evoke alarm and withdrawal; others may be selected as additional attachment figures (for example fathers).

Approximate age (months)	Stage	Description
24 to 48 and over	Formation of a goal-corrected partnership.	The child begins to acquire insight into the mother's (or primary carer's) feelings and goals, which lead to cooperative interaction and partnership.

Attachment and observation

Extensive naturalistic observation, as well as controlled observation, has been used by the field of ethology which Bowlby and his followers drew on to develop their own approach to observations. They also borrowed the infant observation technique from the psychoanalytical field and offered research rigour from the scientific field. Whereas psychoanalytical infant observation was not intrusive, Bowlby and his followers (see Ainsworth, 1969, 1973, 1979, 1985, 1989; Winnicot, 1986, 1987, 1995, 2005) added an intrusive procedure in infant observation. Intrusive observation is concerned with reactions of children where a change is occurring and takes place in a controlled environment (see Ainsworth's experiments with babies and their mothers). The focus is to investigate the pattern of behaviour that will occur if the routine of the baby is disturbed.

Social cognition

Albert Bandura (1971, 1977, 1986, 1989, 2001) argued that human beings develop by using their cognitive abilities in the social and cultural environment in which they live. He suggested the idea of observational learning as an important aspect of development: human beings develop and learn by the examples of others. Children make sense of the world and learn how to behave in particular moments of their lives through observing others (e.g. parents, teachers and other children). Bandura elaborates this idea with examples of children being violent. He presented to young children, in a controlled laboratory setting, an adult beating a doll. The children were then invited to go into a room and play with this doll and with other toys that were there. Observing children's responses, he demonstrated that children imitated what the adult did and that they bit the doll. Bandura concluded that children continuously learn behaviours through the observation of others.

Although Bandura studied development as part of the environment, he did not merely provide a limited description of the environment as an influential factor in human development.

Social cognition and observation

Similar to behaviourism, social cognition has been based heavily on observations but whereas behaviourism has introduced controlled observations in a laboratory context, social cognition moved beyond this and employed psychoanalytical methods using naturalistic observations. For social cognition, observation of others is seen as a way for people to learn and to develop an understanding of the environment. Knowledge is acquired directly via observations.

Ecology

In contrast to Bandura, Urie Bronfenbrenner (1977, 1979, 1989, 1995, 2005), the origina-
tor of ecological systems theory, viewed the natural environment as the most influential
factor in human development. He challenged theorists who study human development and
learning in artificial and laboratory contexts and proposed study within the natural environment. He defined an *environment as [being] a set of nested structures, each inside the
next, like a set of Russian dolls* (1979, p.22). As a result, he viewed the child as developing
within a complex system of relationships, affected by the multiple levels of the surrounding
environment, such as immediate settings within broad cultural values, laws and customs.
His main idea of how children develop within systems is illustrated in Figure 2.1.

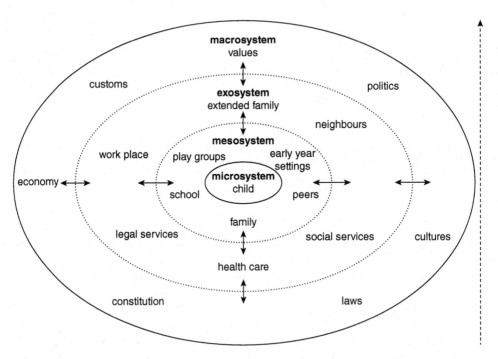

Figure 2.1   Bronfenbrenner's ecological system which illustrates the layers of influence in
a child's life

For Bronfenbrenner, human development involves the interactions of these four
systems – the micro, meso, exo and macrosystems – over time. This approach to child
development emphasises them as active participants in creating their own environments
and their experiences of their interactions with their social context as important aspects.

Ecology and observation

Ecological approaches use mainly naturalistic observations. They are concerned with
direct observation of behaviour in multiple settings such as home, school and social
activities in all four systems – micro, meso, exo and macro – to have a complete picture
of the person's social development. They are also concerned with the direct observation

of more than one person – multi-person systems – in the same place as a way of examining interactions among people.

Cognition

In developmental psychology the school of cognition has been one of the most dominant theories in child development. Cognition is concerned with the *study of the processes involved in cognition – the processes involved in making sense of the environment and interacting appropriately with it* (Eysenck, 1995, p.10). The mental processes through which we attempt to understand the world were defined as:

- thinking and knowing;
- reasoning;
- learning;
- problem-solving;
- using language;
- memory;
- perception.

The two most important theorists who have furthered our understanding of child development in cognitive psychology are Jean Piaget – who emphasised that a child has an active mind inhabited by rich structures of knowledge – and Lev Vygotsky. Vygotsky's socio-cognitive perspectives (1986) focused on how cultural values, beliefs, customs and social interactions are necessary for children in acquiring new ways of thinking.

Piaget

Piaget's theory suggests that children develop through stages. Children develop and construct knowledge (schema) via these stages. According to Piaget (1929, 1952, 1954, 1962, 1968, 1969), the schemata, which are specific psychological structures, change with age. Piaget's cognitive theory suggests that during the first two years of life cognition can be seen in the baby's motor actions towards the environment.

To explain how children acquire schemata and subsequently change these Piaget identifies two important intellectual functions: assimilation and accommodation. Assimilation is the process by which the child cognitively adapts to, and organises, the environment, and which therefore allows growth but not a change of schemata. The process responsible for changes in schemata is accommodation. Accommodation is part of the process of adaptation in which old schemata are adjusted and new ones are created to produce a better fit within the environment. The processes of assimilation and accommodation are necessary for cognitive development. For Piaget, these two processes interact in a balanced way which he calls interaction *equilibrium*. This is a self-regulatory process whose tools are assimilation and accommodation. Children with equilibrium transfer external experiences into internal structures (or 'schemata').

It is not until the end of the second year that children begin to use mental-symbolic processes in order to adapt to their environment (Piaget, 1952). Piaget (1952) made clear that the behaviour of small infants, although not conceptually based, was nevertheless intelligent. By this he meant that infants had ways of meeting their needs, of using their own resources and other resources in the environment, and of adapting those resources to the specific nature of the task at hand. This sensory motor intelligence was embodied not in the mind, but in the actions and movements that the baby made in direct interaction with its environment (Piaget, 1952, 1962). There follows the move into childhood and pre-operational thought. The distinguishing characteristic between infancy and childhood is the use of language and the ability to perform logical reasoning.

Another characteristic that assists development from infancy to childhood is the *object concept* or the concept of *object permanence*. This refers to a set of implicit, common-sense beliefs that we all share about the basic nature and behaviour of objects, including ourselves. When an object disappears from one's sight, adults do not assume that it has thereby gone out of existence, but this skill does not exist at the beginning of our lives and is acquired only gradually. When children acquire object permanence it is then that symbolic representation involves implications for language, attention and social development.

According to Piaget, knowledge is not absorbed passively from the environment but is constructed through interactions and experiences between the mental structures (schemata) and the environment. As a result, knowledge is constructed from a child's actions in the environment. In Piaget's theory there are three kinds of knowledge:

- physical;
- logical-mathematical;
- social.

The Piagetian theory has had a great impact on the early childhood environment. The developmentally appropriate practices in settings and the pedagogical principles that have evolved as a result of his theory have changed the ways that learning in early childhood is viewed.

The following description presents a picture of a classroom that fosters development, promotes learning and is influenced by Piagetian ideas.

CASE STUDY 2.1

Example of the physical environment of a classroom which applies Piaget's theories

The classroom is divided into small learning areas where groups of children may play with sand or occupy themselves in parallel or cooperative play with bricks, Lego or painting, while others are supported by the early childhood practitioner in a group task. Others are engaged in symbolic play or dramatic play. A few children may be at the writing area. One or two are on the floor looking at a big picture book or sitting in a chair in the library corner looking at or reading books, leading, perhaps, to a shared reading with a practitioner or a peer.

Outside, children may be involved with larger materials and apparatus in solitary or cooperative imaginative play or with others in socially agreed play. Children may be painting at an easel or writing. The practitioners move between the various activities, supporting children with their experience of the materials. Occasionally, usually at the start or the end of the session, the class comes together for a group story reading, a shared book experience or a song. Thus a whole range of activities will be taking place supporting children's learning through experience and interactions with materials.

Vygotsky

While Piaget viewed cognitive development as the result of the individual child's interaction with the environment, Vygotsky (1962, 1986) expanded further on that view and emphasised the importance of social interaction for children's cognitive development. He introduced the idea of the *Zone of Proximal Development* (ZPD). Vygotsky (1986) identifies the zone of actual development which *defines actions that have already matured; that is, the end product of development*. This refers to a number of skills that a child has already mastered and which help the child to achieve certain tasks. However, during development, children should preferably be placed in the zone of proximal development where the potential development of a child is situated: *[Children] that have not yet matured but are in the process of [acquiring . . .] functions that will mature tomorrow, but are currently in an embryonic state* (Vygotsky, 1986, p.87). This refers to a range of skills that the child cannot yet handle, but with the help of a more mature or skilled peer or an adult the child can master these skills. In practice, this means that children need social interaction. The help of an adult or of other children is an important and integral part of a child's development.

In Vygotsky's theory there is emphasis on what children *can* do rather than what they *cannot* do. Consequently, learning is constructed as a partnership between the child and the adult.

CASE STUDY 2.2

ZPD with the help of an adult

The following example attempts to demonstrate how the interaction of the practitioner with children helps them to read a picture book. The book is about animals. At the end of each page there is some push-button music playing to the sound of the animal illustrated in the picture.

Practitioner:	*Do you want to look at this book with me?*
George:	[He just nods his head.]
Practitioner:	*So, do you want to look at the book?*
George:	*Yes.*
Practitioner:	[reads the story] On the farm the little dog . . .
	[George interrupts the reading and presses a button to listen to the music.]
Practitioner:	*We have not reached the part where you must press the button for the music. Do you want to wait? It is not going to take long.*
	[George looks at the practitioner and presses the button again.]
Practitioner:	*Do you want me to suggest something to you, then? We can do the following: I will give you the book for you to turn the pages and listen to all the noises, and then, if you want, we can still look at it together.*

(Continued)

(Continued)

[George takes the book and starts to press the button more than three times.]

Practitioner: *You know, if we turn the page like this you should be able to listen to some more nice sounds. Shall we do it like this?* [Taking the book gently from George's hand and turning the page slowly.]

[George sees the new button and presses it. He presses it about three times and then turns the next page by himself, discovers the button and starts the next piece of music playing.]

After he has experienced the whole book, the practitioner asks George if he still wants to look at the book and read it. In this way George discovered that he had to press the buttons in order to listen to the music – the same way in which he learnt how to turn the pages. This happened with some help.

ZPD with the help of a more experienced peer

Another example of ZPD is illustrated in the following extract. In this one it is a mature peer who offers help to another child:

Sophia, Raj and Anka were in the library corner with a large number of books. They were looking at the pictures.

The practitioner said that it was tidy-up time, so all three of them started to put the books and the newspapers back in their places, according to the symbols that had been designed to categorise the different types of books and magazines.

Tidiness is not simply the act of shelving books back in the library, but putting them back according to their themes. These were represented by the use of small pictures: the labels bore different symbols for storybooks, knowledge books, fantasy books, talking books, magazines and so on, e.g.

📖   Storybooks

📄   Talking books

🗁   Magazines

Raj: This is a magazine – it goes with the magazines, next to hairdresser's shop, and this one goes here with the storybooks.

Anka: What about this one?

Sophia: This is a storybook and goes ... oh yes ... here, where the symbol for 'books' is.

Anka: Oh! Here's another one (Anka picks up a talking book and puts it in the right place).

To summarise, both Piaget and Vygotsky are important because they challenge educators to rethink children's cognitive development. They further our understanding of how children think, develop and learn, offering us a view that young children are more capable than we perhaps had once assumed. Both theorists placed an emphasis on what children can do and viewed learning not only as the construction of knowledge, but as an ability to use and apply it appropriately in different contexts. They changed the ways in which we consider children's abilities. Now we can offer a more enriched environment to young children, full of activities and support that enhance their own development and learning.

Cognition and observation

The field of cognitive psychology employs a number of observation techniques which are structured and focus on aspects of development: verbal ability, logical-analytical ability, psychomobility (flexibility of thought), memory (short-term, long-term, working memory recall), analytic-synthetic (ability to create an entity) and psychospatial ability (our ability to perceive environmental patterns). Although they acknowledged that these are not independent from each other and that interaction is necessary, they developed methods to test and observe them separately at an experimental level (Anderson, 1983). In the field of education, the Piagetian tests and systematic observations have changed methods of study.

ACTIVITY 2.2

Piaget and Vygotsky in practice

In the following example from an observation in a setting, try to investigate whether you can identify any of the ideas of Piaget and Vygotsky in practice.

Activity: Planting beans

The practitioner introduced the activity and the diary to a small group of children. They had to write down who put water on the beans and when, and to chart the beans' development through making drawings. Then, with the assistance of the adults, the children started to fill in the notebook according to their daily observations. Every day the group was asked to spend about five minutes checking the beans and then to record their observations in the notebook. In the second week after the planting, when the children had finished checking the plants, they went to the writing area and occupied themselves there. When they had finished, they came back to the practitioner. The child in the following extract wanted to write down her name on her drawing, but did not know how, so she approached the practitioner.

C1:	*Can you write down my name?*
Practitioner:	*What have you done in your drawing?*
C1:	*I draw what I see in the beans.*

(Continued)

(Continued)

Practitioner:	*So what do you say, then?*
C1:	*That this bean* [points to the big blue shapes similar to a circle on her drawing] *has grown so big. Here it is* [pointing to her drawing]. *I wrote my own letters.*
Practitioner:	*And what do these letters say?*
C1:	[As if reading] *'The bean is big'. This is my gardening notebook. Can you write my name?*
Practitioner:	*What are the sounds of your name?*
C1:	*Lisa.*
Practitioner:	*What is the first one?*
C1:	*Lisa.*
Practitioner:	*What is the first one you can hear?*
C1:	*'L'?*
Practitioner:	*Yes. Let's write down the letter 'L'.*

Comment

During this activity we can see Piaget's idea that children learn actively through interaction with the actual plants and they were able to construct a product/knowledge/schema with real-life examples as a context. Children were given roles and responsibilities and through this activity a context was provided for children to learn how plants develop.

In the dialogue with the practitioner and the child we can identify the help the adult offers the child in creating her own notebook and to link sounds to letters.

Within the dialogue above, the ZPD can be identified. The child discusses her request with the practitioner and through the guidance of the adult the child has begun to make sense of letters as symbols.

Summary

The field of child development continues to seek new directions. Information processing views the development of the mind as a symbol-manipulating system through which information flows (Klahr, 1992). This approach helps researchers to achieve a clear understanding of what children of different ages do when faced with tasks and problems. New technological achievements in the medical field, such as MRI technology, have helped neuroscience to understand how the brain develops and functions. There is more evidence available now to explain how parts of the brain are used when a child faces a task or a problem.

Comparing these child development theories, we can conclude that they differ in many respects, each focusing on different aspects of development, but all using observations as their main tool to study children. The psychoanalytical theory emphasises children's social and emotional development. Piaget's cognitive theory, information processing and Vygotsky's socio-cultural theory stress the importance of the social learning environment in children's thinking. They investigate child development in the context of a non-isolated environment and regard the child as an active learner through experience and interaction with that environment – both early and later experiences are important. The remaining approaches – behaviourism and ecological systems theory – discuss factors assumed to affect all aspects of a child's functioning.

Considering the influence of these theories in the field of early childhood education, they can offer a perspective of the child-as-learner, where learning is determined by the child's own development.

ACTIVITY 2.3

The role of psychological theories in your practice

- Reflect on your own practice and consider what (if any) developmental theories influence your practice.
- Discuss how each psychological theory is using observation.

Conditions for learning

Similar to pedagogy, learning is not an activity that occurs in isolation. One of the main principles of the curricula in the UK is to develop an enabling environment for children's learning and development. The setting should not be separated from wider cultural and social contexts. Although practitioners in early childhood are working with a national quality framework (the EYFS in England, the Foundation Phase Framework for Children's Learning in Wales, the Curriculum for Excellence in Scotland, the Foundation Stage Curriculum in Northern Ireland, Aistear: The Early Curriculum Framework in Ireland), he or she should look to develop local conditions for learning that apply to the needs of the immediate setting and takes the environment into consideration.

In such a learning environment, certain skills are not developed in isolation. Piaget viewed human development as an integrated process where feelings, emotions and relationships have an effect on cognitive skills, such as on numeracy and literacy. Learning is the product of many experiences in meaningful contexts.

In designing educational programmes and activities for children the following conditions should be considered.

Emphasis on children's development

The development of a child is central in early childhood education. From a cognitive perspective, the key developmental areas are physical, social, emotional and moral development, language, numeracy, thinking, memory, attention, perception and reasoning. These areas are reflected in many educational policies, curricula and pedagogical practices. As was shown in Chapter 1, in the UK all curricula place emphasis on a child's development as learning outcomes.

ACTIVITY 2.4

Reflect on your curriculum

Consider the curriculum framework in your context and discuss what are the key areas that are important in terms of children's development? What is the role of play? What is the role of observation?

Emphasis on play

Play is important in early childhood. Within the EYFS again there is great emphasis on play which is described as *purposeful*. Similarly, the Foundation Phase in Wales focuses on play, in particular outdoor play, as an important aspect of children's development and learning. In an attempt to understand this, we need to ask *what exactly is play?*

Moyles (1989) defines play as the situation when children do their learning. Play is when children have opportunities to express their thoughts and emotions, to try out new things and possibilities, to put different elements of a situation together in various ways and to look at problems from different viewpoints (Bruner, 1972) and create imaginary situations in which children change the meaning of objects and actions, giving them new meanings (Vygotsky 1966. Kravtsova (2014) suggests that *in play a child is at the same time inside it (i.e. crying like a patient) and outside it (i.e. rejoicing as a player)* (p. 22). Important elements of play are pleasure and enjoyment. Children need play to enjoy themselves as well as to enrich their experiences while interacting with their environment. Play for young children should not be seen as a separate activity that children do at a specific time. It is something that very young children, in particular, do constantly. Consequently, play is oriented by spontaneity. Early forms of play in very young children lack any organisation and are used by children to help them make sense of the world, to communicate with others and to explore their environment.

Although play is a complex term to define a number of authors have stressed the importance of play for children's well-being, development and learning (Brooker et al., 2014; Pellegrini, 2011; Wood, 2010a, 2010b, 2013a, 2013b). One of the most important pioneers of early childhood education (Froebel) who introduced the kindergarten (the nursery) in Germany, based his philosophy on the role of play in early childhood education. A Froebel classroom was rich with play materials that he called *gifts and occupations* and activities were organised in relation to these 'gifts' in what he considered 'natural' ways. Subsequently a number of theorists have examined play in early childhood education. Curricula practices in early childhood education do emphasise the role of play and promote a play-based pedagogy, but what is important is *to maintain an expansive understanding of play and pedagogy, and to hold that space against reductionist policy discourses* (Wood, 2014, p.15). More recently, a number of researchers have examined children's play in the digital era (Arnott et al., 2018; Edwards and Bird, 2017; Yelland, 2018; Yelland and Gilbert, 2017; Marsh et al., 2016) and how play-based pedagogy synergises children's experiences with the digital and non-digital world. The discussion on play in the field of early childhood education is ongoing, but nevertheless what is important to remember is that *in play the child creates the structure meaning/object, where the semantic aspect – the meaning of the world, the meaning of thing – dominates and determines his behaviour* (Vygotsky, 1966/2016, p.14). Thus it is important to place emphasis on play in any search for effective pedagogy in early childhood education *not because children like to play, but also for its voluntary and experiential features, and its importance for identity formation, expression and social learning* (UNESCO 2004, p.1).

Emphasis on children's needs, interests and emotions

Children's needs, interests and emotions are important factors that influence their learning. These derive from developmental needs such as physical activities, social and emotional well-being and opportunities for play. In early childhood education is important to be able to detect and respond to children's needs, interests and emotions if we aim to create an environment where children are able to produce more engaging and fulfilling interactions with materials, activities, their peers and the adults.

Emphasis on children's freedom to choose materials and activities

The importance of children's participation has been emphasised in a number of policies relating to children, such as the UNCRC. The enabling of children as active learners, who are able to take control of their own learning and development, requires an environment where children are given the appropriate opportunities to participate in choosing their materials and activities and offers time for children to develop their play.

Emphasis on children's ownership of their learning

Similarly, children should be given opportunities to explore their own learning. They should not be underestimated in terms of their abilities to translate their interests into activities and thus to explore the world. Children's internal needs, interests and curiosity drive them to form relationships with others and in forming these relationships they discover new ways of learning.

Pedagogy in practice

Developing a pedagogy requires the construction of a practitioner identity with a good understanding of developmental theories as well as pedagogical practices, and an understanding of children's developmental needs.

However, the practitioner has to work within a context. Miller et al. (2003), comparing different curricula across the timeline and in other countries, found that *curricula guidance for the early years has become increasingly centralised in a number of countries* (p.113). Again, the practitioner is asked to be able to work creatively and to improve practice in this sector. This is a difficult task for the practitioner as it requires a very good understanding of current policies and practices, such as EYFS. In your search for pedagogy it is important to look at other pedagogical practices to further your understanding. In studying other effective practices, you should not seek to transfer them to your own practice without adaptation, but adopt a critical approach to compare and reflect on your own practice, and also to enrich your understanding of early childhood pedagogy.

While this chapter aimed to discuss issues around the different views that influence pedagogy, we will return to the discussion of pedagogy and the curriculum in Chapter 11, after building a theoretical and practical understanding of observation as a tool for practice and research.

SUMMARY

This chapter discussed the influential constructions of childhood and philosophical approaches and developmental theories in early childhood in an attempt to search for some principles for forming a pedagogy. The chapter presented a main emphasis on the ideas of Piaget and Vygotsky and how these apply to ECEC. In the search for a pedagogical framework, some conditions of learning were identified with emphasis on children's

- *development;*
- *play;*
- *needs, interests and emotions;*
- *freedom to choose materials and activities;*
- *ownership of their learning.*

The following chapter will discuss observations in this context.

Further Reading

To extend your understanding on childhood and issues affecting early childhood education:

MacBlain, S, Dunn, J and Luke, I (2017) *Contemporary Childhood*. London: Sage.
Owen, A (ed) (2017) *Childhood Today*. London: Sage.

To extend your understanding on child development:

Conkbayir, M (2017) *Early Childhood and Neuroscience: Theory, Research and Implications for Practice*. London: Bloomsbury.
Crowley, K (2017) *Child Development: A Practical Introduction* (2nd edn). London: Sage.

To extend your understanding on contemporary issues influence early childhood:

Yelland, N and Bentley, DF (eds) (2018) *Found in Translation: Connecting Reconceptualist Thinking with Early Childhood Education Practices*. London: Routledge.

To extend your understanding on key thinkers that have influenced early childhood education:

Cohen, LE and Waite-Stupiansky, S (2017) *Theories of Early Childhood Education: Developmental, Behaviourist and Critical*. London: Routledge.

CHAPTER 3

BECOMING AN OBSERVER

Chapter objectives

After reading this chapter, you will:

- understand the aims and objectives of observation;
- address the issue of subjectivity and objectivity in observation;
- understand how to work with others including parents and children as a team to plan observations.

Observation is central to early childhood education as it provides a systematic way of understanding children's development and learning and responding to children's interests.

Introduction

In this book, it is advocated that observation should be an integral part of the daily routine of early childhood education. Nutbrown (2001) urges practitioners

> to watch the children they work with, keeping open minds and responding with sensitivity and respect to what they see. Children need well-educated educators with knowledge at their fingertips, adults working with them who:
>
> *(Continued)*

(Continued)

- *see what is happening*
- *understand what they see, and*
- *act on what they understand.*

Just seeing, just understanding is not enough.

(p.135)

Observation, as a primary tool, is thus a purposeful and daily reflective method for gathering information about children's behaviour, their needs and experiences and their development which requires a skilful practitioner. Observations are more than just watching children and require a set of skills that practitioners need to develop in order to be able to *see*, *understand* and *act* in their daily practice. These skills include a clear understanding of the aims and objectives of the observation, issues around minimising subjectivity and how to involve the whole team, including parents and children. So, this chapter aims to offer guidance on how to become a skilful observer discussing all these factors involved when we prepare for observations. Finally, it offers an overview of the types of observation available to practitioners.

Observation aims and objectives

As observation is a systematic method to collect evidence of children's behaviour, so it is important to set clear aims and objectives. There is a need to distinguish between what is meant by aims and objectives.

Aims are about what you intend to observe and what you want to achieve. They are therefore focused, precise and unambiguous. For example, they are on an area of development such as physical or social development, or on an activity that has been introduced in the setting to encourage children's language interactions, such as the telephone area. Objectives are about specific skills or abilities you want to observe; thus they are achievable, measurable, realistic and detailed reasons for observation, linked with children's development and your practice. In that sense objectives are considered as the steps by which you achieve your aims.

ACTIVITY 3.1

Set the aims and objectives of your observation

You work in the baby room and you want to observe the babies' emotional development. Table 3.1 is an example of the possible aims and objectives when you observe emotional development. Try to develop your own objectives for distress, affection, enjoyment and interest in activities.

Table 3.1   Aims and objectives when observing emotional development

Aim: Emotional development	Objectives
Shows interest in materials	**When exploring materials, possible observed objectives:**
	Directing eyes towards materials
	Touching materials
	Exploring materials for a period of time
	Showing intensity
	Showing apathy
	Showing a lot/little movement
	Touching materials with care
	Kicking materials
	Throwing materials
	Dropping materials
	Showing curiosity
How fear is expressed	**When experiencing unfamiliar faces possible observed objectives:**
	Crying
	Whining
	Clinging
	Hiding behind objects
	Tightening muscles
	Closing eyes sharply for a period of time
	Shouting
	Trembling
	Runs/crawls away
	Puts hands on face (hiding with his/her hands)
	Seeks one of the practitioners
How anger is expressed	**When baby is physically or psychologically frustrated, possible observed objective:**
	Feeling disappointed when child cannot achieve something
	Feeling irritated when child cannot achieve something
	Frowning when child cannot achieve
	Shouting
	Red face

(Continued)

Table 3.1   (Continued)

Aim: Emotional development	Objectives
	Loud words
	Aggression
	Biting
	Beating
	Crying
	Withdrawing
	Screaming

When the early childhood team is planning how individual children's profiles will be built and when developing strategies of evaluating the educational programme and its activities, observations are the tool for collecting this evidence. It is important that members of the early childhood team share roles and responsibilities before they start and clarify and set aims and objectives for the observations. This way the team will remain focused and collect rich evidence to effectively complete each child's profile and to evaluate the educational programme itself.

Aims and objectives for undertaking the observations should be clearly defined as the objectives will determine the nature of the information to be gathered.

Working within a curriculum such as the EYFS, the learning and development goals need to be met, but due to the broad nature of the learning areas it is important to set clear objectives. For example, in the EYFS the prime areas are communication and language, physical development and personal, social and emotional development. These are the broad areas which should be the aims of your observations, with specific objectives needing to be set as in Table 3.1. These will enable the gathering of comprehensive evidence around each goal of your aims and objectives. Clear aims and objectives will also allow you to choose the most appropriate observation technique. As inclusive practitioners aims and objectives ought to be shared with parents and carers of children and modified in the light of subsequent comments.

CASE STUDY 3.1

The Australian curriculum

As mentioned in the Introduction, Australia's curriculum for early childhood education is called Belonging, Being and Becoming: The Early Years Learning Framework. It sets five broad learning outcomes:

1. Children have a strong sense of identity
2. Children are connected with and contribute to their world

3. Children have a strong sense of well-being
4. Children are confident and involved learners
5. Children are effective communicators.

It offers examples of how these outcomes can be observed. Here are the examples provided for the first outcome. The left-hand column provides guidance on what types of behaviours practitioners can collect evidence on via observations.

Outcome 1: Children have a strong sense of identity

- *Children feel safe, secure and supported*
- *Children develop their emerging autonomy, interdependence, resilience and sense of agency*
- *Children develop knowledgeable and confident self-identities*
- *Children learn to interact in relation to others with care, empathy and respect*

Children feel safe, secure and supported	
This is evident, for example, when children:	Practitioners promote this learning, for example, when they:
<ul><li>build secure attachments with one and then more familiar educators</li><li>use effective routines to help make predicted transitions smoothly</li><li>sense and respond to a feeling of belonging</li><li>communicate their needs for comfort and assistance</li><li>establish and maintain respectful, trusting relationships with other children and educators</li><li>openly express their feelings and ideas in their interactions with others</li><li>respond to ideas and suggestions from others</li><li>initiate interactions and conversations with trusted educators</li><li>confidently explore and engage with social and physical environments through relationships and play</li><li>initiate and join in play</li><li>explore aspects of identity through role play</li></ul>	<ul><li>acknowledge and respond sensitively to children's cues and signals</li><li>respond sensitively to children's attempts to initiate interactions and conversations</li><li>support children's secure attachment through consistent and warm nurturing relationships</li><li>support children in times of change and bridge the gap between the familiar and the unfamiliar</li><li>build upon culturally valued child-rearing practices and approaches to learning</li><li>are emotionally available and support children's expression of their thoughts and feelings</li><li>recognise that feelings of distress, fear or discomfort may take some time to resolve</li><li>acknowledge each child's uniqueness in positive ways</li><li>spend time interacting and conversing with each child</li></ul>

(Continued)

(Continued)

Children develop their emerging autonomy, interdependence, resilience and sense of agency

This is evident, for example, when children:	Practitioners promote this learning, for example, when they:
• demonstrate increasing awareness of the needs and rights of others • are open to new challenges and discoveries • increasingly cooperate and work collaboratively with others • take considered risks in their decision-making and cope with the unexpected • recognise their individual achievements and the achievements of others • demonstrate an increasing capacity for self-regulation • approach new safe situations with confidence • begin to initiate negotiating and sharing behaviours • persist when faced with challenges and when first attempts are not successful	• provide children with strategies to make informed choices about their behaviours • promote children's sense of belonging, connectedness and well-being • maintain high expectations of each child's capabilities • mediate and assist children to negotiate their rights in relation to the rights of others • provide opportunities for children to engage independently with tasks and play • display delight, encouragement and enthusiasm for children's attempts • support children's efforts, assisting and encouraging as appropriate • motivate and encourage children to succeed when they are faced with challenges • provide time and space for children to engage in both individual and collaborative pursuits • build on the culturally valued learning of individual children's communities • encourage children to make choices and decisions

Children develop knowledgeable and confident self-identities

This is evident, for example, when children:	Practitioners promote this learning, for example, when they:
• feel recognised and respected for who they are • explore different identities and points of view in dramatic play • share aspects of their culture with the other children and educators • use their home language to construct meaning • develop strong foundations in both the culture and language/s of their family and of the broader community without compromising their cultural identities	• promote in all children a strong sense of who they are and their connectedness to others – a shared identity as Australians • ensure all children experience pride and confidence in their achievements • share children's successes with families • show respect for diversity, acknowledging the varying approaches of children, families, communities and cultures • acknowledge and understand that children construct meaning in many different ways • demonstrate deep understanding of each child, their family and community contexts in planning for children's learning

Children develop knowledgeable and confident self-identities

- develop their social and cultural heritage through engagement with Elders and community members
- reach out and communicate for comfort, assistance and companionship
- celebrate and share their contributions and achievements with others

- provide children with examples of the many ways identities and culture are recognised and expressed
- build upon culturally valued approaches to learning
- build on the knowledge, languages and understandings that children bring
- talk with children in respectful ways about similarities and differences in people
- provide rich and diverse resources that reflect children's social worlds
- listen to and learn about children's understandings of themselves
- actively support the maintenance of home language and culture
- develop authentic children's understanding of themselves

Children learn to interact in relation to others with care, empathy and respect

This is evident, for example, when children:

Practitioners promote this learning, for example, when they:

- show interest in other children and being part of a group
- engage in and contribute to shared play experiences
- express a wide range of emotions, thoughts and views constructively
- empathise with and express concern for others
- display awareness of and respect for others' perspectives
- reflect on their actions and consider the consequences for others

- initiate one-to-one interactions with children, particularly babies and toddlers, during daily routines
- organise learning environments in ways that promote small group interactions and play experiences
- model care, empathy and respect for children, staff and families
- model explicit communication strategies to support children to initiate interactions and join in play and social experiences in ways that sustain productive relationships with other children
- acknowledge children's complex relationships and sensitively intervene in ways that promote consideration of alternative perspectives and social inclusion

Adapted from *Belonging, Being and Becoming: The Early Years Learning Framework for Australia* (2019) produced by the Australia Government of Education and Training for the Council of Australian Government, pp. 22–7.

ACTIVITY 3.2

Set your aims and objectives to meet the learning outcomes of your curriculum

Reflecting on the case study of the Australian curriculum, consider your context and the key outcomes of your curriculum. What aims and objectives can you create in order to collect observations towards gathering information to assess the outcomes for each child?

Observation planning should involve the whole team in the process of agreeing who will carry out the observations and should ensure that all team members gain the valuable experience of undertaking observations.

Clear roles within the classroom setting should be decided, so that the practitioner undertaking the observation knows when to remove him or herself from activities in preparation to observe. It is also important that children know in advance who is the observer in that activity – although, of course, with very young children this cannot always be achieved.

Objectivity: Does it exist?

Reflecting on the quote below, what do you think Nutbrown is trying to say to the practitioners?

> If educators are blinkered, having tunnel vision, they may not have the full picture – so it's not simply a case of understanding what is seen, but it is first crucial to see what is really happening and not what adults sometimes suppose to be happening. Children and the things they do need to be seen in the whole context and adults working with them must open to seeing what exists not what their professional mind tells them they should see.
>
> (Nutbrown, 2001, p.135)

One of the key skills that practitioners should develop is objectivity. This is always a main aspiration. It is a challenging aspect of the observation and takes much practice, thus ensuring as far as possible that we are objective and so record what actually happens and not what we merely assume to be happening. However, the issue of achieving objectivity is a difficult one and can mislead the workforce. As mentioned above, the aim of observation is to record in a systematic way what we actually do. In that sense one might claim that this is objectivity. However, we cannot ignore that how we represent the world or events is related to our perception which in turn is influenced by our own experiences, emotions, self-image and self-perception of what 'reality' is. In such contexts, objectivity is relative. One should seek for subjective 'reality' (Gillham, 2008) and try to collect as much evidence as possible, using a plethora of collection techniques in order to avoid the trap of seeing what we want to see, or assume to have seen, rather than the reality of events. A video recording of the same scenario may well differ from our notes of it, despite the intended honesty of the observer.

The following activity attempts to demonstrate how difficult it is to be objective and to record what actually does take place.

ACTIVITY 3.3

Seeing what exists

Look at the picture and write down what you see. Then show the picture to a colleague or to a fellow student and ask this person to do the same. Now compare your answers. Are they the same? Do you see what it is actually there?

Have you written, 'There are two boys reading books'?

But what do you actually see? You see two boys holding books. Whether these two boys read the books is an interpretation of what is seen. What we can actually observe is the following: two boys are holding and looking at books.

This is a clear example of one of the main challenges when we observe young children. It is difficult to step out of our personal values, beliefs and cultural stereotypes and retain objectivity when we record our observations.

Figure 3.1   Children at the book area

Consequently, the second challenge for the practitioner is not only to step back from personal values, beliefs and culture, but also to step out of the role that these normally signify. There are times when the systematic observer should not interfere with the activity of the child in question. Within the daily life of the classroom the practitioner is faced with a number of tasks and when he or she has to deliver activities with the children, so it is challenging to step out of the 'practitioner' role and become an observer. This is a constant exercise and will be discussed more comprehensively in the following chapters.

It is important that when an observation is taking place the observer judges to what extent the collection of information is 'disturbed'. In such a case the observer needs to stop the observation if the child or children is/are distracted or if the observation is unduly distorted, as attention and concentration on the task will be lost.

The challenging task of observation not only requires objectivity, in addition to training to distance yourself from your normal role as a systematic observer, but also the consideration that your emotions are involved. As Willan (2007, p.109) argues:

> Both child and observer come with their own load of emotional baggage. The child being observed or assessed has feelings, as do the parents, carers and educators around him/her – and so, of course, does the observer. It is important to be aware of the emotional dimension of the observational context, and to try to take it into account as part of the assessment process.

The process of observation takes place in the child's natural environment and the setting where children stay for a great amount of their day. Within this context there are a number of pressures for the practitioners. There is always the pressure for children to be safe, for them to be able to participate and enjoy activities, but there is also the additional pressure of being capable of observing objectively without bringing any values, beliefs or stereotypes into the process. In this context observers should assume an emotionally unbiased attitude towards the subject. However, it is often difficult to achieve such an emotionally unbiased equilibrium. Luff (2007, p.187) adds to this point and elaborates upon another difficulty:

> The processes for learning using documentation are, therefore, highly complex. An additional challenge for English early years professionals is a requirement to work in two potentially contradictory ways. On the one hand, observations can create opportunities to plan according to carefully looking at, and listening to, children's actions and responses; on the other hand, early years professionals are expected to work towards specific pre-set learning outcomes. As skilled professionals, early years practitioners must therefore gain confidence in demonstrating how specified criteria can be met through flexible holistic ways of working, [and] also need to find means of using structured guidelines, such as the EYFS, as frameworks for their observations.

To conclude, objectivity is a difficult skill to be achieved and requires training and practice to become a skilful observer.

Team involvement

As mentioned above, it is essential for the whole team to be involved in the observation process. The team needs to share ownership of this and be clear that all of them work to common aims and objectives. One of the main limitations of observation is that what is observed needs to be recorded – and practitioners will return to this after either a long day of work or after a certain period of time. When the events are subsequently read and analysed, the factors that lead a child to behave in a certain way, or which led to the success or otherwise of an activity, might have been forgotten and the record of the events loses its meaning. Important information might be missing or cannot be remembered. If possible, not only events should be recorded, but the possible reasons for these so that future reviews of the notes, possibly by others that were not involved in the process at the time, are meaningful. In this way valid conclusions can be drawn from the event. Team involvement is important as objectivity is very difficult to achieve. Each of us has our own values and system of beliefs; we are part of a social or cultural group and this influences the way we observe. A plethora of observations (the same ones from different people) will offer a pluralistic portrait of what actually happens in children's development and learning. Such an approach will lead to a closer 'accurate' interpretation of the observation findings.

Team involvement in the observation process can also work as a way of mentoring less experienced practitioners and guiding them in the process through peer interaction. Moreover, each member of the team can bring different expertise and experiences so that putting them together will enrich the observation planning and broaden its scope. Observation planning can also work as a team-building process. During team meetings and involvement there are often opportunities to develop a culture of critical listening, analysis of policy and diverse perspectives, and the creation of positive interactions with all participants. Team involvement in observation planning can become a valid opportunity to communicate information in order to try to solve problems before they arise. Finally, and equally importantly, through ownership of the observation planning by all members of the team an ethos of mutual trust can be built. Members of the team should not feel intimidated, threatened or 'afraid' when observations are taking place as they share ownership of the process.

Parental involvement

In addition to these skills there is also a need to involve parents in the observation of their children. As mentioned earlier, observations can become a valid path of communication between practitioners and the children's families. Parental involvement is important in the assessment of their children. Involving the parents encourages them to feel that they are participating in the life of their children while they are in the setting. Moreover, parents feel more comfortable about their child's daily life in the classroom, and this subsequently minimises the risk of feeling inordinately judged by the early childhood environment. The involvement of parents in the observation planning helps break down barriers between practitioners and parents. Asking for parents' help might assist practitioners to achieve emotionally unbiased skills and to offer a more in-depth insight into other aspects of the children's behaviour and subsequently into the development that is under scrutiny.

Child involvement

As well as involving the parents, it is essential the children can also be heard within this process as participants (see Chapters 4, 5, and 6 for examples). Observations in the daily classroom environment offer opportunities for listening to children's own voices. Clark and Moss (2001) carried out a study aiming to search *for a way to listen to young children [talk] about their lives* (p.11), to demonstrate the effects of listening to children and to suggest ways of doing so. As a result, they developed the Mosaic approach, a way of not only listening to children's distinct voices (a requirement of many curricula as a response to the United Nations Convention on the Rights of the Child, as mentioned earlier), but also as a way of ensuring children's views are respected in an empowering way for the child. Clark and Moss (2001) describe fundamental conditions for empowering children's voices when we create such an environment. Firstly, they introduce a climate of listening whereby children's experiences, interests and views influence their relationships with adults and their environment. Secondly, they stress the importance of allowing time to listen to children. The Mosaic approach involves a time of communication for early child-hood staff in several ways:

- gathering the material will take longer because we are not relying on a single method of communication;
- interpreting the material gathered is time-consuming.

(p.64)

Thirdly, they also emphasise the significant place of staff training, not only in order to listen to children, but also in terms of understanding children's development and the ways in which children make attempts to communicate to learn the skills that they will use throughout their lives.

To conclude, children's involvement as participants in the observation process gives them a sense of belonging and a sense of connection with what happens in the setting. In an era when early childhood education is searching for ways for children to be participants in all aspects of their lives and listening to children is now embedded in practice, child involve-ment is required as it can create a warm and welcoming environment where all children are respected, valued and collaborate with practitioners in curriculum planning and decisions. In such an environment the curriculum becomes meaningful to children so that children can engage in activities that can have an impact on their development and learning. Important elements of children's involvement are:

- recognition and value of children as knowledgeable beings;
- valuing children's contribution and the role they can play;
- mutual trust;
- respect and responsiveness to each child's opinion, social context, diversity and culture;
- shared decision-making;
- equity.

ACTIVITY 3.4

What skills do you need to become an observer?

Read the following extract and try to identify the main skills that practitioners should develop in order to become competent observers. Which of these skills do you feel you already have?

One of the greatest challenges is the need to be objective and unbiased. We must not allow objectivity to be influenced by pre-conceived ideas about the child's attainment.

Observation can also be a time-consuming process. It does need to be carefully organised and managed within the setting or classrooms so that everyone is aware of their role and responsibility, in relation to observation and assessment. It is essential to involve all those working with children in the observation and assessment process and this needs careful organisation, management and training for all those who are going to be carrying out these processes. Devising ways of integrating observation into practice within a reception class, particularly if there are no additional adults working with you, requires creativity and a commitment to the value of this as an essential tool for your practice. Observation can also be demanding for practitioners. These demands can take the form of being surprised or threatened by the information gathered through observation. When gathering observation data it is also likely that one will be observing the adults working with children more carefully than usual and this may also engender a sense of fear and anxiety within the adults. A final challenge to practitioners is that of interpreting or analysing the information that has been gathered. You need to use your understanding of child development, along with your knowledge, to interpret what you see and hear and take the child's learning forward or change your own practice. This is often best achieved through discussions with all those involved in the setting, including nursery nurses, teaching assistants, key workers and other practitioners. A key factor in this process of interpretation is ensuring that the evidence you are working with is gathered objectively, and accurately, taking account of the challenges that are identified above.

(Hamilton et al., 2003, p.61)

Observation planning

As mentioned in the previous section, the process of becoming a skilful observer is complex and challenging. It requires constant self-development, self-assessment, responsiveness, awareness and positive attitudes towards the diversity of different social contexts and cultures, addressing individual needs and the overcoming of personal emotional boundaries. Thus it is important to invest time and effort in observation planning before embarking on it. During the planning stage the aims and objectives should be described clearly so all involved in the process (children, parents, team members) know what they are doing and feel confident about this. Team, parental and child involvement are essential in your observational planning.

Good observation planning should consider the following questions:

- What are the aim (s) of the observation?
- What steps (objectives) do we need to take in order to reach our aim/aims?
- How can we gain more information in relation to a particular child or children?
- How can we gain more information in relation to the implementation of the curriculum?

- How can we involve the children?
- How can we involve the team so all of them feel comfortable and confident?
- How can we involve parents?

The next step is to choose your observation techniques and develop them to fit your own context (this will be explored in Chapters 4, 5 and 6). Once your observation recordings have been collected you need to analyse them systematically and, finally, the last step is to decide which ways you will employ to record and document your observations and findings (see Chapter 7 and 8) in an ethical manner (Chapter 9).

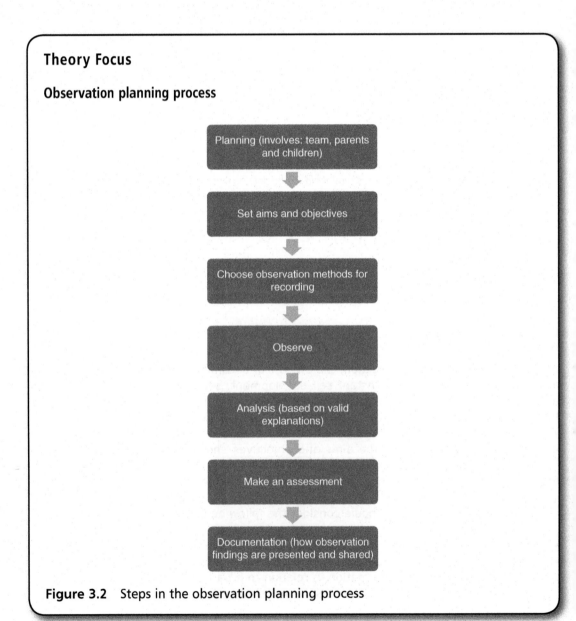

Theory Focus

Observation planning process

Planning (involves: team, parents and children)

⬇

Set aims and objectives

⬇

Choose observation methods for recording

⬇

Observe

⬇

Analysis (based on valid explanations)

⬇

Make an assessment

⬇

Documentation (how observation findings are presented and shared)

Figure 3.2 Steps in the observation planning process

Types of observation

There are three main types of observation that have been developed from the field of social research and which can be used in early childhood settings' day-to-day practice. These are: unstructured (participant) observations (discussed in Chapter 4), structured (non-participant) observations (discussed in Chapter 5) and semi-structured observations (discussed in Chapter 6). The Theory Focus box below describes these methods and their techniques as well as offering a brief evaluation.

The role of the observer

As discussed throughout this chapter becoming a skilful observer requires a set of skills that can be developed through training and practice. Martin (2019, p.68) suggests that a professional observer:

> *knows when to observe*
>
> *knows how to observe*
>
> *knows why to observe*
>
> *knows whom to observe*
>
> *knows where to observe*
>
> *has the skill to record using a variety of formats and methods*
>
> *has the ability to organise observational data*
>
> *can analyse the observational data, preferably in a process of co-inquiry*
>
> *can identify his [sic] perspective, lenses and filters when involved in any part of the observation process*
>
> *can address issues of bias and show sensitivity to cultural and other perspectives and to diverse lifeways*
>
> *can share observational data and its analysis in a meaningful way.*

These can become guiding questions in your observation planning so you can meet what Malaguzzi (1993) suggests in the *hundred languages of children*:

> *There are hundreds of different images of the child. Each one of you has inside yourself an image of the child that directs you as you begin to relate to a child. This theory within you pushes you to behave in certain ways; its orients you as you talk to the child, listen to the child, observe the child.*

THEORY FOCUS

Three types of observation: advantages and disadvantages

Table 3.2 Three types of observation: advantages and disadvantages

Methods	Description	Purpose	Advantages	Disadvantages
A. Unstructured observation (participant observation – Chapter 4)	The observer is part of the normal daily life of the group being observed. Normally the observer belongs to the group (for example is an early childhood practitioner). It is naturalistic observation in the sense that events are observed as they occur.	It aims to capture what children do in that setting on a particular day, as they participate in the activity. Notes are kept to be checked afterwards with other team members. The aim is to collect evidence which will support the description of an activity event or behaviour. Other materials may be used such as photographs, videos, drawings or other relevant documents to support the description of the event.	Provides useful insight into activities, behaviours. It is not time-consuming as it happens as the events occur. Requires minimum preparation. Captures unexpected behaviours or changes in an activity.	It is difficult to interpret if not supported by other evidence as it relies on memory. It might be based on the perspective of the observer only (lack of objectivity). It can be very detailed and descriptive and it might distract from its significance. It is time-consuming. Information collected can be large and messy and requires too much organisation.
B. Structured observation (non-participant – discussed in Chapter 5)	Observation has a clear focus on exact behaviours, events or activities.	It is mechanistic, as specific techniques are used, but it offers rigour through good information on an activity, event or behaviour.	Evidence collected is normally numeric and is easy to interpret. Captures sequences of events, behaviours or activities.	Numerical information can be superficial and does not offer an in-depth approach to why certain events, behaviours occur.

Methods	Description	Purpose	Advantages	Disadvantages
(All the following techniques are part of the structured non-participant observations.)			It does not require a lot of time (including the planning). Information collected can be easily organised and categorised.	
B. 1 Narratives: (a) Anecdotal records (b) Running records	Written description of an event, child's behaviour or activity. Anecdotal: brief narrative describing an event, behaviour or activity. Running: a sequence of written descriptions of a particular event, behaviour or activity.	They aim to record specific behaviours, events, activities and their progress over a period of time. Aim to discover why certain events or behaviours occur.	Offer rich information as the observer records everything that happens. The observer can capture significant, unexpected events, activities or behaviours.	They offer a complete picture of what has happened. They can be messy if not organised carefully. They rely on memory and attention of the individual so need to be cross-referenced with other materials, information. They are time-consuming. They require special training. Observer needs to remove him/herself from the children and this has an impact on the ratio of the classroom.
B. 2 Rating scales: (a) Graphic scales (b) Numerical scales	A scale of events, behaviours recorded before, during or after the event.	It aims to rate the child's behaviour, involvement, participation in a certain activity or event.	Once designed, it does not take time from the observer. It is easy to design. You can observe more than one child at a time.	It is limited only to the focus of the scale.

(Continued)

Table 3.2 (Continued)

Methods	Description	Purpose	Advantages	Disadvantages
			It can be used by several observers for the same child. Children can participate in this method as self-observers.	You might miss other behaviours. Scale can be difficult to use if not all observers have understood the rating.
B. 3 Checklists	They capture a list of behaviours or developmental steps.	They aim to identify whether or not a child or children has/ have acquired certain behaviours or developmental characteristics.	Offer an overview of the development of a child or group of children.	They focus only on certain developmental characteristics or behaviours.
			Once designed, they can be used again.	They do not offer a rationale for why certain characteristics or behaviours occur.
			They can be used by several observers.	
			They can be used by children who can participate in self-observations.	They need to be cross-referenced or supported by other methods.
B. 4 Diagrammatic: (a) Histograms (b) Tracking (c) Sociograms d) Bar charts and pie charts	This is a purpose-specific technique and captures a certain behaviour or aspect of development.	It aims to observe whether a certain behaviour or developmental aspect has or has not occurred.	It can be used by children as self-observers.	It is limited to only one aspect of behaviour or development.
			Once designed, it can be used again for another group of children.	It does not offer an explanation as to why a behaviour is occurring.
			Offers an overview of a behaviour or aspect of development.	It needs to be cross-referenced with other methods.

Methods	Description	Purpose	Advantages	Disadvantages
B. 5 Sampling: (a) Time sampling (b) Event sampling	Captures samples of events, activities or behaviours. It is concerned with frequency (how often or rare) and duration.	It aims to observe certain behaviours over a period of time or over different activities.	It does not take much time. Children can participate as self-observers. Information can be collected for one child or a group of children at the same time with minimum effort from the observer. Offers useful information on intervals and frequencies.	It does not offer an explanation as to why an event or a behaviour has occurred. It needs to be used in conjunction with other methods. It is limited only to observable behaviours and other behaviours might be missed.
C. Semi-structured observation (Chapter 6)	The observation has clear aims and objectives, but the methods are 'open' so unpredicted events can be captured.	It aims to capture events that cannot be predicted. It aims to discover why certain events or behaviours occur.	Provides in-depth information about the context and circumstances of a behaviour, event or activities. Helps you identify problems, good practices, strengths and weaknesses that you might have not considered.	You might miss events or behaviours you considered normal and to be expected. It is time-consuming as you need to spend time in the setting. It can be messy. It requires careful interpretation and cross-checking with other members of the team or other materials.

ACTIVITY 3.5

Questions to consider before observation

During the preparation for your observation take some time to think about the following:

1. Have I reviewed the context/curriculum that is implemented?
2. What are the goals of the setting?
3. What are their principles of practice?
4. What are their learning outcomes?
5. Do I have the necessary permissions for my observations?

SUMMARY

This chapter has addressed the key issues of becoming a skilful observer. It is important that all early childhood education practitioners have training in order to become skilful observers as observation is not just watching. In the daily routine of practice, and as a systematic observer of children, you will need to develop objectivity, an absence of emotional bias and thus step out of the role that you normally hold. As will be highlighted in Chapter 9, part of the observation planning is the ethical considerations of the planning and this should be based on team, parental and child involvement – and confidentiality is an essential element in the whole process. Before we explore this, it is important to study the observation techniques available to practitioners. The next three chapters attempt to discuss the variety of observation techniques that are available to the professional.

Further Reading

For a step-by-step guide on observations:

Sharman, C and Cross, W (2015) *Observing Children and Young People* (4th edn). London: Continuum.

To learn more about developing professionalism:

Waring, M and Evans, C (2015) *Understanding Pedagogy: Developing Critical Approach to Teaching and Learning*. London: Routledge.

Websites

For some useful approaches to observations visit:

https://www.teachwire.net/news/7-useful-approaches-to-early-years-observations

CHAPTER 4

UNSTRUCTURED (PARTICIPANT) OBSERVATION

Chapter objectives

After reading this chapter, you will be able to understand:

- what unstructured (participant) observation is and its origins;
- the advantages and disadvantages of this type of observation;
- how they can be used in your daily practice.

Unstructured (participant) observation happens when the observer is immersed in the daily experiences of the children and offers rich narratives of what actually happens and when.

Introduction: What is it?

Unstructured observation (or participant observation or naturalistic observation) is a method common in research. It has its origins in a type of research that is called ethnography. Ethnographic studies require the researchers to immerse themselves in the particular social context they are researching by making observations of what people in that context say or do. The key characteristic of ethnography is that the researcher 'lives' in the natural environment of the researched context and gets an understanding of this environment. Thus this type of research is often called naturalistic as well. As the researcher wants to know this particular context, they tend to observe what they think it might be of significant importance and thus use unstructured (participant, naturalistic) observations. They keep detailed notes of their observations alongside other materials such as artefacts, photos, videos or documents that might help them to gain an in-depth understanding of the particular context they study. However, the main tool to collect information (data) is the use of unstructured (participant) observation. The benefits of using participant observation in research is that it assists the researchers to find out what actually goes on in this context.

There are different types of unstructured observation available to researchers, but the type of observation is characterised by:

1. *The researcher established a direct relationship with the social actors [the people involved]*
2. *staying in their natural environment;*
3. *with the purpose of observing and describing their social actions;*
4. *by interacting with them and participating in their every day ceremonials and rituals; and*
5. *learning their code (or at least part of it) in order to understand the meaning of their actions.*

(Silverman, 2011, p. 17)

(For more information on using observation for research see Chapter 12.)

Due to the nature of the unstructured observation (hereafter it will be referred as participant observation) it requires good knowledge of the context that is researched and this method has been used commonly in education by teachers to collect evidence for assessment purposes. This method is also often used in early childhood education by practitioners as they have a very good knowledge of their setting and the children who are attending.

In this type of observation, the practitioner records what happens when it happens. In the daily practice of an early childhood setting practitioners engage in a variety of activities with children, but if something happens the practitioner thinks is relevant in relation to a child's behaviour or an activity then he or she will record it as it happens. In participant observation the observer is part of the group and is involved with them, meaning the observation takes place during the event. For example, say new toys have been brought in a room with babies and the participants are taking them out and showing them to attract the babies' attention and interest. One of the children is crawling towards the toys and picks up the wooden car and instead of putting it to his mouth, as the child would normally have done, instead places the wooden car on the floor and starts playing. In such an event the practitioner might want to record this play and determine what behaviours or pattern of behaviours might be exhibited during this play. So in that instance participant observation is the best choice.

In early childhood education participant observation is part of the daily routine. When practitioners work with children they either record an event by writing down quick notes at the time of the event, or later after the event. These brief and immediate notes are part of an ongoing daily practice. The event is recorded when the practitioner is working with the children directly and he or she does not withdraw in order to observe. These recordings are usually brief comments about a child's behaviour during an activity, or are comments on how the activity was implemented.

ACTIVITY 4.1

Capturing the unexpected

George has just arrived from a playgroup back to the childminder's home. He is sitting on a chair in front of a table and playing with a toy train that contains three carriages connected to each other magnetically. Suddenly, he stops, raises his right hand and starts hitting his left hand shouting 'No', 'No', 'No'. He repeats this four times. As the childminder sees this, he picks up the camera and records the incident, thinking this is unusual behaviour for George. The way he hits himself appears to be painful and he is hurting himself, thus the childminder decides to video record the event (see the sequence of video screenshots in Figure 4.1 of how the incident developed).

Figure 4.1

- Can the childminder make a conclusion from this incident?
- What will be the next steps for the childminder after this participant observation recording?

How to do participant observations

Although participant observation is unstructured and naturalistic (record the event when it happens, where it happens), it is important to have strategies and a system in place that help you record the event/s in an accurate and faithful way.

To develop your skills as a participant observer requires you to be prepared all the time to record something that happens. However, there might be instances where you will keep some notes after the incident has happened, but this needs to be immediately afterwards. Lofland et al., (2006, pp.112–15) suggest some guidelines for the effective use of participant observation:

- **Be concrete.** Give specific concrete descriptions of events, for example who is involved, where the incident took place, what materials were used. They warn us to avoid characterising and keep out any judgments such as 'John was trying to build a tower'; it should be 'John is putting wooden bricks one on the top of another'.
- **Distinguish comments from recording events.** Make sure that what you have recorded is the exact event and you have not added any of your own comments. For example, 'John was trying to build a tower' entails the practitioner's comment based on observing John to try to put wooden bricks one on the top of another – what actually happened.
- **Interpretative idea.** These can be notes offering your analysis of the situations as they occur, for example 'John was trying to build a tower'.
- **Personal impressions and feelings.** Always ask whether what is recorded is your subjective reactions and to what extent your own impressions and feelings have altered the way this event is recorded. For example, you have been waiting for a very long time for John to start building a tower with wooden bricks and in your observation when you show John playing with the bricks you assumed he was trying to build a tower.
- **Look for additional information.** An incident that has been observed always needs to be checked either with another practitioner or by asking the child (if a child is involved) directly if this is what you think it is.

The recording of participant observation can take a written form as in a notebook or in the shape of sticky notes or by using digital media such as videos or photographs. Normally practitioners use all these methods in their daily routine. It is not an uncommon practice, as will be explained below, for practitioners to take a video or a photo and then add a brief narrative to it.

Written participant observation

There are different types of written participant observation:

From memory. These are notes that you write down after the event has happened as it was impossible to write them when the event was happening. However, as mentioned earlier, you need to write them down soon after the incident and should include details such as where it happened, who was involved, date and time of the day. Remember that when you revisit this observation later you should not have to ask yourself 'what does this mean?', 'why did I make this observation?' It is helpful to add some personal reflections (analytical notes) of why you found this incident important at the time.

CASE STUDY 4.1

Observation from memory

This morning when John arrived in the nursery he went straight to the table with the little wooden animals. He started playing alone and suddenly started thrashing the little wooden animals on the wall. I approached him to ask why he was doing this and he stopped and walked away from me. The same incident happened again just before lunch time.

My notes. I am not sure why this happened twice so far, but this is out of character for John. I do need to keep an eye to see how it will be for the rest of the day and if this behaviour is repeated again.

Jotted notes (or scratch notes or snapshots or Post it observations). These are very brief notes written on a piece of paper such as sticky notes. Lofland and Lofland (1996) explain that these are 'little phrases, quotes, key words'. Normally, especially with the use of photos in early childhood settings, it is common practice to take a photo and then add a brief phrase to explain what happen has happened. These days there are software and applications that help you to record your jotted notes in a digital way.

CASE STUDY 4.2

Jotted observation with the use of digital media

9th October

Mario has managed to balance himself and walk all the way for the first time.

Figure 4.2

Full observation. This is detailed observation that is recorded when the event happens. To assist you with this observation, it might help to have pre-prepared forms to quickly record occurrences. The following information can be included:

Name of the observer: _____

Name of the child: _____

Date of observation: _____

Starting time: _____

Finishing time: _____

No. of adults present: _____

Area of observation: _____

Description of the activity observed: _____

Additional comments: _____

I think _____ (In this section you add your thoughts that occurred during the observation, so that they might help you later to interpret your recordings.)

Note: It might be helpful to create in-trays: one for activities, one for events and one for each child in your setting where you put the observation recordings for activities, events or named children. This helps to categorise and organise observations and limits the messy factor of participant observation. This obviously speeds up the recording process and facilitates the filing of recordings. Therefore, when the recordings are re-visited, all the information will be included, making retrieval and interpretation much easier.

CASE STUDY 4.3

Full participant observation

Kenzie is four years and eleven months old. He has been absent from many of his classes. The aim of the observation is to identify whether or not these frequent absences are affecting his ability to make and sustain friendships.

Aim: To look for evidence of social play and participation

Observation 1

Name of the observer: Emily
Name of the child: Kenzie, 4 years and 11 months

Date of observation: 9/7
Starting time: 10:30 a.m.
Finishing time: 10:34 a.m.
No. of adults present: 1 adult
Area of observation: Free play outdoors

Description of the activity observed:

It is an outdoor play time and Kenzie is in the corner of the playground kicking leaves that have fallen from a tree. He is on his own, smiling and his arms are waving freely as he kicks the leaves. Liam, who has been playing with a group of three other boys, approaches Kenzie and says 'Come and play. It's me, Jack and Tommy'. Kenzie drops his head, looking towards the floor and his arms and legs remain still whilst Liam is speaking to him. Liam returns to his group of friends without Kenzie, who continues to droop his head and remain motionless.

Additional comment:

Prior to Kenzie being approached by his peer, he was involved in play. Kenzie appeared to be joyfully content with solitary play and there was a definite change in his body language when Liam joined him. This event seems to support the concerns raised as Kenzie refused to answer Liam and preferred not to make any eye contact.

Observation 2

Name of the observer: Emily
Name of the child: Kenzie, 4 years and 11 months
Date of observation: 9/7
Starting time: 11:40 a.m.
Finishing time: 11:45 a.m.
No. of adults present: 1 adult
Area of observation: Writing area

Description of the activity observed:

Kenzie is sitting at a table with three other children. There is a tub of wax crayons close to him on the table and he has a picture of a lollipop lady in front of him which he has been asked to colour in. He is looking down at his lollipop lady picture and his tongue is moving from side to side as he holds a red wax crayon to the paper. Toby says to Kenzie: 'I need a green, can I have a green crayon?' Kenzie remains silent and lifts his head to face Toby. Kenzie reaches out his left arm towards the tub of crayons, scoops the tub in the crook of his arm and pulls it towards his body. His eyebrows are lowered and his lips are puckered tightly.

Additional comments:

Kenzie is choosing not to communicate with Toby. He is capable of expressing himself and could well have asked Toby to wait until he had finished with the green crayon and put it back into the tub or

(Continued)

(Continued)

given it to Toby. He does not want to share (something that he did earlier in the sand area as well). He makes eye contact on this occasion.

Observation 3

Name of the observer: Emily
Name of the child: Kenzie, 4 years and 11 months
Date of observation: 11/7
Starting time: 11:15 a.m.
Finishing time: 11:20 a.m.
No. of adults present: 1 adult
Area of observation: Outdoors play

Description of the activity observed:

During outdoor free play, Kenzie is sitting on a tricycle. He is pedaling, raising his head and 'La-La-ing' a tune loudly. Tommy and Claire run over to Kenzie and Tommy shouts excitedly, 'We are playing trains! Come and make a big, long train.' Kenzie stops pedalling and while Tommy is talking, Kenzie is looking and smiling at Tommy as he is getting off the tricycle. Both of his arms are up in the air and he is shouting, 'Yeah, big train, yeah!' The three children run off together and form a line by standing one behind the other. They are all running around in a line, laughing and making 'Woo-hoo' noises.

Additional comments:

Since the last observations, it appears that there is progress in terms of making friendships. Other members of staff report that he seems to have settled in well and engages in most activities. He has a lot of free play with Tommy. He has even started to bring items to the Show and Tell time at the beginning of the morning session, which also demonstrates an important social step forward.

Digital participant observation

With a variety of accessible electronic media now widely available, the early childhood team can use a number of techniques to improve the observation process. The digital camera or the digital video recorder can be used to add another dimension. The photographic evidence or video recording evidence cannot replace the traditional observation techniques such as narratives, checklists, sampling and diagrammatic methods (see Chapter 5), but they can be used as additional tools in the observation process. They offer accurate information about events as they capture everything. The Mosaic approach (mentioned in Chapter 3) provides an excellent example of how media techniques were used as a useful method of gathering information about children's progress through the activities. In the Mosaic approach, it was demonstrated how media techniques became a powerful tool to encourage children's participation in contributing to data collection. They adopted media techniques as *participatory techniques* for use with children to enable them to be actively involved in the observation process (Clark and Moss, 2001).

However, when using digital observation (photographs or videos) we might want to consider that, for some children and practitioners, photographs or videos can make the observation intrusive as they might object to being visually recorded. It also eliminates the anonymity and confidentiality factor, while behaviour may be affected and spontaneity lost. It is also worth mentioning that digital media for observation serve as representations of a narrative and we cannot ignore the fact that they illustrate a narrative sequence; their interpretation is subject to individual experiences. Pink (2007, p.21) addresses this in the following extract:

> *Visual research methods [in our case visual observation techniques] are not purely visual. Rather they pay a particular attention to visual aspects of culture. Similarly, they cannot be used independently of other methods; neither a purely visual ethnography nor an exclusively visual approach to culture exist.*

Bentzen (2009) also cautions us on the use of visual media in observations as taking away information we might be able to gather that require the activation of our senses:

> *Our brains enable us to see in ways that far exceed the camera's ability to 'see'. But observation becomes complicated precisely because we do more with sensory information than the camera is able to [. . .] what and how much information perceived varies from person to person, and even within the same person from one time to another. So it is that two individuals can be visually aware of the same object but visually aware in different ways.*
>
> (pp.5–6)

This point will be elaborated in Chapter 8 when the uses of digital media are discussed.

ACTIVITY 4.2

Do an observation

Write down what you see in the sequence of photos shown in Figures 4.3 and 4.4. Compare what you have written with one of your fellow students or practitioners. Are you able to identify whether your recording is similar or different? In what ways?

(Continued)

(Continued)

Figure 4.3 Harry plays with soldiers and pirates

Figure 4.4 Balancing

At a practical level, digital technologies can be used to facilitate how you file your observations. Saving the observations in folders with your explanations means they can be easily shared via a USB stick either with other members of staff or with parents to take home. (Of course, first ask the parents if they want it and if they have the facility. Avoid overwhelming them with information that they might not want to see.) Using digital storage space enables you to share more information than with paper copy files. By saving observations in a digital device you are able to easily see the child's progress throughout the year; in addition, those parents who like a wealth of information can also have access.

There are also several applications (apps) available now which can be uploaded to a digital device, such as tablets for digital observations (see Chapter 8). Although these apps are not observations they can be very helpful tools for practitioners and their settings. Although the use of digital media has many positives, as will be discussed in Chapter 8, there are legal and ethical implications of using them. Online information about children's activities, development and learning carry the risk that they may be seen by third parties who are not related to the children and who might expose the children's and families' privacy and personal information. However, the use of digital media can be integrated into the everyday routine of an early childhood education setting and some have already done so. Software packages, mobile apps, online computing services, intranets and other platforms need to be used alongside security systems to protect children's personal information from the observations. If you are using digital media to facilitate your observations you do need to be proactive to ensure that your information is protected. As digital information can be stored indefinitely it is essential to make sure that there are systems in place to ensure that the information you have collected, used and shared with the parents is protected (see Chapter 9 for more information).

ACTIVITY 4.3

Do participant observation

In your early childhood setting, undertake at least three participant observations. Share your observations with a more experienced colleague or a fellow student. Was it difficult to find time to observe events and, if so, how did you overcome this?
  Remember:

* be factual and objective;
* record when and where it happened;
* record what was said and done;
* record facial expressions, body language, tones of voice, gestures.

Evaluation of participant observation

There are a number of advantages when practitioners are using participant observation. As you observe events while they unfold these recorded daily events can provide the practitioner with a useful insight into a child or an activity. Special training is not required, as the practitioner writes down his/her perception of an event as it occurs. This type of observation is unstructured and observers write down what appears to them to be most interesting and relevant at the time. It does not require planning or organisation and it is useful as events such as unexpected behaviour or an unexpected change within an activity are recorded. Finally, as participant observation records unexpected events, these can provide you with new information about a child or an activity which, with further information, might assist you to develop new ideas about your future planning of your activities.

However, there are obvious limitations to this method. Participant observation will not give a complete picture of the events and requires the participant to rely on their memory as events will be recorded either after they have happened or when they happen. This means that it can be difficult as you are involved with the children and subsequently you might become biased and not 'see' what actually happens or exists (see Chapter 3 section on objectivity).

As Devereux (2003) points out, participant observation can be messy and difficult to manage. It should be categorised and filed immediately otherwise useful evidence could be lost. An additional disadvantage to this type of observation technique is that the recorded information could be examined long after an event, thus allowing the potential for an inaccurate and biased interpretation of events.

However, despite the disadvantages of using participant observation, it is a very simple and immediate tool to employ in collecting information as events occur and can be used to capture unexpected events during the day.

ACTIVITY 4.4

Evaluate participant observation

Can you list any further disadvantages of participant observation?

SUMMARY

This chapter discussed one of the most popular observation methods in early childhood education, participant observation. This grew out of the field of ethnographic research where researchers immerse themselves in the situation they are studying. It has found popularity within education and is heavily used in early childhood. There are two main types of participant observation: written and digital, although a combination of the two can offer a more complete profile of what is observed. However, participant observation cannot offer a complete picture of events or a child's development and learning, thus it should be used alongside other evidence collected with other observation methods. The following chapters therefore discuss structured (non-participant) observation (Chapter 5) and semi-structured observation (Chapter 6).

Further Reading

For extensive examples on observation techniques, see the work of:

Bruce, T, Louis, S and McCall, G (2015) *Observing Young Children*. London: Sage.

Websites

Visit this website as it has video recordings of children playing and you will have an opportunity to practise your observation techniques:

https://study.sagepub.com/walleranddavis3e/student-resources/child-observation-videos

CHAPTER 5

STRUCTURED (NON-PARTICIPANT) OBSERVATION

Chapter objectives

After reading this chapter, you should understand:

- the most common used structured observations (narratives, rating scales, checklists, sampling, diagrammatics);
- how, when and why to use these techniques;
- the strengths and limitations of each technique;
- the available most commonly used structured observation tools used in early childhood practice.

Structured (non-participant observation) is a detached approached that requires training and preparation. It can be extremely helpful in the daily practice as it captures events behaviours on targeted areas of your curriculum.

Introduction: Structured (non-participant) observation

This type of observation is systematic and requires a number of techniques as will be described below. Structured (hereafter it will be referred to as non-participant) observation requires the practitioner to step outside their normal role – and not be involved in interacting with the children or the activity as it happens – acting instead as a distant objective observer of the child or an activity.

Preparation and organisation are required for non-participant observation and it needs to be planned in advance. As was shown at the beginning of Chapter 1, most curricular approaches in the UK, such as the EYFS in England or the Foundation Phase in Wales, require the practitioner to create a profile for the child based on ongoing observations against the learning areas that are described. For the practitioners to be able to meet these requirements and to be able to complete the profile effectively a systematic preparation for this type of observation is crucial. The following sections aim to offer a detailed account of all the different types of non-participant observation techniques available to the early childhood practitioner (see the Theory Focus, Table 3.1, in Chapter 3 for an overview of the types of unstructured observation with a brief description of their advantages and disadvantages for each):

- narratives (or written observations);
- rating scales;
- checklists;
- diagrams (histograms, tracking, sociograms, bar charts, pie charts);
- sampling (time and event sampling).

Preparing for non-participant observation

To become a systematic observer of children, you must first step out of the role you normally hold. Once you have decided when your observations will take place, you must withdraw from your role in the class and take on instead the role of the systematic observer. You should position yourself close to what you want to observe, but not interfere with the child/children in question or with the activity you are observing. Your presence as an observer should be discreet. You must not announce to the children that you are doing an observation and the children should be left alone. If children have been involved in the observation planning (see Chapters 3 and 9 for more information on this) then there is no need to announce this each time. Sit closely, however, so that you can see and hear what happens. However, if a child interrupts your observation, it is better to stop rather than gather patchy and inaccurate information.

The best time to undertake observations will be determined by the aims and objectives. For example, an investigation of activities popular with children on arrival will be conducted. If you wish to observe children's language development, this could be done through a variety of observations at different times of the day.

Similarly, the type of activity to be observed should relate to your aims and objectives. You may, for example, wish to investigate the social interactions of a child during story time.

However, there will be cases where the type of activity to be observed is not always implicit in your aims and objectives. For example, your aim could be to observe social skills and your objective is to investigate whether or not the child in question forms good relationships with peers. In these instances it is important to refer back to the initial team meetings and reconsider the planning notes, as discussed in Chapter 3.

Preparation of the observations is crucial as it speeds up this process. The systematic way of recording your observations will become effective as you categorise, file, retrieve and then analyse them.

The observation techniques are explained in the following sections and include an evaluation of each one.

Narratives or written observations

This is the most common observation technique used by practitioners. As was shown in the Theory Focus table in Chapter 3, there are two types of narrative or written observations:

1. **Anecdotal records** (example in Table 5.1, p.110): A brief narrative that describes an event, behaviour or activity when it occurs, but is not planned beforehand. The event that occurs normally is recorded as it seems unexpected and attracts the interest of the practitioner as it is considered to be important. This technique is similar to participant observation, but the difference is that the participant does not participate in the activity and steps out of the normal role as practitioner, becoming an observer from a distance rather than interacting with children and observing at the same time as in the participant observation.

   Example: In the observation in Table 5.1 the practitioner observed the incident as Bella attempts for the first time to experience the foam soap.

2. **Running records or specimen records** (example in Table 5.2, p.111): In several textbooks this technique is alternatively called: running record or specimen record or narrative record. No matter which term you use the nature of this observation is the same. It is a written record of an event as it occurs, but the aims and objectives of the observation have been decided beforehand and the observer writes down what they see over a specified period of time.

   Example: In the example of a narrative observation shown in Table 5.2 the focus has been identified beforehand and the activity has been designed as the practitioner wants to observe how Sally is developing her skills when interacting with jigsaws.

When written observations are used the usual process is for observers to remove themselves from the activity and observe from a discreet distance, avoiding interacting with or interrupting the children or the activities. Each observation is brief (no more than five minutes) and requires an accurate recording of exactly what happens at the time. This is written in the present tense. As discussed in the participant observation chapter, it is helpful to have forms already prepared. Again, these will include the following information as illustrated in the sample form shown on p.110. Additionally, with the availability of digital media, videos or photographs can be used but it is important to include some narrative in the digital recordings so you know the context and the reason why they were captured.

Table 5.1   Observation of Bella – an example of anecdotal records

Child's name:	Bella
Adult observer:	Kelly
Area of provision:	Foam play
Date: 13/03	Time duration: 10 min

What happens:

The children have a tray each with foam soap; there are various different utensils both practical such as spoons and bowls and a selection of toys to support each child's individual interests, e.g. Peppa Pig figures, cars, small dolls, etc.

Bella begins by pushing her hands into the foam and squeezing it between her fingers.

B: *It's squishy.*

Bella rubs her hands together as though washing them.

KP: *Are you washing your hands Bella?*

B: *Yeah, it's Peppa Pig and George.*

Bella continues.

KP: *Do you know what colour the foam is Bella?*

B: *Don't know.*

It has been snowing so the KP attempts to make links with the weather.

KP: *It's white Bella, I think it might look like snow; do you think it looks like snow?*

No response so the practitioner attempts to extend Bella's learning in another direction.

KP: *What does it smell like?*

B: *Poo poo, it smells like wee wee.*

B: *This is fun, this is fun KP.*

Another child puts his hands on his face.

B: *It looks like a beard.*

Possible lines of development: Continue to make links through activities to encourage Bella to make comparisons between what she is doing and other experiences.

It is helpful to add comments immediately after the observation has been completed, but care should be taken not to include any of your own comments during the observation itself. It is worth reiterating that observations should only include what actually occurs. Initial thoughts about what has been observed will give a good basis for later interpretation and analysis.

Table 5.2 Observation of Sally – an example of running records or specimen records

Child's name:	Sally
Date of birth:	xxxx
Age in months:	36
Adult observer:	KP
Activity:	Shape, Space and Measures & ICT
Date: 09/05	Time/duration: 10 mins

What happens/happened:

KP has introduced a program on the Kindle to a group of five children. The program encourages fine motor skills by matching shapes, in this case different sized and shaped fishes. The aim of the activity is to manipulate the fish at different angles to make them fit the corresponding shadowed shape. The activity builds upon Sally's interests as the KP has observed Sally choosing to do jigsaws within the setting, from her own observations and from speaking to Sally's foster carer.

This is the first time Sally has accessed this program. Sally struggles initially to identify which shape fits into which space, but with help from KP Sally begins to identify the correct shape but then struggles to move the shape across to the corresponding shadowed shape. KP gives Sally a pen to see if this makes the manipulation of the virtual shape any easier. Sally does not want to use the pen and attempts to move the shape once again with her finger. This time Sally is able to move the shapes across to the correct shape. Now the shape must be twisted and moved to enable the shape to fit. Sally maintains her attention and after a few attempts the first fish is slotted into place. Sally readily allows other children to have a turn, but watches them while carefully attempting to offer suggestions on how they might move the fish, but does not physically interfere. Between the five children they take turns and complete the program together. The other children move onto a different activity; Sally asks KP if she can do another puzzle.

Personal social emotional development	Physical development	Communication language	Literacy	Mathematics	Understanding the world	Expressive arts development
Self-confidence and self-awareness.	Health and self-care.	Understanding. Listening and attention.	Reading. Writing.	Numbers, shape, space and measure.	The world. People and communities.	Exploring and using media and materials.
Making relationships. Managing feelings and behaviour.	Moving and handling.	Speaking.			Technology.	Being imaginative.

(Continued)

Table 5.2 (Continued)

Personal social emotional development	Physical development	Communication language	Literacy	Mathematics	Understanding the world	Expressive arts development
Age and stage						
				30–50 months	40–60 months	30–50 months
30–50 months				Uses shapes appropriately for tasks.	Completes a simple program on a computer.	Shows skill in making toys work by pressing parts or lifting flaps to achieve effects such as sound, movement or new images.
Demonstrates friendly behaviour, initiating conversations and forming good relationships with peers and familiar adults.						
30–50 months						
Can select and use activities and resources with help.						

Playing and exploring	**Active learning**			**Creating and thinking critically**		
Finding out and exploring.	Being involved and concentrating.			Having their own ideas.		
Playing with what they know.				Making links.		
Being willing to 'have a go'.	Keeping on trying.			Choosing ways to do things.		
	Enjoying and achieving what they set out to do.					

Next steps:

- Repeat the activity to develop Sally's skills.
- Speak to Sally's foster carer to try this activity at home.
- Identify other ICT programs Sally might like based on her interests.
- Attempt the activity with a 3D representation to see if the results are similar.

ACTIVITY 5.1

Do a written observation

Look at the photographs in Figures 5.1 and 5.2 and write down what you have observed.

Share your recordings with a fellow student or a more experienced colleague. Have you recorded the same information?

Figure 5.1   Children drawing

(Continued)

(Continued)

Figure 5.2 Ben's attempts on the slide

CASE STUDY 5.1

A written observation

Name of child/children:	Vicky
No. of adults present:	1
No. of children present:	2
Activity:	Cooking
Area:	Writing area
Date of observation:	04/02
Start time of observation:	1:45 p.m.
Finishing time of observation:	1:50 p.m.
Aim:	Social development
Objective:	To what extent Vicky has developed her ability to play successfully with others?

Observation

Two children (Vicky and Zara) and the practitioner (Maria) are in the writing area and they write down a recipe on a sheet of poster paper.

Maria: *So, we need one glass of olive oil and do you remember what else we wrote?*

Zara: *Sugar?*

Maria: *Can you remember how many glasses of sugar we need?*

Vicky: *Three and four glasses of that . . .* [she points to the water]

Maria: [pointing to the word 'water'] *Here, it says 'water'. We need four glasses of water.*

Maria: *What else did we say?*

Vicky: *Two glasses of that.*

Maria: *What is it?*

Vicky: *I don't know. Zara: Is this semolina?*

Vicky: *. . . semolina.*

Maria: *And how many glasses of semolina do we need?*

Vicky: *. . . two?*

Zara: *Where does this say 'two'?*

Vicky: [points to the poster] *Here.*

Maria: *Yes. If you look here, we need two glasses of semolina.*

Comment (a brief comment may be added here):

The children were working together with Maria in order to make sense of the recipe. Zara was helping Vicky, and with the help of the practitioner, they were trying to cook. The children show some evidence of working together towards a common purpose.

Evaluation of written observations

As this observation aims to record everything that happens, the observer records anything and everything that happens (such as dialogues, movements, emotions) and this offers rich evidence of the children's behaviours or the implementation of activities. Some advantages of this technique are that the recordings are:

*   accurate;
*   complete;
*   comprehensive.

However, as the observation proceeds, the information recorded can be taken out of context and is open to biased and inaccurate interpretation. A further disadvantage is that the observer may have omitted some relevant information, thus presenting an incomplete and patchy picture of the event. In a busy environment, where the observer is an integral part of the team, it may not always be possible or practical to release the team member in order to undertake an uninterrupted observation.

ACTIVITY 5.2

Reflect on how you do written observation

In your early childhood setting undertake at least three written observations. Set clear aims and objectives for undertaking these. Be clear with yourself at what point of the day you anticipate undertaking them.
   Evaluate the process, for example:

* Have I included all the relevant information and details?
* Have I included any judgements or comments?
* Could I have missed significant events?

Rating scales

Rating scales can be a valid technique for recording certain behaviour or aspects of development. This is a helpful technique as each behaviour is rated on a scale of a continuum from the lowest to highest (or vice versa) and it is marked against certain points along the scale. The observer makes a judgement about where on the scale a child's behaviour is. The most common rating scales in early childhood settings are:

* the Ferre Laevers scales of involvement and well-being (as will be explained later in this section);
* the Early Childhood Environment Rating Scale – Revised (ECERS-R) that aims to evaluate quality of provision for children aged 2½ to 5 years in early childhood settings;
* the Infant Toddler Environment Rating Scale – Revised (ITERS-R) is the partner scale for the 0–2½ age range.

Both these scales include a number of statements (indicators) that aim to evaluate the quality of the early childhood environment in terms of:

Space and furnishings (e.g. room layout, accessibility of resources, display)

Personal care routines (e.g. welfare requirements such as health and safety and provision for sleeping)

Language and reasoning (e.g. supporting children's communication, language and literacy development, critical thinking)

Activities (e.g. provision of an exciting and accessible learning environment, resources to support specific types of play)

Interaction (e.g. supervision, support for social interactions)

Programme structure (e.g. opportunities for children to access their own curriculum, planning schedules/routines to meet children's needs)

Provision for parents and staff (e.g. partnership with parents, staff training and development)

(Source : **http://www.ecersuk.org/4.html**)

- Professor Kathy Sylva, Professor Iram Siraj-Blatchford and Brenda Taggart as part of the EPPE Project have developed these scales (the ECERS-E) to include other aspects of early childhood education such as literacy, mathematics, science and environment, and finally diversity;
- Classroom Assessment Scoring System (CLASS) that focuses on the quality of classroom interactions in three domains: emotional support, classroom organisation and instructional support. It is an observation instrument and includes four cycles of 15-minute observations of teachers and children. These observations are then rated using a manual of behaviours and responses. However, it requires training before it is used. (For more information see: **https://curry.virginia.edu/classroom-assess ment-scoring-system**)

ACTIVITY 5.3

Personal study

Visit the **http://www.ecersuk.org/4.html** and study the Early Childhood Environment Scales. How can they be used in your context? What are the benefits using these scales?

There are two main types of rating scales: graphic and numerical. These scales are simple to make. Firstly you should identify the behaviour you want to observe, then you draw a line and mark off a number of interval points along the line. Normally we use five interval points (that either describe the frequency of a behaviour such as always, often, sometimes, rare or never, or duration of a behaviour such as 2–3 times, 3–5 times and so on; see the examples below). Although creating rating scales is a simple technique, the observer should know the children very well in order to be able to make judgements and to interpret the children's behaviours. This technique can be used by children as well, if it is designed in a way that children have participated in the designing process so that they too fully understand. Children are normally the best judges of their behaviours if they are given the opportunity to express themselves.

Examples

Graphic scale

Aim: Social development
Objective: Children wait for their turn during play

> Always: Child always waits for his/her turn
>
> Often: Child often waits for his/her turn
>
> Sometimes: Child sometimes waits for his/her turn
>
> Rare: Child rarely waits for his/her turn
>
> Never: Child never waits for his/her turn

So after using this scale to observe a child several times in different areas and activities you may have the graphic scale shown in Figure 5.3 for one child:

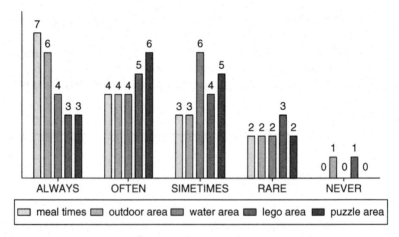

Figure 5.3   Child waits for his/her turn

Alternatively a child self-observation graphic scale could look like this:

Times during the day	Always	Often	Sometimes	Never
Meal times	☺			
Outdoor area		☺		
Lego area		☺		
Puzzle area			☹	
Water area				☹
Storytelling time			☹	

Symbols to choose from:

  Objective: Wait for my turn

☺ Always

😐 Often

☹ Sometimes

👎 Never

It is important that these symbols would be very carefully explained to children before their use. Children can add a card of one of each symbols chosen (as shown above) to the chart according to their view on whether they were waiting for their turn or not. So for example over a period of a week you can collect the charts for each day (as the table above shows as an example) and you can have a graphic scale as the example in Figure 5.1. This way children are able to carry out a self-observation and self-evaluation of their behaviour and consequently they are actively participating in the observation process.

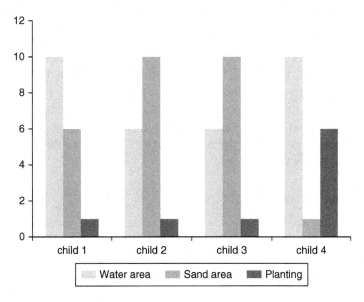

Figure 5.4   Activities children liked during the day

Numerical scales

Numerical scales are normally used where certain behaviours or aspects of development are scored. For example, if you want to investigate children's feelings towards a certain activity, this can be done numerically.

☺ This activity made me happy (smiley face scores high: 10)

😐 This activity was OK (smiley face scores medium: 6)

☹ This activity did not interest me (scores low: 1)

Again these symbols would need to be very carefully explained to children prior to use.

Using this information you can obtain an overall picture (in the form of a bar chart – see Figure 5.4) of whether children liked a certain activity. As a practitioner, in the area you want to evaluate you could set up a box containing small cards (like tokens) with little phrases on them, and ask the children to put one of the cards into the box every time they use the area. At the end of the day you can collect the box and find out how many children have used a certain area and according to the cards children have put in the box you can assess whether this is a popular area or not.

CASE STUDY 5.2

Ferre Laevers' rating scales of well-being and involvement

As was mentioned earlier there are a number of rating scales available to be used in early childhood education. A commonly used and popular type of rating scale is the Ferre Laevers scale of well-being and involvement (Laevers, 1997, 1998, 1999, 2000). The work of Ferre Laevers is concerned with the question of quality in early childhood education. In an attempt to understand what makes an educational setting a quality one, he proposes that the activities offered and the children's involvement in those activities are key factors of quality. Consequently, along with Moons, he has developed rating scales for well-being and involvement around Ten Action Points as an inventory of ten types of initiatives that will between them measure these two factors (Laevers and Moons, 1997). These scales are also known as Leuven scales (see examples on pp.122 and 123) which was the university that Laevers was working in when he created the scales.

The Leuven scale for well-being

Signals:

1. *Extremely low*

   The child clearly shows signs of discomfort such as crying or screaming. He or she may look dejected, sad, frightened or angry. The child does not respond to the environment, avoids contact and is withdrawn. The child may behave aggressively, hurting him/herself or others.

2. *Low*

   The posture, facial expression and actions indicate that the child does not feel at ease. However, the signals are less explicit than for level 1 – or the sense of discomfort is not expressed the whole time.

3. *Moderate*

   The child has a neutral posture. Facial expression and posture show little or no emotion. There are no signs indicating sadness or pleasure, comfort or discomfort.

4. *High*

   The child shows obvious signs of satisfaction (as listed under level 5). However, these signals are not constantly present with the same intensity.

5. *Extremely high*

   The child looks happy and cheerful, smiles, cries out with pleasure. He or she may be lively and full of energy. Actions can be spontaneous and expressive. The child may talk to him/herself, play with sounds, hum or sing. The child appears relaxed and does not show any signs of stress or tension. He or she is open and accessible to the environment. The child expresses self-confidence and self-assurance.

The Leuven scale for involvement

Signals:

1. *Extremely low*

   Activity is simple, repetitive and passive. The child seems absent and displays no energy. He or she may stare into space or look around to see what others are doing.

2. *Low*

   Frequently interrupted activity. The child will be engaged in the activity for some of the time he or she is observed, but there will be moments of non-activity when the child will stare into space or be distracted by what is going on around him or her.

3. *Moderate*

   Mainly continuous activity. The child is busy with the activity, but at a fairly routine level and there are few signs of real involvement. He or she makes some progress with what he or she is doing, but does not show much energy and concentration and can be easily distracted.

4. *High*

   Continuous activity with intense moments. The child's activity has intense moments and at all times he or she seems involved. He or she is not easily distracted.

5. *Extremely high*

   The child shows continuous and intense activity revealing the greatest involvement. He or she is concentrated, creative, energetic and persistent throughout nearly all the observed period.

(Adapted from Laevers, 1994, 2005a, 2005b, 2009; Laevers and Moons, 1997; Laevers et al., 1997)

(Continued)

(Continued)

Examples of Leuven Scales are shown in Figure 5.5.

Name of Child: CHILD H G			Age of Child: 4 YEARS			
Observer: RJ4KS			Gender: FEMALE			
Date: 29/6/15			Subject: IPAD ACTIVITIES			
Adult Led: Yes/No			Child Initiated: Yes/No			
Observation of Engagement using Leuven Scale of Engagement						
Activity	Time	Extremely Low	Low	Moderate	High	Extremely High
Elmo 123	9:25			3		
Endless Reader	9:27			3		
Peppa Pig Shopping	9:29			3		
Endless Wordplay	9:31			3		
	9:33			3		
	9:35				4	
	9:37				4	
	9:39				4	

Brief description of setting and activity: She plays this game routinely. She opens games & closes them. She is engaged with Endless wordplay but she has played this so many times, she is mentally challenged by the game anymore. She has intense moments at 9:35, moving away from everyone. She changes again. She is usually engaged with the activities but not more than four or five minutes

Name of Child: CHILD 1B				Age of Child: 3 YEARS		
Observer: RONICE				Gender: MALE		
Date: 29/6/15				Subject: IPAD ACTIVITIES		
Adult Led: Yes/No				Child Initiated: Yes/No		
Observation of Engagement using Leuven Scale of Engagement						
Activity	Time	Extremely Low	Low	Moderate	High	Extremely High
Peppa Pig Shopping	9:05					5
	9:07					5
	9:09					5
	9:11					5
Peppa's Paint box	9:13				4	
Max & Ruby /water /diet	9:15					5
	9:17					5
	9:19					5
	9:21					5
	9:22					5

Brief description of setting and activity: There are five children around us. However, instead of being a distraction, they are collaborating. They are working together to get all the items in the trolley. He celebrates when he finishes. He enjoys water beat by himself. When he gets it wrong, the other children to correct him.

Figure 5.5 Scales of involvement examples

Checklists

Checklists are a very useful observation technique. It is a relatively difficult technique, compared to narratives, as careful planning and preparation are required. Checklists can be used to record the activities of a single child or a group of children. They can also be used to record the progress of an activity for evaluation purposes. They are a useful tool for the practitioner, offering specific information and providing a starting point for planning activities for individuals or for groups of children.

The learning areas of the curriculum you are working with can be your starting point for creating checklists. For example, within the EYFS the learning areas that are described can provide a helpful starting point in creating a checklist as the example below demonstrates. However, they cannot stand as an independent comprehensive checklist and should not be used as such, so they need to be developed further. The learning areas of your curriculum can become objectives of your checklists, but not the checklists themselves (see the discussion on aims and objectives in Chapter 3).

Example: The Early Learning Goals of the EYFS (DfE, 2017, pp.10–12)

Personal, social and emotional development:

Self-confidence and self-awareness: *children are confident to try new activities, and say why they like some activities more than others. They are confident to speak in a familiar group, will talk about their ideas, and will choose the resources they need for their chosen activities. They say when they do or don't need help.*

Managing feelings and behaviour: *children talk about how they and others show feelings, talk about their own and others' behaviour and its consequences, and know that some behaviour is unacceptable. They work as part of a group or class, and understand and follow the rules. They adjust their behaviour to different situations, and take changes of routine in their stride.*

Making relationships: *children play cooperatively, taking turns with others. They take account of one another's ideas about how to organise their activity. They show sensitivity to others' needs and feelings, and form positive relationships with adults and other children.*

(DfE, 2017, p.11)

You want to focus on Making Relationships as your objective for this learning area, so you can start creating your checklist with the characteristics that are provided in the EYFS.

Table 5.4 below is an example of a checklist that has been created for three-year-old children for Personal Social and Emotional Development, and the action points that the staff implemented after discussing the information from the checklist.

During a staff meeting discussing the checklists for this area, practitioners realised that the majority of the children had not yet developed the ability to wait for their turn. Thus they decided to take some action and introduced activities and areas to support children in turn taking. Here is the Action Plan:

1. In the outdoor area introduce a traffic light system where children have to wait for the lights to change. Once children experience how to play with the traffic system they will increase the duration of the red traffic light which means they have to wait.
2. Introduce two activities where the number of children that can participate is limited to only three. Then introduce a list with children's names on a clipboard on which the children will have to put their names down if they want to participate in an activity in which only a limited number of children can participate.
3. Create a post office area where one child at a time is behind the 'desk for selling stamps' and the other children need to take numbered cards if they want to be the 'post person'.
4. Set up more cooking activities and the use of a timer that children have to set according to the waiting times of the recipe.

Designing a checklist is not an easy task. Things to keep in mind when you create one include:

- length – keep it short;
- include items that are representative of the particular behaviour under study;
- include items that are representative of the age of the children you are observing;
- ensure that it can be understood by the whole team.

Table 5.4 Checklist for Harry

Child's name: Harry

Aim: Making relationships

Objective: Taking turns

Behaviours I want to observe:	Evidence (you can add a tick if this behaviour happens or you can allow space to write a brief comment):	Date:
Child can wait for his/her turn to use a toy	Harry asked to take one of the bicycles that other children used and sat next to me until one was free	08/11
Child can wait for his/her turn to be part of an activity	✓	10/11
Child gives up when he/she has to wait for a toy for more than five minutes	Harry was waiting to use the swing but after two minutes put his head down and complained, then started walking towards the water area ✓	02/11 03/11 05/11
Child gives up when he/she has to wait for more than five minutes to be part of an activity	✓	06/11
Child waits for his/her turn without fuss when he/she waits to take a toy or take part in an activity	Harry started talking with Leon when they were waiting to take turns on the swing	13/11

(Continued)

Table 5.4 (Continued)

Child makes a fuss when he/she has to wait for a toy or to take part in an activity	Harry cried when he could not be first on the line for going outdoors	11/11
		12/11
	Harry complained during musical chairs activity when a chair was not available for him	13/11
Child offers his turn to another child	Harry chose to take part in the cooking activity but gave his turn to Emily	16/11
Child occupies him/herself with another toy or activity until his/her turn arrives	No	11/11
	No	12/11
	No	13/11
Child stares when he/she has to wait for his/her turn	✓	03/11

EXAMPLE

Look at the checklist below which attempts to record a child's behaviour during storytelling time.

1. Which of the items below capture listening behaviours?
2. Are there any additional items to be added to the list?
3. In what ways is this a useful tool for the early childhood workforce?

Name of child:
Date:
No. of adults present:
No. of children present:
Activity:
Story time area: Carpet
Aim: Language development
Objective: Listens and responds

1. Looks at teacher directly
2. Child pays attention
3. Facial movements: 3(a) Smile 3(b) Impressed 3(c) Apathetic
4. Uses body language: 4(a) Movement 4(b) Direction 4(c) Emotion 4(d) Relaxation 4(e) Interest
5. Asks questions
6. Joins in discussion
7. Answers questions
8. Predicts events from the book

ACTIVITY 5.4

Create your checklist

Using your curriculum learning goals as your guide, create a checklist for social development. How are you going to tackle the objectives in your checklist: 'Child works as part of a group or class by showing sharing fairly'? or 'Child complies with rules'? Consider the timing of your observation and specific items to include in your checklist.

In the literature a key element in the observation process and planning is children's participation. The early childhood workforce needs not only to involve children in the process of observation planning, but also to involve them in the actual observations. As illustrated in Chapter 3, the Mosaic approach has demonstrated a way of involving children in the observation process by using videos and cameras.

Involving children like this can be done in two ways: self-observation and observing others. In both cases, a number of observation techniques (see the Theory Box, Table 3.2 on p.90) are available. Self-observation by children provides a way of recording in detail children's views and opinions about themselves. A number of techniques can be used, for example drawings, digital media, photographs, videos and sketches made by children. However, if the techniques are designed in a way that is accessible to children they are capable of using a number of observation techniques, as will be demonstrated in the sections below through examples and case studies.

Checklists can become a useful tool for children who use them for self-observation if they are developed in collaboration with the children themselves.

CASE STUDY 5.3

Pictographic checklist

Aim: To assess children's social development during free play
Objective: Interactions during outdoor play

Table 5.5   Child self-evaluation checklist

Social play	Pictographic presentation of items	Child self-evaluation
Prefer to watch others when they play		

(Continued)

Table 5.5   (Continued)

Social play	Pictographic presentation of items	Child self-evaluation
Prefer to play on my own		
Prefer to have my own toys		✓
Prefer to play with others		✓
Prefer to join in when others have organised the play		
Prefer to be part of organising the play		✓
Prefer to share toys		✓

Note: When pictographic lists are developed to be used by children all images need to be very carefully explained to them.

Evaluation of checklists

Observation checklists can be quick, easy and efficient tools if they are carefully con-structed. Checklists can be re-used and adapted – gaps in the checklist may be identified, children may demonstrate unanticipated behaviour or the setting may have particular needs to be incorporated into it. Observation checklists can be used discreetly when the child is present. A number of different observers can use the same checklist to ensure that the information gathered is consistent, accurate and reliable. However, no checklist will be comprehensive and they should always be subject to additions and modifications. Finally, they can become a participatory tool for children to observe either themselves or others, so it increases the participation of children in the daily life and routines of the early childhood setting.

A major disadvantage of using a checklist is that if an unforeseen event occurs during an observation an important piece of information about a child or an activity may not have been covered by it. As this method requires knowledge of and expertise in child development the participation of children and parents in its preparation may be limited. Although checklists provide a breadth of information they may lack a depth of detail. It may be best to use them in conjunction with other techniques to ensure that enough information is gathered.

Diagrammatics

This is a focused and purpose-specific observation technique which includes a number of different methods:

- tracking;
- the use of sociograms;
- the use of histograms;
- the use of bar charts and pie charts.

Tracking

Tracking is used to record the amount of time a child spends on an activity of their choice or an activity that they have been asked to do. It does not explain *why* a child spends time on an activity or what a child did – it focuses only on time so in order to find out the reason you will need to carry out other types of observations, such as written.

It is a useful tool when you want to:

- observe children's attention span;
- investigate the play areas preferred by children;
- assess how many times children visit an area;
- keep track of the use of different areas within the classroom.

Tracking can offer quantitative evidence of the above. However, it does not help you to explain why a particular behaviour has occurred. For example, you may want to observe the physical development of children, so you can use tracking to investigate in what ways children are active during the day. You can track where they go (e.g. tunnel area, playground, etc.). Children can participate actively in this. For example, in each area you can put a sack and different coloured stones or Lego pieces. Children each have their own colours and when they are using an area they add their coloured stone or Lego piece into the sack. At the end of the day you can count how many times a child has used each area. However, there is always the risk that children might forget to do this or are putting more than one stone or Lego piece in each time, so practitioners should monitor this during the day.

EXAMPLE

You are planning to change the learning areas of your class. You want to investigate which areas are the most popular among the children during free play so that you can enrich these. Areas not used by the children can subsequently be removed or replaced. You plan to carry out observations for one week and you are going to use tracking to do this. On completion the findings show that the Lego area was the least popular among the children, so you decide to alter this area and enrich it with other construction materials instead (see Figure 5.6).

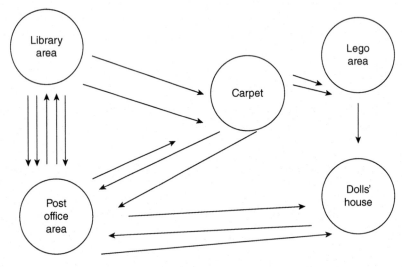

Figure 5.6   Diagram of tracking technique

Sociogram

The focus of this technique is social development. It is a helpful tool to investigate how children interact with others during the day. It investigates the child's relationships with other children or adults and can demonstrate the child's popularity with other children.

The main advantage of this technique is that it speeds up the process of observing social development. However, in the same way as tracking, it does not explain the reasons *why* something happens and can only tell us *what* happens. Sociograms can also offer misleading information as children's relationships can rapidly change.

EXAMPLE

The aim of the observation is to investigate how children form relationships with adults and peers. The specific objective is to investigate which children have formed smaller groups of friendships within the bigger class group. You show children three pictures: a smiley face, a sad face and a neutral face. The children are then asked to choose a picture that describes how they feel when they play with other children as illustrated in Table 5.6.

Table 5.6 Example of the sociogram technique

Children	Gregory	Alison	Gren	Raj
John	☺	☺	☺	☹
Katie	☺	☺	☺	☺
Mathew	☺	☹	☺	☺
Eric	☺	☺	☺	☺
George	☹	☺	☺	☺
Ahmed	☺	☺	☺	☺
Alia	☺	☹	☹	☹

ACTIVITY 5.5

Understanding a sociogram

From the sociogram in Table 5.6, can you make any interpretations?

- Can you identify which child has the most friends among the children that were asked?
- Can you identify which child has the least friendships among the children that were asked?

Histograms

Histograms are a helpful technique to follow the development of a child over time. They can provide patterns of a behaviour that occur over a period of time. Histograms are a special form of bar chart where the information gathered is represented continuously rather than in discrete categories. This means that in a histogram there are no gaps within the columns representing the different categories. The main advantage of histograms is that you focus on a child's particular behaviour over a longer period of time as the example below shows.

EXAMPLE

Oscar is 31 months old. The practitioner who works closely with him wants to examine his language. Here are the summaries of three weeks of various observations:

(Continued)

(Continued)

Week 1: A selection of photos of various activities and things around the house were collected to encourage Oscar to talk. Two copies of everything were produced and one copy tacked onto the actual object wherever possible. The practitioner has worked with Oscar for around a month with interventions to support Oscar's language development; however, he already knows how to use one-word utterances to ask for what he wants and although he was encouraged to use two-word combinations, there were no improvements over the month.

Week 2: Oscar has enjoyed looking through the photos and will ask the practitioner to point to various people in the photos. A further resource pack has been developed that also goes home with Oscar so that his family can duplicate the activities at home. Oscar will ask 'what doing?' when looking at the photos. The practitioner then explains what is happening in the photo. Oscar will copy usually the last word that is spoken. The practitioner tried to break the sentence down and encourage Oscar to copy each word first, and he happily does this task. Then the practitioner asks him to repeat a combination of words limited to two and three words at a time. Occasionally he will manage to copy two words but very rarely three words at a time.

Week 3: The practitioner has developed a 'now and then' board to work alongside the photos. Oscar likes to put the photos on the board, but does not work with the board in the way that the practitioner intended. The practitioner started using the board with Oscar so that he can see what has been planned in short, two-action sequences, but this has not helped when Oscar does not want to take part in an activity and he is still disruptive during activities such as story times.

The practitioner then used all the information from the observations to created a histogram for Oscar's use of language over these three weeks to examine whether there was progress in his language development (see Figure 5.7).

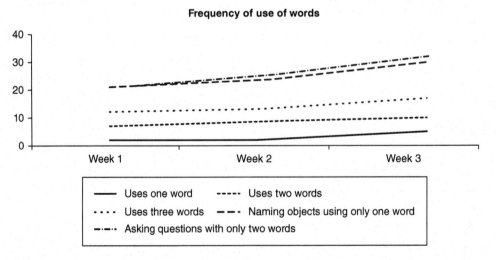

Figure 5.7   Histogram of Oscar's language development on the observed items over three weeks

Once the practitioner developed the histogram then she was able to plan for future weeks – below is an example of some of the actions:

Next steps:

1. Continue to try and use the now and then board with Oscar to encourage the use of three words.
2. Introduce a visual timetable to help Oscar understand the routines of the day and carry on repeating three-word sentences.

CASE STUDY 5.4

Alia, aged two years and three months, has been finding it difficult to adapt to life in her classroom. A month after joining the class she is still crying every day and asks for her mother. The practitioners have decided to observe her over a period of time to discover those times when she cries the most. The practitioners observed Alia over a week during free play, arrival time, storytelling time, outdoor play, snack time, playing with toy animals (which was her favourite activity) and singing time. As Figure 5.8 shows she cried the most during this week over arrival time and singing time.

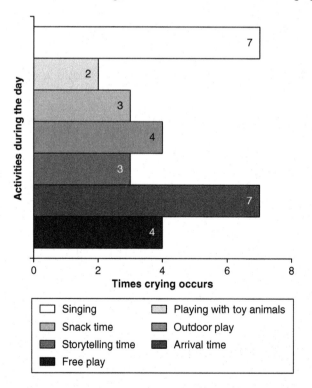

Figure 5.8 Histogram of adaptation to life in early years classroom

ACTIVITY 5.6

Based on Alia's histogram create an action plan

Can you plan some activities to help Alia's transition from home to early childhood setting? How are you going to follow this up with an observation plan?

CASE STUDY

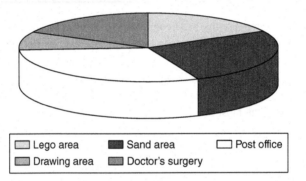

Figure 5.9   Pie chart illustrating activities boys prefer during class

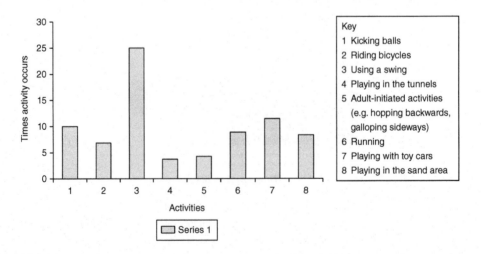

Figure 5.10   Bar chart illustrating activities boys prefer during outdoor play

Bar charts and pie charts

These can both be useful as techniques for collecting information about both individual and groups of children. They can be produced to offer a visual presentation of the results from your observation recordings – how children come to the setting, for example. Others might include what children eat in school, which areas boys prefer using during the day, which areas girls prefer during the day, or what boys do during outdoor play.

Sampling

The aim of sampling is to identify how and when a particular behaviour occurs. The emphasis of sampling is on the duration of a particular behaviour. For example, you may want to investigate how long a two-and-a-half-year-old child pays attention and focuses on storytelling or how often a three-year-old visits the sand area.

Time sampling

The observer records whether or not certain behaviours occur over a period of time. The focus of time sampling is on the duration of a particular behaviour. As time sampling records behaviours over a period of time, the frequency of the chosen behaviour is highlighted.

The main advantages of time sampling are

- it takes less time and effort than other techniques;
- it helps you to remain objective as you know the behaviour that you are looking for;
- you can collect data on a number of children or a number of behaviours at the same time, and it provides information at intervals throughout a given period of time;
- it shows the frequency of behaviour.

However, time sampling is not open-ended. You may miss important behaviours as you are merely recording their frequency and not actually describing the behaviour. Time sampling is thus limited to observable behaviours that occur frequently. This usually focuses on a type of behaviour and may therefore give a skewed view of the behaviour of a child as the example below demonstrates.

EXAMPLE OF TIME SAMPLING OBSERVATION FOR ALICE

Start date: 10/10
Finish date: 20/10
Method: Time sample to try to establish any triggers to Alice's distress, conducted over a week, for one-hour intervals at various times during the day
Area of development: PSED: Managing feelings and behaviours
Number of children present: Four children including Alice

(Continued)

(Continued)

Initials of the children present: NK, BN, SP, AM
Age: 11 months
Gender: F

Background information and aim of observation: Alice has been in the setting for around two months and appears to be struggling to settle in. Alice attends the setting and the key person (KP) began on 18 October to try to identify possible reasons for Alice struggling to settle within the setting (see Table 5.7). The aim of the observation is to identify any possible antecedents affecting Alice and to identify solutions in collaboration with Alice's mother.

Table 5.7 Time sampling observation

Date	Time	Description of what is happening
18/10	7:10 a.m.	AM arrives with her mum. She enters the setting and happily allows her mum to pass her to her key person (KP). She waves goodbye to her mum. KP takes AM to the play room and sits with AM on her knee.
	7:30 a.m.	KP selects toys that AM has shown she likes and places them on the floor. KP sits on the floor with AM still on her knee.
	7:50 a.m.	KP places AM next to her on the floor so she is still in close proximity. AM begins to cry. KP tries to engage AM in play by producing favourite toys and talking in a soothing voice. AM continues to cry until her KP picks her up five minutes later. AM stops crying instantly and begins to smile again.
	8:00 a.m.	BN enters the room. AM is still on KP's knee, but starts to cry. This continues for around five minutes. None of the other children are near her in proximity.
18/10	10:45 a.m.	KP places AM on the floor with toys, but remains in close proximity. Another of the KP's children needs their nappy changing. KP leaves the playroom; the other KP is present and tries to distract AM when she begins to cry.
	10:55 a.m.	KP re-enters the room and AM is still crying. KP sits next to her and cuddles her, but does not pick her up. AM continues to scream. KP leaves it five minutes then picks her up; AM stops crying.
	11:05 a.m.	AM still sat on KP's knee.
	11:15 a.m.	KP takes AM into the outside play area. KP sits down and places AM next to her. AM smiles and begins to explore the area.
	11:25 a.m.	AM turns around to smile at KP, but continues to play independently. She crawls to the sand pit and takes part in parallel play with the three other children. AM smiles at the other children and tries to engage them socially.

Date	Time	Description of what is happening
	11:35 a.m.	KP gets up and leaves the area. AM immediately begins to cry and tries to crawl after her.
18/10	2:00 p.m.	The children are playing with play dough. KP takes AM across to the craft table and demonstrates how to squeeze and manipulate the dough. AM is standing at the table and KP has her arm around her. AM smiles and tries to copy.
	2:10 p.m.	AM has lost interest in the activity. KP steps back to see if AM will choose where she wants to go next. AM begins to cry and crawls across to KP and hugs her leg. KP bends down and talks soothingly to AM and encourages her to look at the toys. AM continues to cry and then begins to scream. AM sits on the floor and stamps her legs up and down. AM only calms down when KP picks her up.
	2:20 p.m.	AM is still upset and is making little whimpering noises; KP continues to soothe her.
	2:30 p.m.	AM has now settled and has a bottle of milk.
	2:40 p.m.	KP attempts to place AM on the floor and surrounds her with items from the treasure basket. The KP sits next to AM and talks to her. AM smiles and begins to play.
	2:50 p.m.	The doorbell rings, AM begins to scream. KP cuddles her, but AM cannot be consoled.
19/10	9:00 a.m.	AM has had a similar morning to yesterday and KP is still trying to calm her down, as she had to change another child's nappy and AM was distraught.
	9:10 a.m.	KP puts AM's coat on and takes her outside. AM sits on KP's knee for a few minutes then pushes herself to go down. AM walks to the sand pit and plays with the sand. AM stands in a position that allows her to keep KP in sight.
	9:20 a.m.	AM walks across to the small climbing frame and watches the other children playing. AM smiles as they come down the slide. AM walks across to the play kitchen and plays, opening and closing the doors.
	9:30 a.m.	Another child takes a book to KP and KP begins to read the story. AM walks up and stands at the opposite side to the child so they can both see the book. Both children point to the pictures as KP is reading.
	9:40 a.m.	KP decides to do the planned music session outside as all the children are enjoying being outside. The children join in and AM smiles and claps her hands and is still standing independently.

(Continued)

Table 5.7 (Continued)

Date	Time	Description of what is happening
	9:50 a.m.	All the other children choose to go inside and due to ratios KP has to take AM inside. Within minutes AM begins to cry. KP has to help the other children take off their outdoor clothing and so by the time this has finished AM is distraught.
20/10	1:00 p.m.	This morning followed a similar pattern to the past few days with KP spending more time outside. KP has decided to bring the sand tray inside the setting and placed it next to the large glass doors to give it a feeling of outside. AM has just had her lunch and is sat on her KP's knee. KP takes her across to the sand tray and stands her next to it. AM smiles and immediately begins to play in the sand. KP sits nearby, but not close enough to touch AM.
	1:10 p.m.	AM looks at her KP and smiles and continues to play. AM then brings various toys and resources across to KP to look at, but always returns to the sand tray.
	1:20 p.m.	AM is showing signs of losing interest, so KP introduces water to the sand. This renews AM's interest and she carries on playing.
	1:30 p.m.	AM has now had enough and has approached KP, but is stood next to her and does not appear to want to be picked up. Another child has selected a book to look at and both children look through the book with KP.
	1:40 p.m.	The other child goes to the sand tray. AM watches her for a few moments and then follows her. AM plays alongside the other child and keeps watching and trying to copy the other child's movements.

CASE STUDY 5.6

There are concerns that Val is demonstrating some aggressive behaviour. The practitioners have decided to observe her, in order to find out how frequently Val displays inappropriate behaviours that cause some distress among the other children.

In preparing for the time sampling it is important to define what inappropriate behaviour is. So the practitioner, with reference to the curriculum she is working within, highlights some specific behaviours that can be easily observed and measured, and to simplify and speed up the process she gives a number to each observed behaviour as follows (see Table 5.8):

1. turn-taking;
2. taking toys from other children before they have finished with them;

3. hitting other children;
4. pushing other children;
5. shouting at other children.

Alternatively you can use a key for your chosen items, such as the first letter of each item. It is up to you to decide how best you are going to code your items. Then you will need to decide when to record them – for example departure time, outdoor play, literacy activities, etc. The emphasis in this observation is to record *when* Val demonstrates inappropriate behaviour.

Table 5.8 Example of time sampling technique

Activity	Time	Behaviour observed
Departure time	8:45 a.m.	1 4 5
	9:15 a.m.	2 3
Outdoor play	11:15 a.m.	5 5 4 3 3
	2:20 p.m.	3 1
Storytelling	10:30 a.m.	1 3
Drawing area	3:00 p.m.	3 5 4 2 2
Dancing activity	11:45 a.m.	4 4 4 4 4 5

Event sampling

The observer records a specific, pre-selected behaviour. Event sampling is used to study the conditions under which particular behaviours occur. It may be important to learn what triggers a particular kind of behaviour, e.g. biting.

Event sampling helps you to keep the event of the behaviour intact. This can make analysis easier and is objective, as behaviour can be defined ahead of time. It is also helpful for recording infrequent behaviours. However, it can take the event out of context and, as it looks at specific behaviours, it can be lacking in detail.

CASE STUDY 5.7

Table 5.9 Example of event sampling technique

Behaviours	Departure time	Outdoors play	Storytelling time	Gardening activities
Turn taking	**	*		****
Hits other children	****	********	****	***
Pushes other children	*******	*****		**
Shouts at other children	*	****		*

Event sampling can help you to investigate what behaviours occur during different times of the day and with time sampling it is possible to determine how many times it occurs. In this way, you can develop strategies to encourage certain behaviours and discourage others.

SUMMARY

This chapter has explored the variety of non-participant observation techniques that are available to early childhood practitioners. As discussed in Chapter 4, in order to have a complete picture of a child or an activity, the use of just one method is not enough and you need to gather evidence from a number of sources to complete a profile for a child for either statutory or informal assessments as well to evaluate your environment. Non-participant observation offers rich information and there is a variety of methods:

- *narrative or written techniques;*
- *rating scales;*
- *checklists;*
- *diagrammatic techniques;*
- *sampling.*

All these tools complement each other and can be used in your daily observation routines so that interesting and relevant children's behaviours are not missed. In addition, evidence can be collected regarding your environment and the interactions that occur. Although there is a distinction between participant and non participant observation there will be occasions where it is necessary to use semi-structured observation. This is discussed in the next chapter.

Further Reading

For extensive examples on observation techniques, see the work of:

Bruce, T, Louis, S and McCall, G (2015) *Observing Young Children*. London: Sage.

To extend your understanding on how these scales have been used you can also read:

Siraj, I, Kingston, D and Melhuish, E (2015) *Assessing Quality in Early Childhood Education and Care: Sustained Shared Thinking and Emotional Wellbeing (SSTEW) Scale for 2–5 Year Olds Provision*. London: UCL and IOE Press.

Siraj, I, Kingston, K, Neilsen-Hewett, C, Howard, SJ, Melhuish, E, de Rosnay, M . . . Luu, B (2017) *A Review of the Current International Evidence Considering Quality in Early Childhood Education and Care Programmes – in Delivery, Pedagogy and Child Outcomes*. Sydney: NSW Department of Education.

Websites

For more information on the Early Childhood Environment Rating Scale – Revised (ECERS-R):

http://www.ecersuk.org/4.html

CHAPTER 6

SEMI-STRUCTURED OBSERVATION

Chapter objectives

Reading this chapter will help you understand:

- the nature of semi-structured observation;
- how, when and why it is used;
- through examples how you can integrate semi-structured observation into your practice.

Semi-structured observation is used to capture not only specific aims, but also unpredicted events that might offer you information on evaluating a particular aspect in practice or a particular child/children's behaviour/s or experience/s.

Introduction: what is it?

The previous chapters introduced the roles and uses of participant and non-participant observation. It was pointed out that participant observation is used when the observer is an active participant and observes something that happens while the activities unfold. During participant observation the observer chooses to capture a moment that is judge to be significant. By contrast, in non-participant observation, the observer steps back and keeps a distance from what is intended to be observed.

However, there might be occasions in your setting where phenomena (such as certain children's behaviours) the occurrence of which you cannot explain and you cannot capture with the use of participant or non-participant observation. In this instance, although you develop some specific aims and objectives for your observation plan, you leave an 'open' aim to allow you to capture the unexpected that might help you to find out why and how the particular phenomenon happens in your setting. This is where semi-structured observations are useful as they can help you to give structure to key elements of what will need to be gathered and the elements of which processes need to be observed while at the same time allowing you to collect information that cannot be predicted as observed outcomes.

This type of observation is derived from the field of ecology (see Chapter 2). Ecologists are interested in studying human interaction with their environment and how this interaction affects the behaviours and experiences of individuals. The key emphasis from an ecological perspective is to study behaviours and interactions as they occur and how the environment impacts (negatively, positively or neither) on people's behaviours. However, they are also interested in how humans have had an impact on their environment and how the interactions with the environment determine behaviours and experiences.

In early childhood education, as will be shown in the case studies below, semi-structured observation can be a useful tool for gathering information about predetermined aims and objectives in relation to your pedagogy or a child's development, learning, play and experiences, but at the same time allows you the opportunity to collect information that you might have not anticipated when you were setting your observation aims.

How is it used?

Semi-structured observation uses a combination of methods from non-participant and participant observation. Normally the team of practitioners identify the focus of the observation and have a number of clear aims regarding what they want to be observed, but they also want to leave open what might happen that they cannot predict in advance. So they choose methods from the other two observation techniques that will help them address this. In that sense semi-structured does not have its own techniques as, for example, in participant observation, but is a 'bricolage', a synthesis of methods and techniques that offers elements of structure where the key aims are identified in advance and elements of fluidity and openness for any 'surprising', unforeseen or unpredicted behaviours or events that might happen.

The steps to be undertaken when you use semi-structured observation as illustrated in Figure 6.1 are firstly to identify the area, aspect, issue, event or behaviour you want to find more information about. Secondly, the team decides the protocol of the semi-structured observation that all will use. Thirdly the period of observation is determined. Finally, individuals analyse their recordings, followed by a team meeting where all the findings from the individual analyses are put together, compared and constructed so conclusions can be made in order to address the next action points.

In the case study below you can see how the semi-structured observation process was employed to address changes in a nursery.

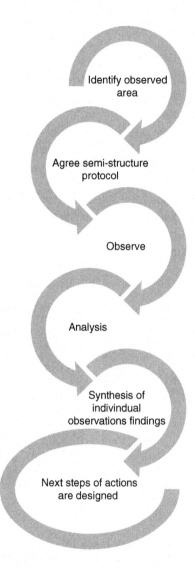

Figure 6.1   Semi-structured observation process

Semi-structured observation process: how do we use tablets in the nursery?

The nursery has decided to introduce tablets instead of cameras for children to use for recording (taking photos or videos and then voice recording their comments on their activities). The practitioners want to observe how this new initiative is received by the children and how the practitioners are using it. They have decided that they want to know:

(Continued)

(Continued)

1. What happens, how and when children are using the tablets.
2. Are they used for playing activities?
3. Are they used for learning activities?
4. How are children behaving when they are using them?
5. How are practitioners interacting with the children when the tablets are being used?
6. How children interact with each other when the tablets are being used?

They also wanted to focus on how the tablets were used in the science area, the arts area (they had introduced a ripping and tearing game in which a number of materials could be ripped and torn such as leaves and different types of paper to encourage eye–hand coordination) and the outdoor area with a focus on the new 'My garden' area they had introduced.

Figure 6.2 Science area

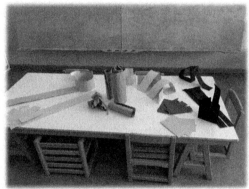

Figure 6.3 Arts area: ripping and tearing

Figure 6.4 Our garden area

After an initial team meeting, they decided to employ semi-structured observation and developed the protocol shown in Table 6.1. They choose the event sampling technique and the written observation from the non-participant observation and set clear aims of what will be observed and when, but they decided to use participant observation to capture the unexpected.

Table 6.1 Example from the semi-structured protocol

Practitioner name: Liz Date: 22/02		Child/children involved: Marisa, Stefan, Gene	
Event sampling: **Behaviours aimed to** **be observed**	**What will be** **observed**	**Observation**	**Notes (if any)**
	Is it play activity?	*Yes*	
	Is it learning activity?		
	Who is taking part?	*All three*	
	Timing and space of the activity	*11:45 in the garden area*	
	Who is deciding what resources will be used?	*Marisa leads*	
	Who is deciding who will have the tablet?	*Marisa*	
	How is the tablet used?	*She takes photos of the plants*	
How children **interact**	Are children motivated to use it during the activity?	*It appears yes as she takes a lot of photos* *Gene and Stefan ask Marisa to take more photos and point out which plants to take photos of*	
	Is there any body language?	*Pointing to plants, moving so they will not disturb Marisa in taking photos*	
	Do they seem to find it helpful?	*Yes*	
	Do they seem to find it difficult?	*No*	
	For how long did they use it?	*10 min*	

(Continued)

Table 6.1   (Continued)

Practitioner name: Liz Date: 22/02		Child/children involved: Marisa, Stefan, Gene
Capturing focused areas How tablets used in these areas by children and participants (written observation)	Science area	N/A
	Arts area (focusing on the new project on ripping and tearing game)	N/A
	Our garden area	*Marisa came to see me and asked if she can take the tablet to take some photos in the garden area with Stefan and Gene.*
Capturing the unexpected (use participant observation)	*Stefan asked Marisa for the tablet and asked if they wanted their photo to be taken. Once he took the photo, Marisa and Gene left the garden area. Stefan took the tablet, sat on a bench and tried to see if there were any games to play. I approached him and reminded him of the rules regarding how we use these tablets.*	
My initial thoughts	*All three seemed to enjoy taking photos with the tablet and appeared in control of the activity with no need of help from the adults. A reminder of the rules about how we use the tablets was needed. Maybe do a poster?*	

Two months after the tablet was introduced into the nursery, the practitioners gathered in a staff meeting to evaluate progress. Analysing their individual observations they found that as the tablets were kept in a drawer, the children did not used them on their own initiative, but only if the practitioners were offering them. They also found that when children were using the tablets their recordings were richer and offered them valid information for evaluating the activities. In addition, there was more information about children's language development as there was the option of recording their thoughts alongside the videos and photographs.

Thus it was decided that the tablets would be kept within visual reach of the children while trying to keep at least one tablet in the 'Science and Arts' areas so when the children were visiting these areas they could see the tablet and use it on their own initiative. For the outdoors they decided to keep a table next to the door that children were using to go outside. They also decided that they would carry on with the semi-structured observation protocol for another month to see whether these steps of action had been effective.

As it can be seen in this observation protocol there is a set of categories/behaviours that offer a structure to the observer, aiming to capture certain key events that are of interest to the setting with event sampling method and the written observation, focusing on certain areas with the use of non-participant observation and any unexpected events or behaviours with the use of participant observation.

The structured observation (non-participant) has clear aims, but the non-structured (participant) has the element of openness as it captures unexpected behaviours or events.

ACTIVITY 6.1

Do a semi-structured observation

- Reflecting on your context can you think of any issues where you can implement a semi-structured observation?
- What are your specific aims going to be?
- What observation methods will you be using to meet them?
- How will you capture any unpredicted events?
- Will you plan to use any digital media for these observations?
- If so, what these will be?

Example

To help you you with this activity Table 6.2 is an example from observing Amy, a three-year-old girl, outdoors. The team had developed a semi-structured observation protocol as they were interested in certain areas in the outdoors and how they were used.

Table 6.2 Semi-structured observation for Amy when outdoors

Practitioner name: Emily	Child's name: Amy	Date: 29/1
Wanted outcomes	Children use the water area	*Amy has not used the water area today.*
	Children use the swing	*Amy spent ten minutes in the swing.*
	Children use the benches	*Amy sat with Kerry on the bench for five minutes and pretended they were drinking tea bringing the tea pots from indoors.*
	Children initiate to water the plants	*Amy did not participate on the planting activities today.*
	Children initiate to do some pottery	*Not today.*
	Children initiate to construct with the tools	*Not today.*
	Children initiate to use the microscope to study leaves	*She showed some initiative but then got distracted and left.*
Other notes (capturing the unexpected)	*Amy was approaching the area that the microscopes were kept and asked to use one. However, Kelly came and asked her if she wanted to play butterflies and Amy looked at her and said yes. They both went to pick up some paper to create their wings and Amy said 'No! no! butterflies . . . monsters! Let's be monsters! Let's be evil monsters.' Kelly said she did not want to but Amy shouted in an angry manner 'I want to be a monster and eat you.'*	
My initial thoughts	*This is unusual for Amy to shout in anger to Kelly with no apparent reason. It does not cause concern at this stage but I need to look if other instances might occur.*	

CASE STUDY 6.2

Semi-structured observation established from research: The Learning Story

A good example of semi-structured observation is the Learning Story. As was discussed in the Introduction, Margaret Carr, an internationally well respected academic from New Zealand, has introduced the Learning Stories. Learning Stories is a framework that derived from the project Assessing Children's Learning that she led, and serves as a way of observing and documenting children's learning (Carr, 1988, 2001) within the Te Whāriki curriculum (see Introduction and Chapter 11). She explains:

Learning stories are similar to the narrative style observations [. . .] but they are more structured. They are observations in everyday settings, designed to provide a cumulative series of qualitative 'snapshots' or written vignettes of individual children displaying one or more of the five target domains of learning disposition. The five domains of disposition are translated into actions: taking an interest, being involved, persisting with difficulty or uncertainty, expressing an idea or a feeling, and taking responsibility or taking another point of view [. . .] Learning Stories have been sufficiently wideranging in their focus to acknowledge the unpredictability of development and to both map and enhance participation repertoires.

(Carr, 2001, pp.96–101)

She goes on to say that Learning Stories are designed to acknowledge the unpredictability of development-unexpected, but at the same time to capture children's learning dispositions in a way that *reflect the learning better than performance indicators* (p.101). There are four steps in the process of Learning Stories – she calls them the *four Ds: Describing, Documenting, Discussing and Deciding* (Carr, 2001, p.101).

Describing is about defining the learning, developing and applying constructs that are relevant to the local learning opportunities. Discussing is about talking with other staff, the children and the families in order to develop, confirm or question an interpretation. Documenting is about recording the assessment in some way: using text, pictures and /or collected work. Deciding is about deciding what to do next: spontaneous responding, and informal or formal planning.

(p.107)

Activity 6.2

Compare the four Ds with semi-structured observation

Can you see any similarities or differences between the four Ds and the semi-structured process?

Initially when this work was developed the use of photos was not as extensive in early childhood education, but more recently with the wide use of cameras in early childhood education Carr and Lee (2012) have proposed that Learning Stories can now include photographs. Their book *Learning Stories: Constructing Learner Identities in Early Education* provides a range of examples of Learning Stories in written text format as well as in photographic sequences (see Further Reading).

CASE STUDY 6.3

Andrea's Learning Story

Child's name: Andrea (2 years and 6 months)

Practitioner: Liz

Date: 3/4

Table 6.3   Andrea's Learning Story

Strands of the Curriculum (Te Whāriki)	The dispositions	Examples of cues	A Learning Story
Belonging	TAKING AN INTEREST	Finding something of interest here – a topic, an activity, a role. Recognising the familiar, enjoying the unfamiliar. Coping with change.	*Andrea is playing with a baby doll. She says: 'baby crying . . . baby crying'. She holds her in a hug and starts rocking the doll. She looks at her doll and says 'she is wet'. She pretends that she is changing the doll. She lifts the doll again and say to her 'better now?'*
Well-being	BEING INVOLVED	Paying attention for sustained period, feeling safe, trusting others. Being playful with others and/or materials.	
Exploration	PERSISTING WITH DIFFICULTY	Setting and choosing difficult tasks. Using a range of strategies to solve problems when 'stuck' (be specific).	*Then she puts the doll in the pram and says: 'Let's go shopping now'. She takes the pram outdoors and as she is passing one of the practitioners she says 'My baby wants candy'. The practitioner pretends that she is giving her a candy and Andrea pretends that she feeds her baby doll.*
Communication	EXPRESSING AN IDEA OR A FEELING	In a range of ways (specify). For example: oral, language, gesture, music, art, writing, using numbers and patterns, telling stories.	
Contribution	TAKING RESPONSIBILITY	Responding to others, to stories and imagined events that things are fair, self-evaluating, helping others, contributing to programme.	*She goes outside, goes around the playground in circles and then comes back and takes the baby doll back to its original place and goes outside again.*

(Continued)

Table 6.3   (Continued)

Short-term review	What next?
Andrea today showed that she has started to engage with role play and signs of complexity in her play using oral language as well as body language. Question: What learning do I think went on here (i.e. the main point(s) of the learning story)?	*Bring more toys that will encourage Andrea to develop her play, involved more actively in Andrea's play if she asks.* Questions: How might we encourage this interest, ability, strategy, disposition, story to: • be complex • appear in different areas or activities in the programme. How might we encourage the next 'step' in the Learning Story framework?

Source: Carr and Lee (2012).

CASE STUDY 6.4

James' Learning Story

Child's Name: James, 9mths, 3wks

Date: 8 Oct

Observer: Julie

A learning Story

 James crawls to the puzzle area where Leigh (3.5 yrs) is completing a puzzle. He looks at what Leigh is doing, then chooses a puzzle and starts to work with it, He takes a piece out and attempts to put it back in. He tries quite a few times to position the piece correctly by lifting it out, repositioning it, and putting it back in. Eventually, the piece goes in the right way.

Leigh (the older child) finishes her puzzle, looks around for something to do, then yawns and goes to lie down on sofa. James crawls across the floor and up the steps, and crawls to the sofa and stands near Leigh.

Leigh doesn't respond, so James crawls towards some books and looks at them.

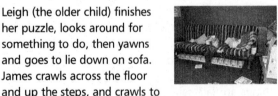

When Leigh later moves to playdough area, James follows her, and they play together there for ten minutes or so.

Short-term review	What next?
James is enjoying being able to move independently and chooses his own activities and company.	Encourage James to play alongside other children.
Although he and Leigh are unable to communicate verbally, it is clear he wants to be in her company,	Let him experience different types of puzzles, different textures (playdough, fingerpaint, sand, clay & waterplay), read him short stories and picture books.
James is enjoying exploring the playcentre and particularly likes puzzles, books, and playdough.	James also enjoys music, particularly the drum and the small shakers. This might be an opportunity for further play with other children.
(Leigh makes no attempts to discourage him, and the two children finally play together.)	

Source: Ministry of Education (2004), Assessment for infants and toddlers, New Zealand, p.7.

ACTIVITY 6.3

Create your learning story

Based on your context and your curriculum can you create a Learning Story that is based on the outcomes and dispositions of your curriculum?

You can start practising using the examples provided below. For example, if you work with the EYFS you can create a Learning Story as in the example below. Can you think of other ways?

The Early Learning Goals	Children learn when	Learning Story
Listening and attention	playing and exploring – children investigate and experience things, and 'have a go'.	
	active learning – children concentrate and keep on trying if they encounter difficulties, and enjoy achievements.	
	creating and thinking critically – children have and develop their own ideas, make links between ideas and develop strategies for doing things.	

If you work in the Wales curriculum an example is provided below. Can you think your own?

Learning Goal	Skills	Learning Story
Creative movement	Explore and express a range of moods and feelings through a variety of movements	
	Develop their responses to different stimuli such as music, pictures, words and ideas	

(Continued)

(Continued)

Learning Goal	Skills	Learning Story
	Develop their control by linking movements to create a series of changing body shapes and pathways	
	Work on their own and with others to pretend, improvise and think imaginatively	
	Work on their own, with a partner or in a small group to develop their own and others' ideas and help them to reflect on them	
	Perform movements or patterns, including some from traditional Welsh dances and from other cultures	

If you work in Scotland an example is provided. Can you create your own?

Capacities	Attributes	Learning Story
Successful Learners	Enthusiasm and motivation for learning	
	Determination to reach high standards of achievement	
	Openness to new thinking and ideas	
Confident Learners	Self-respect	
	A sense of physical,	
	mental and emotional well-being	
	Secure values and beliefs	
	Ambition	
Responsible Citizens	Respect for others	
	Commitment to participate responsibly in political, economic social and cultural life.	
Effective Contribution	An enterprising attitude	
	Resilience	
	Self-reliance	

If you work in the Northern Ireland curriculum an example is provided. Can you create your own?

Areas of Learning	Children learn and develop through	Learning Story
Early Mathematical Experience: Development of Space	Experimenting with a wide range of materials Exploring and investigating the properties of materials	
	Being given time to consolidate their understanding of concepts Hearing mathematical language being used as a natural part of conversations with adults	
	Being encouraged to use mathematical language as they talk about their experiences and findings with adults and peers	

Evaluation

Semi-structured observation can help you bring to the surface issues that were not expected or predicted in a targeted area of your setting or when focusing on a child/children for whom you might have concerns. This can be used in your daily practice when you want to watch an event, initiative or action closely that might become a potential problem or where opportunities for development might be missed. You can also untangle issues that already known, but difficult for practitioners to manage so you can identify ways for it to be resolved. It also can help you to gather rich information on targeted areas of your curriculum, as was shown in the case of Learning Story.

However, semi-structured observations are time-consuming as you do need to develop a protocol of what will be observed, how it will be observed and identify all participants who need to be involved. You can also involve children and parents in the process as in the other methods of observation. Semi-structured observation can be accompanied by discussions with the children and the parents during the analysis stages, as will be shown in Chapter 7.

SUMMARY

Semi-structured observation can provide information on a targeted aspect of your practice such as behaviours that arise, a change in circumstances, an event or activities. Semi-structured observation offers in-depth information about the classroom context (such as physical materials, routines, activities), the interactions that take place between practitioners and children or between children, the play experiences, the learning experiences and any specific curriculum requirements. This is because, although there are some specific aims and objectives, they always entail an element of openness to capture the unpredicted, unexpected events that might happen.

Further Reading

To develop a good understanding of Learning Story read:

Carr, M and Lee, W (2019) *Learning Stories: Constructing Learner Identities in Early Education* (2nd edn). London: Sage.

CHAPTER 7

ANALYSING AND DOCUMENTING OBSERVATIONS

Chapter objectives

After reading this chapter, you should be able to:

- understand the process of analysing the observation recordings;
- distinguish between a valid and faulty explanation of observation recordings;
- understand the importance of documenting your observation recordings;
- explore different ways of documenting your evidence;
- understand how analysis and documentation inform your formative and summative assessments of children.

Analysing and documenting observations is an essential aspect of observation planning. Each early childhood team should find their own ways to document the observation findings that are meaningful to their context.

Introduction: Analysing observations – a collaborative process

This chapter discusses the final steps in your observation planning process. So far we have discussed the purpose of observation, addressing key issues of team, parental and child involvement, as well as the importance of clear aims and objectives. Issues around aims and objectives have been addressed. Chapters 4, 5 and 6 discussed in detail the observation methods and techniques available in order to gather your evidence. The next step is analysis of the recordings and documentation which is explored in the following sections. Before how observations are analysed and documented is discussed, however, it is important to define what the terms mean in this book for the early childhood education context:

- **Analysis** is a systematic and organised examination, evaluation and interpretation of what observation has recorded in order to learn more about children's learning and development and our practice, so we can arrive at conclusions that will inform our assessment process.
- **Documentation** is the organised and systematic way the observation findings that lead to accurate conclusions and assessments are recorded and classified to be presented and shared in a format that will be understood by all involved in early childhood education (children, practitioners, parents and everyone else who has an interest such as inspection bodies) *in a way to get to know better what the children, in their own way, already know* (Turner and Wilson, 2010, p.8).

What has been recorded in the observations, either in a written format with participant, non-participant or semi-structured methods or by the use of digital media (see Chapter 4), does not necessarily mean they 'tell' us something about a child or our curriculum. It needs a form of evaluation, interpretation and explanation and this is the role of the analysis. *Meaning does not come from seeing or observation alone [. . .] it is produced in acts of interpretation* (Dahlberg et al., 1999, p.147).

Although it is common practice now to use both observations in written text format and digital media (visuals such as photographs, videos and apps) where the written narrative accompanies the visual or vice versa), this chapter aims to discuss how the written text observations can be analysed. Chapter 8 will discuss how digital media observations can be analysed and recorded. Some of the principles of analysing apply to both, but visual observations collected by digital media require different analysis techniques and will be explored in the next chapter.

Whether you use written text or digital media observations, or as it is the norm now in early childhood education a combination of both, the analysis in the whole observation planning process should be inclusive and involve all participants, children and their parents. For example, you might have a child for whom, after several observations over a period of time, you have concerns about his/her emotional outbursts in the setting. The child is happy one moment and plays collaboratively with other children and yet, suddenly, he or she can start screaming and throwing toys all over the place. Before you arrive at any assessment of why this behaviour occurs it will be helpful to present your findings to the parents and ask their views on why this might happen and perhaps collect more information from the parents as well as the child him/herself. Asking children to explain their actions in a sensitive and child-friendly way offers many explanations that we as practitioners might not have captured with our observations. Also, children might offer an explanation that the practitioner could not predict. Remember that children start to establish a sense of self from an early stage in their lives and develop their ability to see the perspectives of others.

Steps of analysis

Analysing the observation findings is a way of try to make meaning of all the recordings you have gathered over a period of time. Analysis is a complex process and requires the employment of a systematic approach. It is important to be able to analyse your observation recordings as this will inform the assessment process and shape your documentation. Martin (2019) explains the difficulties of the analysis stage and offers some stages to assist you in the process:

The analytical process is very demanding, but very rewarding. The stages seem a challenge at first, but practice increases your professional skills and they will gradually take less time. If you encounter problems, you may need to go back a stage or two. There are six stages:

A.   Review material
B.   Develop a plan for your analytical process
C.   Review what information the particular method is revealing
D.   Reduce the amount of material
E.   Summarise the data
F.   Make inferences and check them

(p.529)

In line with these stages, the following sections offer eight practical steps to guide you through the analysis process:.

Step 1: Carefully read all your observation recordings

In the daily life of the early childhood setting and especially with the wide availability of digital media to take photos, videos and audio recordings, you can end up with vast amounts of information. At this stage you need to filter so you can keep the recordings that best present a complete picture of either the child under focus or the education programme. In order to interpret your observation, and while examining its collection, it is important that the recordings are read thoroughly and filtered. You need to develop a set of questions to be able to filter your observation recordings:

1.   Is there any missing information (e.g. place, time, name of observer, children present) that make the observation incomplete?
2.   Is this observation recording complete and can I cross reference it with another recording?
3.   Has the observation method been used in an appropriate and relevant way?

4. Does the observation include any judgments, comments that actually are not recording what happened, but what the observer thought happened?
5. What observation recordings will be included? And why? This question will be guided by what you are looking to discover from these observation recordings. For example, if you wanted to find out why a child has emotional outbreaks (as in the example above) then you need to make a decision as to which observation recordings are relevant to help you find out more about this child.

Step 2: Making meaning of your observation

Once this initial filter has been conducted then a series of questions can help you to start making meaning of your observation recordings:

* What does this observation tell us about each child's experiences and progress?
* What does this observation tell us about each child's interests, skills, development and learning achievements?
* What information do you still need to assess for each child in order to complete the profile?
* How will this observation help you to share information with the children, parents, practitioners and other services in order to promote partnership?
* How will this observation help you to evaluate the implementation of your activities within your curriculum?
* Has your observation met the aims and objectives of its design?

Step 3: Decide who will be involved

As analysing can be time-consuming, it is helpful to decide once you have filtered your observation recordings to consider who will be involved in the analysis. How many practitioners? Will you involve parents and children at this stage? And if yes, why? What is your plan to share the filtered observation recordings with the parents and the children? Do you need to invite any specialists such as a health visitor, educational psychologist?

Step 4: Examination, evaluation and interpretation

The next step is to investigate whether there is any interpretation that can be applied to the specific event that you have recorded. Early childhood education practitioners are busy people. They have to look after the children, provide a high-quality environment and interactions for children and implement the curriculum. So, during the hectic pace and workload of the day they may have collected data without attempting any interpretation of them. Once an observation has been conducted, a brief evaluation, explanation or interpretation as regards initial thoughts must be performed as soon as possible thereafter. Memory deteriorates with time . . .

THEORY FOCUS

Explain, evaluate interpret

- **Valid explanation:** can a possible explanation be derived from the behaviour you have observed?
- **Faulty (or biased) explanation:** can a possible explanation be derived from your personal opinion?
- **Conclusions:** is a judgement based on valid explanations made from accumulated observation recordings?

A valid explanation is one where it is only possible to reach a conclusion derived from the behaviour recorded. These explanations should not be biased and should not be derived from personal opinions.

Example

Observation recording: *Vicky would not let Kelly borrow her orange pencil.*

A valid and accurate explanation may be one that says:

Vicky had not finished using her pencil so she did not give it to Kelly.

A biased or faulty explanation may be the one that says:

Vicky does not know how to share.

In the above example we do not have enough evidence to support whether Vicky wanted to share or not, so making such an interpretation would be based on our personal knowledge of Vicky as a child and not from the recorded observation.

It is easy to draw an inappropriate conclusion on the basis of the evidence. During the process observers must take immediate decisions about what to record, so the results may be superficial or form an unreliable account, with no chance of an exact repeat of the behaviour. Often faulty conclusions can also be made when information about prior activities cannot be obtained. Therefore it is helpful for observations to be repeated either by another person or at different times during the day or on different days, so that reliability can be checked.

ACTIVITY 7.1

Make an interpretation of an observation

Look at the photo in Figure 7.1 of the boy (George) and write down what you see.

Figure 7.1   Boy on a bike

Is your observation recording similar to this? Observation recording: George is sitting on the bike.

Here are two explanations:

1.   George can ride a bike.
2.   George knows how to sit on a bike.

Which one is faulty and which one is valid? What conclusions can you validly draw?

Observations can provide highly accurate, detailed and verifiable information. However, as mentioned in Chapter 3, observations are susceptible to bias. This can occur either because of the observer's lack of attention to significant events, or because the observer has recorded something they thought they saw rather than what actually occurred. So before you arrive at any conclusions, the next step in the process of analysing observation recordings is to check their reliability.

Step 5 Check your explanation, evaluation, interpretation

Once you have arrived at what you think are valid interpretations of your observation it is important that you check these alongside other practitioners or/and parents or/and children where you think it is appropriate.

CASE STUDY 7.1

Helen's explanations of Joshua's observations

Helen (the key worker for Joshua, a three years and four months boy attending the nursery) has been observing him for a period of two months as concerns were raised about his visual development. Joshua had difficulties holding toys, once bringing them close to his eyes, and he was rubbing his eyes very frequently. Once outdoors he was not accessing all areas as were the other children but preferred to sit on his own. During story time, he always sat very close to the practitioner and although he enjoyed it, he was not taking any storybooks to read on his own. His parents had taken him to an eyecare specialist, but they said that he was not having any problems. However, Helen had her concerns as she could not explain some of Joshua's behaviours. After interpreting her observation recordings, she arrived at the explanation that Joshua might have some some issues with his vision and there were several observations where Joshua was observed to show signs of eye crossing.

Helen decided before acting any further to show her findings to the other practitioner that was working with Joshua as well and get her views. She also decided to invite and speak to his parents at this stage, but she decided not to approach Joshua as this might hurt his feelings and self-confidence. Once all these discussions had taken place Helen and the parents decided that the observation recordings raised issues for concern, but they were not in a position to arrive to any conclusions and a visit to the eyecare specialists was essential. Two weeks later Joshua arrived at the nursery in the morning wearing a pair of 'funky' (as he called them) pair of glasses. Helen then decided to carry on observations on Joshua to see if these behaviours had been eliminated now that he was wearing glasses.

In this case study, Helen came to the interpretation that it might be Joshua's vision that was triggering some of his behaviour, but although he visited the specialists she could not come to a safe conclusion from her observation recordings. Consequently, she decided to carry on observations to make sure that the valid conclusion was that these behaviours were due to Joshua's visual development and not other reasons.

Step 6 Arrive at conclusions

Conclusions should be based on a number of valid and accurate explanations of the observation recordings. In your conclusions you need more evidence to back up your final statement. In Case Study 7.1 above Helen did not have enough evidence to conclude that Joshua's behaviours were only due to his vision so she decided to carry on with with observation to arrive at an accurate conclusion. As mentioned above, making conclusions is always the product of judgements that are made from a number of valid inferences from the observed event(s). For example, in the case of Vicky above, if we had a number of different observation recordings that demonstrated that Vicky did not give any toys or objects to other children at different times of the day or during different activities we could then conclude that she does not know how to share. On the other hand, in the case study of Joshua, Helen carried out more observations and arrived at the accurate conclusion that since he started to wear his glasses these behaviours were not observed again and he actually became very active outdoors, playing with the other children and spending more time outdoors than before. The assessment of a child or your educational programme consists of a number of accurate conclusions.

Step 7 Make an assessment

Making an assessment of children on your educational programme is a product of the process of analysis of your observation recordings. The collection of accurate conclusions that derive from valid explanations, evaluations and interpretations of your observation recordings will lead you to make assessments. In the introductory Chapter 1 the main types of assessment were described: formative and summative. Both types are the product of accurate conclusions.

In making an assessment it is important that all the early childhood team is involved, as well as parents or carers and, where appropriate, children themselves. *The quality of the observations and of the analysis of these observations will determine the quality of assessment made* (Lally and Hurst, 1992, p.79).

Lally and Hurst (1992) have developed a framework for analysing the recordings of observations. They suggest a series of statements that will enable staff to start discussions around children's assessments:

> - *Acknowledge the previous experiences of the child and place observation in the context of this knowledge.*
> - *Make use of their observations to inform their assessment record of the child.*
> - *Raise further questions about the child's experiences. (These may be in connection with the role of the provision or of the involvement of other children or adults with the child. In this way, one observation can be seen to inspire further investigation.)*
> - *Use the information to plan to support the child's future learning.*
> - *Communicate with one another, as analysis of observations is shared.*
>
> (p.90)

Obviously, when working within your curriculum, you operate under a framework for either formal assessment as is the case with the English EYFS or the Wales Foundation Phase or informal as in the case of the Scottish and Northern Ireland curricula. No matter what curricular approaches you are working to, you will always be required to create assessment profiles (formative or summative or both) of children's development and learning, either scoring children on a set of strands as in the case of the EYFS or skills ladders as is the case for the Foundation Phase or learning goals. Prior to the completion of the assessment scales that are either required statutorily from your curriculum (as in the case of the EYFS and the Foundation Phase) or decided in your own context by all the early childhood team, there are steps to undertake in order to help you after having analysed the observation recordings and arrived at accurate conclusions.

Firstly, having the development of the child as a guide, focus on an individual child and create a specific profile of his or her development. Within your framework, you can make comparisons as to what extent the child has met certain developmental areas, what the strengths of the child are and where you need to focus more in order to enhance this child's development. For example, looking at a child's personal, emotional and social develop- ment, the EYFS assessment scales can become your criteria for investigating where this child is developmentally. Similarly, The Foundation Phase Profile skill ladders can be your guidance. Consequently, with a mixture of observations providing cumulative data, you can begin to build a profile of the child's progress through the curriculum. This will help you to plan appropriate activities to support this child's development and learning.

Secondly, you can refer back to the aims of the observations that reflect the learning goals of your curriculum and try to compare your observation recordings with the aims of the learning goals. This will enable you to evaluate whether or not your activities have been implemented effectively, based on a child's progress.

The final step is to decide on the way these assessments will be documented.

Step 8 Documenting observation findings

Documentation in early childhood education, as mentioned earlier, is the way that we syn- thesise, present and share a number of observation recordings as well as assessments either of children or of our educational programme. It should be based on moments of play, *significant learning situations, processes of learning, or experiences* (Martin, 2019, p.473), and written and/or visual narratives about what happens in the life of early childhood edu- cation. Documentation can be presented in many different ways and formats as will be shown below (see also Chapter 8).

In early childhood education documentation is used in a variety of ways and purposes. It can be used for record-keeping of assessment (formative or summative) or to showcase a project, activity, play or learning experience. Although, there is a plethora of its uses in early childhood education, it is suggested that documentation should be used to make children's play and learning experiences, as well as the educational programme, able to be seen in evidence. It also should be used as a tool for reflection on your practice in order to develop your practice further.

Documentation involves holistic data gathering using a variety of methods, including (but not limited to) video/audio footage; photographs; selected examples of artefacts (such as children's work and teacher plans/outlines); programmatic documents (including policies and statements of vision and mission); and interview transcripts. This provides those involved in documentation (teachers, children, parents and other stakeholders) with important opportunities to think deeply about, and take note of, the perceptions, values, circumstances and so on that have contributed to, and perhaps detracted from, the approach/programme's success.

(UNICEF, 2016, p.10)

There are two main methods of documentation: for each child such as portfolios and pro- files, and the collective capturing of significant moments of the daily life of the setting or a project that developed over a period of time, shared joint play or learning experiences (documenting your pedagogy).

Documenting a child's profile

This type of documentation normally has the format of an individual portfolio or profile that can include notes about each child, photographs of significant moments in the setting, samples of art works or any other work, formative or summative assessments, achievements, parents' comments and the child's stories. It might be required for statutory purposes, as in the case of EYFS profile, and thus be formal, or it might be informal where each early childhood setting is using it as a way of keeping records of children. No matter what your context, whether it requires formal or informal documentation, it is important to have a form of documentation for each child's play, learning, experiences and development as a tool for monitoring children's progress. Documentation for each child can be in the form of:

- photo books;
- journey books;
- curriculum-based portfolios that include the learning outcomes and how a child is meeting them (as in the case of EYFS);
- scrapbooks with photos and observations and children's collages;
- story books that include the narration of children's activities;
- digital apps-based, video and audio portfolios (see Chapter 8).

Examples are provided in Figures 7.2 and 7.3.

Figure 7.2   Photobook: studying shapes

Figure 7.3   Journey book: learning to look after plants

Documenting the pedagogy

This approach to documentation was developed in the early childhood settings of Reggio Emilia in Italy (see Case Study 7.3 below) and is widely used not only as a tool to showcase practice, but also to reflect on your practice as it *provides an evidence-base of events and interactions occurring within the setting, which can then be used to prompt teacher/practitioner reflection and analysis. Used effectively, this form of documentation can provide important insights into various aspects of pedagogy (including values; perceptions; interpretations; pragmatic concerns; programmatic factors; the place of children and other stakeholders and so on)* (UNESCO, 2016, p.10). It has a variety of formats and the documentation can be displayed either indoors or outdoors. Some examples of the documentation of pedagogy are:

- arts-based displays in formats such as collages, bricolages, posters, scrapbooks, mood boards;
- realistic displays with children's photographs during an activity, project or a visit: these can either be the final product of a project/activity or how the project/activity was developed;
- digital visual displays that can include all the above as they have the capacity to rotate a number of photos or small videos.

There are many different and inventive ways as to how observation findings can be documented (see Further Reading for resources on documentation), as demonstrated in the examples and case studies which follow.

Figure 7.4 Outdoor display: children's experience of coloured water in bottles

Figure 7.5 Arts display: bricolage – our village project

Figure 7.6   Mood board of the ripping and tearing game

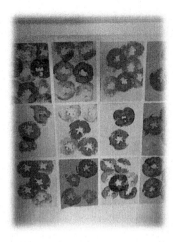

Figure 7.7   Poster: drawing with sponges

CASE STUDY 7.2

The Mosaic approach: polyvocal documentation

The Mosaic approach, as mentioned in Chapter 3, aimed at emphasising that *listening [to children] is an active process, involving not just hearing, but interpreting, constructing meaning and respond-ing* (Clark and Moss, 2001, p.7). Core to this approach is that *the documentation [. . .] is then subject to review, reflection, discussion, and interpretation by children and adults in a process of participant meaning making* (Moss, 2010, p.xi). Children were involved in the process of planning their learning by listening to their own voices and by providing their perspectives on their lives. The Mosaic approach aimed at enabling them to co-construct the activities (Clark and Moss, 2001, 2011). In this study, the discussion of documentation was determined by creating a dialogue among children, practitioners, older children, parents and researchers. The involvement of all par-ticipants was central. Dialogue about the documentation was shared in the following ways.

The idea of creating portfolios as tools of documentation was introduced. These portfolios were open and new tools or materials could be added with the participation of adults, parents and children. Whenever children's or adults' skills and interests were developing, these were added to the portfolio. The important aspect of these portfolios was the data collection tools, developed to enable children to express their views, ideas and feelings (Clark and Moss, 2001, 2011). Observation recordings were cen-tral in the Mosaic approach. Child conferencing – which took the form of a short interview – and tours with the child, map-making, as well as photographs and videos, were the basis for collecting information

(Continued)

(Continued)

around children's interests and skills. Thus children's participation was central throughout the child-conferencing technique. The Mosaic approach is multi-method and allows for the plurality of views of all involved (polyvocal). How it is constructed is illustrated in Figure 7.8.

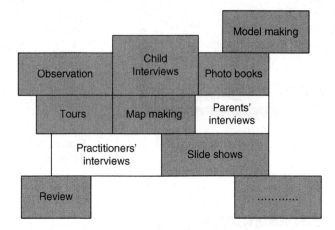

Figure 7.8 The Mosaic approach: multi-method and polyvocal

Source: Clark and Moss (2011).

In order to create these portfolios, three important aspects were taken into consideration:

1. The tools used throughout the process of collecting information about children's perspectives of their own lives.
2. The view of the child as an 'expert' on his or her own life.
3. The involvement of all participants, especially parents and key workers, was highly valued.

As a result, the Mosaic approach suggested a new way of documenting the observation of children. It is not only reliant on observation, but uses a number of other methods to construct documentation. Working in an educational setting, assessment for children should not only focus on the developmental and educational goals, but should start from the child's perspective and emphasise the child's life experiences and voice.

ACTIVITY 7.2

Reflect on the Mosaic approach

Reflect on your own practice, which is underpinned by the curriculum you work within, and consider how you could adopt the Mosaic approach:

- Will this be possible with the workload in your setting?
- Will it promote children's and parents' participation? If yes, in what ways?
- What are the benefits using this approach?

CASE STUDY 7.3

Reggio Emilia: pedagogical documentation

Reggio Emilia is an alternative and flexible pedagogical approach to a pre-defined and pre-described curriculum, in which children, parents and teachers are working together through a variety of activities.

> *Pedagogical documentation [. . .] is fundamentally related to the attempt to see and to understand what happens during the pedagogical experience and seeks to do this without reference to a rigid framework or scheme of predefined expectations. [. . .] pedagogical documentation does not claim what is documented is a direct representation of what children say and do; it is not a true account of what has happened. [. . .] [but it is] understood [. . .] in an interpretive process [. . .] not only for teachers but for children.*

(Dahlberg et al., 1999, 2007, p.xxv)

Children express their ideas and lead the activities according to their interests. One of the main questions about the Reggio approach concerns the way in which children's meaning-making can be assessed. The concept of pedagogical documentation in Reggio Emilia is a way of collecting children's experiences during activities through materials, photographs, videos, notes and audio recordings. This information becomes visible to others (children and parents) through exhibits, DVDs, books, posters and pamphlets. The teachers act as recorders/documenters for the children, helping them to revisit their actions and self-assess their learning. In the Reggio Emilia classroom documentation is an integral part of the procedure and it aims for a pedagogy in which children are listened to. Rinaldi (2005, p.23) stresses two important aspects of documenting children's activities:

1. [Documentation] makes visible the nature of the learning process and strategies used by each child, and makes the subjective and inter-subjective process a common parsimony.
2. It enables reading, revisiting and assessment in time and in space and the actions become an integral part of the knowledge-building process.

An example of pedagogical documentation is shown in Figure 7.9. These photographs were taken in an early childhood setting in Barcelona that was implementing the Reggio Emilia philosophy and pedagogical documentation. They used individual profiles for children in the form of a scrapbook, but also displays on the walls to share these activities with the whole setting and also with the parents.

(Continued)

(Continued)

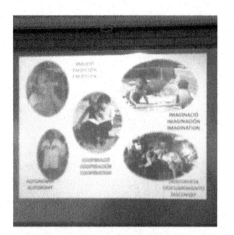

Figure 7.9   Sharing visual displays (Reggio Emilia style)

CASE STUDY 7.3

Te Whāriki: Documenting learning and development

In Chapter 6 we discussed Learning Stories as an example for semi-structured observation. A collection of learning stories can be kept in a synthesised way in a child's portfolio and becomes documentation as in the examples below.

'Ruby and the supermarket'

Learning Story 1

Date: xx/xx

Teacher: Sue

Several children were busy in the sandpit, making puddings. Ruby was very sure of exactly the ingredients she needed for her pie – 'Bananas, apples, chocolate, ice cream' – but she indicated that she didn't have them all.

'Perhaps we could go shopping?' I suggested.

So we set off. First we went to the 'fruit shop'. 'Need two apples,' said Ruby. We found the 'apples' and handed over the money. Ruby had a bucket with a little bit of sand, and each time she bought something, she fished in the bucket and handed over some 'money'. 'What else does Ruby need?' 'Get some bananas.' She used a lot of language.

(Continued)

(Continued)

The game went on for some time. (The others left us for different activities.) We visited a different shop for the ice cream and chocolate and then another one for a handle for the door and some screws. (On our travels, Ruby noticed the door of the sleep room and announced that we needed 'a handle and some screws'.)

We made our way back to the sandpit to make the pie after our busy shopping trip.

Learning Story 2

Date: Same day

Teacher: Jo

Today, just like every other day, Ruby amazed me with her articulate nature. I observed Ruby and Sue discussing a trip to the shops and was very keen to pay attention as these imaginative interactions with Ruby are often so filled with rich language and with scientific and mathematical concepts. They're a real joy to watch, even when you're not taking part! Apples and kiwi fruit were on the agenda today. Today, Ruby's plan was for a short visit, with just enough time to get two shiny red apples and two brown kiwi fruit. 'All finished now,' said Ruby once she had made her purchases. Seeing my opportunity, I approached. 'Would you like to draw a picture of your shops and food, Ruby?' 'Okay,' said Ruby, running over to the table. 'Apple', she said as she drew circles on her paper in red crayon. 'Is this the colour of your apples, Ruby?' I asked. 'Yes', said Ruby. 'Red'. 'Well done, Ruby. What else did you buy?' 'Kiwi fruit – look, there', she said, pointing to her picture. Before long, we had drawn the shops as well as some pictures of her mum and dad. Ducking inside for a moment, I brought out an apple that had been cut in half. Showing it to Ruby, I explained how the apple had been cut and asked whether she would like to draw a picture of the inside of the apple. 'No, peel it', was the response. 'Why?' I asked. 'So Ruby eat it', was the delightful answer I received as Ruby began chewing away on the apple! Well, I never! What learning happened here? Ruby's thirst for knowledge is very much an aspect of her personality. Her make-believe play provides an information exchange within a responsive social context. Ruby's use of language in her play as she responds, imagines, questions, describes, creates and decides shows her independence, confidence, and sense of responsibility for her own learning. Her awareness of scientific and mathematical concepts was evident as she talked about colours and numbers and explored past events.

What next?

Well, a trip to the shops with Ruby is a must. My interest couldn't be greater. Is she wonderfully help-ful? Does she enjoy gathering groceries? I'm sure I will soon see. Keep a lookout for Ruby's follow-up story, soon to come – a visit to the real shops!

Children's learning is greatly influenced by the role of the family and significant others. The atti-tudes, skills and knowledge developed in the early years are the basis for learning in later years.

(Hogben and Wasley, 1989, p.22)

Learning Story 3: The supermarket

Date: xx/xx (3 days later)

Teacher: Jo

'Read Ruby's stories', said Ruby on spotting me early this morning. And so the much anticipated supermarket adventure began. After hearing and seeing her latest story, Ruby showed a keen interest in this shopping trip to the supermarket. She gobbled up an explanation of the need for a 'shopping list' of things to buy, and then we settled to the task at hand. 'Crackers, bananas, and a paper' were 'musts' for Ruby. Mille was a keen helper, happy to help budget as long as she could join us in the adventure. Checking the usually forbidden kitchen cupboards was an amusing task, which they followed by asking all the teachers for further suggestions. 'Shopping list', they announced proudly, waving it around. This time-consuming challenge was of huge interest to these shoppers, who giggled a lot. 'Panadol,' suggested Lorraine, holding her head! (Ha, ha.) 'Shelley', said Ruby, so we went in search of Shelley. 'Bubbles' was Shelley's shopping item of choice and so the journey continued. With our list in hand and warm hats on, we set off with excitement at an all-time high and delightful smiles shining from our faces. The walk was not without challenge as I managed to get the double pushchair stuck in the supermarket entrance bars. After holding up a lot of busy shoppers, we got through and were off again. What a hoot!

Once inside, the fun really began as we searched the aisles for the items on our list, then placed them in the pushchair, a very tricky task when holding a banana. But what clever helpers! With all our items in hand, we paid, waved and left the supermarket, keen to return another day. Munching on our bananas, we returned to the centre, put our shopping away, and sat down for a rest and chat. 'What did you think about our trip to the shops, Ruby and Mille?' I asked. 'Fun shopping!' said Ruby. 'Shops, yeah. Walk', replied Mille. An all-round success, I would say.

What learning happened here?

Reading her learning story and looking at photographs of herself gave Ruby the opportunity to revisit her learning and interests. It also cemented her feelings of confidence and independence and her awareness of how much we value what she does. Our discussing going on a trip to the supermarket enabled Ruby to take responsibility for her learning and to express her ideas and feelings, two very significant learning dispositions. As I had suspected, Ruby was wonderfully helpful on the trip. She persisted with the difficulty of lifting heavy items and gained enjoyment from leading this learning opportunity.

What next?

We will offer Ruby more opportunities to explore her interests and extend already cemented learning.

(Adapted by the Ministry of Education (2004) Assessment for Infants and Toddlers, New Zealand, pp.8–9)

CASE STUDY 7.4

Laevers' scales of involvement and well-being: documenting well-being

As mentioned in Chapter 5, Ferre Laevers at the University of Leuven introduced the Scales of Involvement and Well-being in 1976. The instrument was developed at the Research Centre for Experiential Education (Leuven University, Belgium). The aim is that these scales measure and monitor children's involvement and engagement in activities as well as their well-being.

The scales aim to:

- *serve as a tool for self-assessment by care settings;*
- *focus on quality, taking into consideration the child and his/her experience of the care environment;*
- *achieve appropriateness for the wide range of care provision.*

There are three steps in the process:

- *Step 1 – assessment of the actual levels of well-being and involvement.*
- *Step 2 – analysis of observations.*
- *Step 3 – selection and implementation of actions to improve quality of practice in the early childhood setting.*

This documentation process is mainly based on numerical evidence, interpreted by the team involved in the process. They do not provide as rich information as the other methods of documentation, but are helpful as a self-evaluation tool in your practice.

To conclude, how each early childhood education setting decides to document observations should be consistent, understood by all involved in the process (team, parents, children) and at the same time be accessible by all participants. It is essential that the documentation process should be the product of participation, shared among all involved, helpful, useful and focused on the aims and objectives of the planning process. It also needs to be practical and linked with the setting's curricular practices.

No matter which practice you decide to implement, it is important to reflect on the use of documentation and consider:

1. Do we know why we use documentation? Who is the documentation for?
2. Are our methods of documentation sustainable in terms of time management and do they reflect our skills?
3. Do they promote communication with parents in a summary form?
4. Is our documentation reflecting the child's progress throughout his/her enrolment in our setting?

5. Is the information in the documentation useful, meaningful and making links with our curriculum?
6. How does the documentation help us to forward plan?
7. Have we all agreed to use a specific way of documenting so we can ensure coherence and consistency across the setting?
8. How are we going to include children in the documentation process?
9. How are we going to include parents in the documentation process?
10. Is documentation meeting curricular requirements?
11. Have we chosen a documentation practice that will not take us away from working with children?

ACTIVITY 7.3

What is the role of assessment and documentation in your context?

Reflect on your own setting and discuss:

- How much assessment is formally documented in your setting?
- Who has access to this documentation, and how?
- Is this type of documentation accessible to the parents and the children?
- What methods do you use to document your observations?
- Are you including profiles and how?

S U M M A R Y

This chapter concludes the steps in observation planning as discussed in Chapter 3. It discussed how observation recordings are analysed and how important it is to make valid explanations of the recordings in order to arrive at conclusions on what the recordings 'say' to us. It also discussed different documentation practices such as the Mosaic approach, pedagogical documentation, Learning Stories and Ferre Leavers Scales of Well-Being. All demonstrate how the observation process can be documented in a way which enables the participation of children and parents. There are also examples of how documentation can be used to share information with any individual interested in children's development and learning in an informal or formal way, the early childhood workforce and parents. Finally, a key limitation of observation was addressed – in early childhood settings observation cannot be the only method of collecting evidence as it cannot tell the whole story. Thus it is essential that observation planning is the outcome of team, parental and child involvement. However, more and more practice now uses digital media and visual observations are tending to become part of the daily routine of early childhood education. The next chapter will discuss how we analyse and document digital media observations.

Further Reading

For more information on documentation with a particular focus on visual documentation:

Luff, P (2007) Written observations or walks in the park: documenting children's experiences. In Moyles J (ed.), *Early Years Foundations: Meeting the Challenge*. Maidenhead: Open University Press.

To further your understanding of the Mosaic approach read:

Clark, A and Moss, P (2011) *Listening to Young Children: The Mosaic Approach* (2nd edn). London: National Children's Bureau.

To further your understanding on pedagogical documentation:

Rinaldi, C (2006) *In Dialogue with Reggio Emilia: Listening, Researching and Learning*. London: Routledge.

To further your understanding of how pedagogical documentation can be used in different contexts:

Fleet, A, Patterson, C and Robertson, J (2017) *Pedagogical Documentation in Early Years Practice: Seeing Through Multiple Perspectives*. London: Routledge.

To further your understanding on assessment:

Pascal, C and Bertram, T (2015) Participatory methods for assessment and evaluation. In Furmorhino, J and Pascal, C (eds), *Assessment and Evaluation for Transformation in Early Childhood*. London: Routledge, pp.73–92.

Websites

To explore assessment in an international curriculum visit Assessment for Learning: Te Whāriki:

https://tewhariki.tki.org.nz/en/assessment-for-learning/

CHAPTER 8

OBSERVATION AND DOCUMENTATION IN THE MULTIMODAL AGE

Chapter objectives

After reading this chapter, you should be able to:

- understand the changing nature of observations and documentation in the multimodal age;
- understand how to use the multimodal observations to make meaning of what is observed;
- understand what is multimodal documentation.

With the increased use of digital media in early childhood education and the increased availability in the market of software and applications, it is important to know how to use them and also how to analyse and document the rich visual/audio information they offer.

Introduction: what is it?

Traditionally in early childhood education observations of young children included text paper-based formats such as written notes, children's drawings and other artwork. However, with the availability of digital media such as cameras and touch screens (tablets) it is common practice now to use digital media to capture moments of practice in the setting and moments of children's play or learning.

Digital media (photos, videos, audios), accompanied with some written text to explain what has been captured, can assist the daily observations in early childhood. Moreover, and as discussed in Chapter 4, there is now a variety of software and applications (apps) available to early childhood education that serve as platforms to document what traditionally was done via paper on photo or journey books and scrapbooks. These applications offer the opportunity to record observations instantly and to add videos, photographs, audios and notes to link your observations with the curriculum and to document children's progress. It is also claimed that this documentation can be shared instantly with the parents who can add their own observations and comments on the children's profiles (see, for example, *Tapestry*, an online learning journal at **https://www.tapestry.info/index.html**, or 2Build a Profile at **https://2simple.com/2buildaprofile/**).

> These multi-media forms of 'digital documentation' offer new possibilities to recognise, represent and value children's multiple signs of learning [and play] in new ways, and to shape these narratives with parents and children [. . .]The portability of new handled technologies (e,g. iPads) supports the recording of observations 'on the go' and 'in the moment', offering the possibility to generate images, video clips and audio recordings on the spot, rather than requiring documentation to be compiled retrospectively.
>
> (Flewitt and Cowan, 2019, pp.2–7)

Such devices and applications have also added a new dimension to how observations are recorded. For example, the traditional participant observation written in paper-based format by memory, on jotted notes or through a full observation now can be done by taking short videos or photographs, adding a comment or a note (written or audio) and tagging your learning outcomes to this with the help of the application. This way of doing observation has the advantage that you can always revisit the observation recording to review and analyse. The technology has opened opportunities for observation and documentation to become multimodal where the visual, movement, sound and text come together to create documentation, either of individual children or your pedagogy.

In researching the use of the digital media in early childhood education Yelland (e.g. 2016, 2018) proposes that in early childhood education the *multimodal contexts (oral, aural, linguistic, visual and kinaesthetic) with both printed and digital resources are essential to being able to function effectively in contemporary societies* (2018, p.849). Such a view can be extended to the observation planning process. Observations in the digital era can be multimodal using a range of tools such as text-based and digital-based methods. This multimodality can be reflected in the way documentation is presented.

As seen in the Mosaic approach, Learning Stories from Te Whāriki and the pedagogical documentation of the Reggio Emilia approach, visual documentation has been a popular way of recording observation findings. In the multimodal age, these innovative and interesting approaches to documentation can be extended by using images, photos and videos to make an activity or a behaviour not only visible (with the use of photos), but also place it in the moment it happened in an animated way that makes it vivid and real. Documenting in the multimodal age offers a direct representation of the daily life of the setting and at the same time is accessible to children of all ages as it *speaks* in a lively *visual language* that children of all ages can understand and narrate in their own words. It can also be shared with the parents who can thus get a real feeling of what happened, when it happened. In a research study funded by the Froebel Trust, Flewitt and Cowan (2019) worked in three nurseries to examine how they might use these applications with children from the ages of three to five in order to utilise the opportunities offered by the digital technology. They found that, although it is used in early childhood education, there is still a lack of research into how it can be effectively used *to develop participatory research methods that blend the perspectives of practitioners with young children* (p.9). Among their key findings they demonstrated that practitioners, parents and children valued the use of digital media for observation and documentation purposes. There is still limited advice and guidance at the research level, however, as well as at the policy level. Thus this chapter aims to offer you guidance on how to use multimodal observation and documentation in your practice.

Before that is explored, however, (and based on the above discussion) in this book multimodal observation and documentation are defined as:

> **Multimodal observation:** is a recording of a narrative of an event, activity, a child's play or learning experience, in the format of photograph (or sequence of photographs), video, audio, text-based or a combination of all that is done with the use of technology.
>
> **Multimodal documentation:** is the organised and systematic synthesis of multimodal observation findings that lead to accurate conclusions and assessments either of a child or your pedagogy in the format of a combination of visual, audio and text-based recordings and findings that lead to accurate conclusions and assessments that technology is used as a platform to be presented and shared in a way that will be understood by all involved in early childhood education (children, practitioners, parents and everyone else who has an interest such as inspection bodies) *in a way to get to know better what the children, in their own way, already know* (Turner and Wilson, 2010, p.8).

How is it used?

Multimedia observations, as well as written-based observations, require systematic planning on how they will be used in daily life. In Chapter 3, the principles for good observation planning were discussed (see Figure 3.2) and the same principles apply here as well. However, when you use multimodal observation, the technology that will be used and which software or application that will be chosen needs to be decided and for you to be familiarised with it prior to using it to record your observations. Exploring the potential of the technology you will use is an important part. Then you need to decide which of the functions of the technology you will employ and why. As was discussed in Chapter 4, and as will be explored in the next chapter, you need to be proactive to ensure that your information is protected so issues of how the observation recordings will be stored and who will have access to them need to be addressed in advance.

The software and applications normally have prepared formatted observations. For example, structured observations such as event sampling or checklists are available for when you do your observation. So, instead of completing them in the paper-based format you can complete it on the tablet and store it immediately in the child's profile. Most of these applications have created semi-structured observation schedules for you that will assist the collection of information on focused aims and objectives, but also allow space for capturing the unexpected, as in the following example from Tapestry (source: **https://www.tapestry.info/index.html**).

Care Diary

One of its functions is the Care Diary for infants and toddlers. In the Tapestry website they promote this application as follows: *The Tapestry Care Diary allows you to record the daily care routines you provide for your children. You can record all of these details for individual children, or select multiple children to quickly record information without repeating yourself.*

Among other observations, they have prepared a time sampling app to check sleeping patterns for individual children and as a group:

Time sampling: sleep checks – individual log

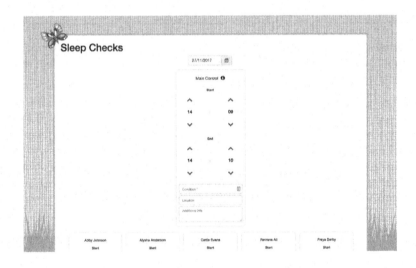

Figure 8.1   Time sampling: sleep checks for the whole group

They have also prepared for written observations:

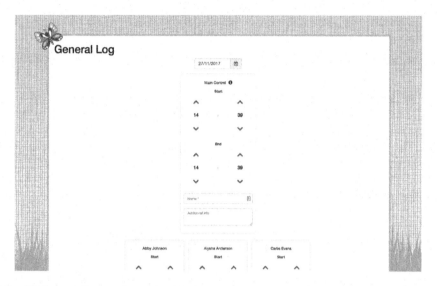

Figure 8.2   Written observation

It is important to note that although these apps and software have been prepared for your observations, *you are still the observer* and you will need to have developed skills in observation as well as a very good understanding of how to do observations and what methods of observation exist. Remember, you will do the observations and the analysis as the software will not do it for you!

When using a multimodal approach to observation always ask:

- *why* will be observed? – refer to aims and objectives of observation planning;
- *how* will it be observed – refer to the chosen observation methods;
- *what* will be observed – refer to the actual observation recording;
- *who* will observe – refer to the key observers (is it the child or the practitioner?);
- *what does it tells* us about what happened in order to be documented – refer to analysing the observation recording;
- *what needs to be documented?*

With the use of multimodal observation you can have all the methods that traditionally were recorded in a paper-based format:

- participant observation: full observation with videos, snapshots of photographs, short videos or observations;
- non-participant observation: visual or audio narratives, rating scales, checklists, diagrammatics, sampling;
- semi-structured observation: as in the case study of Tapestry above.

> **Important note**: When multimodal observation recordings and documentation are used you need to ensure that the information is stored, used, and shared in a safe and secure way so no third parties can have access.

As with the paper-based observations, it is important to be aware that when multimodal observation recordings, such as photographs or videos, are used to share observations, *they still require interpretation* as different people or different children will not 'see' them in the same way. As mentioned in Chapter 4, the use of digital media as a tool for observation is a way of selecting observation recordings and of reconstructing reality, but reality for each of us is perceived differently. So in the next section, how we arrive at multimodal documentation is explained.

Analysing and documenting multimodal observations

The use of multimodal media when observing can lead to a collection of much material as it is so easy to take numerous videos, audio recordings and photographs. Similar to the paper-based analysis process that was explained in Chapter 6 the same steps in the analysis process apply to the multimodal observations. You always start with a careful review of your observation recordings, decide who will be involved in the process in order to make meaning, evaluate your observation recordings, before finally checking your evaluation in order to create your documentation. However, due to the nature of multimodal observations there is some variation on how to conduct the analysis. In the following paragraphs some practical steps on how to analyse your multimodal observations are offered.

Step 1: Review, filter and organise

It is important to organise and filter these materials on a daily basis otherwise, if you leave it all for a long period of time, you will end up with vast amount of recordings that will not be manageable to handle. So the first step is to review your materials frequently. In this process, if it is appropriate, you can ask for the help of the children themselves by choosing which materials they think they find relevant, as in the example below.

Example

A group of three children (aged from three years to four) are working on natural materials to create a collage with the theme: 'Our Neighbourhood'. The practitioner takes short videos during the making of the collage as a way of undertaking participant observation instead of writing down what the children doing. Once the collage was finished the children decided to display it in the class and the practitioner started a discussion about which materials they enjoyed most, which ones they found easier to handle and what they liked in the making of the collage while audio recording the conversation. While the discussion unfolded the practitioner showed them the videos and asked them which one they think mostly represented their emotions during the activity. After watching all the short videos the children decided which one they wanted to keep. The practitioner then asked them to audio record short narratives on why they decided to choose this video. Finally, she took a photograph of the collage on display with the children around it. Once this was finished the practitioner filed the chosen video and children's recordings as the observation recording of the activity under the title 'Observations for Our Neighbourhood Collage'. She also added a brief note:

I need to visit this observation to analyse how language was used to express emotions.

Consequently, she visited the multimodal observation recordings from this activity alongside some others to analyse how children use language to express their emotions. Her findings were then tagged to the Personal Social and Emotional Development for each child's record and also tagged to the group records. Thus the use of a multi-photo sequence of the application documented how children expressed their emotions with language.

As can be seen in this example the short videos from a digital camera are replacing the text-based jotted or scratch notes and full written participant observation in the format of audio and visual recordings. Although there were several, with the children's help they chose the one they considered to be representative of how they felt about the activity. In this example, we also see how children can be in control in their own observations by choosing the materials they would like to use. In an earlier study Cheeseman (2006) cautioned that with the availability of cameras, we might run the risk that we use materials (mainly visuals) that children might not consent to be used:

> *We are tempted to make assumptions that children don't mind this, that it is part of being in early childhood centre. We have always listened into children's conversations [as well as taken photos of children] and used these materials to inform our future planning. The public display of these conversations [and photographs] within the documentation may represent an assumption on behalf of the teacher that children consent to this practice.*
>
> (p.194)

The use of multimodal observations can thus engage children as well as parents to be part, or in control, of the process of what is included in the documentation where all involved feel comfortable as to how recordings are presented, especially those that are visual.

Similar to the analysis of text-based observations the first stage of the analysis process is to review and filter your materials. It is important to have organised your media observations in a logical and chronological sequence. With the technology available now this is easy as the devices add the dates and, in many cases, the place that the photos, videos or audios were taken. Review all the materials you have digitally recorded and then select the ones that will become the focus of your analysis. In order to select the ones that will be analysed consider how this recording will help you to meet the aims and objectives of your observation planning.

For example, in the language and literacy activities you are working with children so they can start creating songs. During lunchtime and when sitting in the chair Paul (three years and eight months) turns to Emily (practitioner) and says that he's thought of a song and asks permission to sing it to her. Emily encourages him and at the same time records the song. Emily saves Paul's song under the file 'Observations for Language and Literacy'.

It is also important to select digital recordings where attributes such as quality of sound, focus and clarity of the visual image or audio recording will assist in formulating an idea of what this digital recording is capturing. There are occasions as the digital recordings are taken while the practitioner is working with children (see digital media in Chapter 4) that the quality of some of the recordings have been lost due to an unexpected noise or, for example, while you were taking a video a child decided to pass in front of the camera and start talking to you so the video of the activity is not clear.

Once you have filtered your recordings you can move to the next step.

Step 2: Blend digital and paper-based observations

Although technology can help you with the observation process in early childhood education, practice is not completely free from paper-based observation or other paper-based evidence such as children's story-making, artefacts, drawings, collages and attempts at handwriting. Thus it is proposed that once you have filtered your multimodal observation you should try to see whether there is any other evidence that you can relate to the recordings from the multimodal observation. Once these are selected then you can blend them to start preparing an interpretation and assessment which will synthesise your multimodal documentation.

In the above example Emily stored Paul's song in the file under 'Observations for Language and Literacy'. Then she went through Paul's paintings and tried to find if there were attempts from Paul to create alphabet letters in his drawings. She found two where Paul clearly was drawing straight lines and linking them with a line in the shape of an H. She took a photo of this drawing and added it to the file as it might be evidence of his attempt to write. She also made a note to check his art work from this point on to see whether there were any other similar attempts to write.

CASE STUDY 8.1

How do we move through the environment?

In a nursery a group three- to four-year-old children have been working towards experiencing different materials from the environment. The main aim of this project was physical development. The specific objectives were to find out:

1. How children use the two body sides together (bilateral coordination)
2. Eye–hand coordination
3. In-hand manipulation
4. Whether children engage in constructional play and activities (how effectively they construct things) and, if so, how?
5. How children use different tools (such as pens, crayons, brushes, cutting with scissors)

The project duration was about a month. The children and the practitioners had been collecting materials from nature and making their own small collages, animal figures with clay and drawings to experiment with them. They went for walks in the park to collect leaves, small branches and everything else that was of interest to the children.

Figure 8.3   Our collages with materials from the nature

The practitioners kept videos of how children were using their bodies in relation to open spaces, focusing on how children move outdoors and indoors and how they coordinate their hands when creating collages. During the project they decided to use a projector to display the children's artefacts on the walls and encouraged the children to walk in front of these displays, making different moves using their whole bodies either to point on the images, or to rotate their bodies around their shadows, or to use their bodies to move like the leaves. (The main objective of this activity was to show how the children used their bodies in the space.)

Figure 8.4   Let's turn on the projector

(Continued)

(Continued)

Figure 8.5 I play with the shadows

Once the project was finished all the practitioners involved had a meeting to filter which materials they will use when entering the interpretation stage. They decided to look for any other evidence related to this project beyond their videos and photographs and their notes, so they selected paintings by children where they were drawing using crayons the shaping of their hands. They also chose to analyse the clay sculptures of hedgehogs that took place after the children were playing with the mud in one of the walks in the park. They considered this activity required very detailed hand–eye coordination, in-hand manipulation and the use of tools and construction abilities which were part of the key objectives of this project. They believed that analysing how the hedgehogs were made would provide them with information on how effectively children use different tools, such as clay and brushes, the quality of the finished constructions such as how well they were painted, whether they had been finished and whether they had used other available materials. (The key objective was how children engaged in construction activities.)

Figure 8.6 Making our hedgehogs with clay

Once they had collected the relevant recordings they blended them together and moved onto the analysis stage to see where each child was in relation to their physical development.

ACTIVITY 8.1

Observe development

In the above case study practitioners focused on the physical development of the children. What other areas of children's development could have been observed? What observation recordings will you choose to evaluate another area of development? Why?

Step 3: Analyse (make meaning): explanations, evaluations and interpretation

When all the materials have been selected and organised in a logical and chronological order then you try to make meaning of what has happened. As discussed in Chapter 7 when you try to make meaning of your observation (see Step 2, p.157) the same questions apply here as well. Evaluate and interpret your observation recordings, no matter what the format is (digital or paper-based) as you will always need to seek valid explanations that will inform your assessment, either for a child's project or your pedagogy. In the above case study, the practitioners evaluated each child's physical development across the objectives they had set and found that all children, with the exception of one, were developing very well. They decided to offer extra support to this child to enhance personal confidence, especially in the construction play activities and the use of tools. They also evaluated the project and found that it encouraged children to explore the world around them, to be creative and to encourage social interactions. Although during the project they felt they used a range of materials when examining the recordings of the observations, however, they found that the materials were limited to leaves and small branches and there were 'missed' opportunities to explore other materials such as cones or little stones and to use a microscope to study the materials.

ACTIVITY 8.2

Set steps of action

With reference to the case study and the practitioner analysis of the observation recordings:

- What do you think their next steps of action should be for the child that does not appear confident with the construction play activities and the use of tools?
- What do you think their next steps of action should be so they do not 'miss' opportunities?

Although the principles and steps of the analysis process of paper-based observation recordings apply to multimodal observation recording with some variations, it is important to emphasise that the visual and audio observation recordings do not 'speak' for themselves and do not 'tell' the same thing to everyone. Visuals, such as videos and photographs, and audio recordings *do not make meaning* on their own, but *they do have the potential to make meaning* through explanation and interpretation.

Analysing audio recordings

Audio observation recordings, by their nature, can be translated from sound to textual recordings where you can analyse with the same techniques as the paper-based observation recordings. In the above example where Paul sung a song to Emily and she recorded it, she went and listened to it later to write down to examine the language Paul used. However, the richness of having the sound helps you to investigate what was the mood or tone of the recording, how the intonation was used or whether something was said for example loudly or in an angry manner. When analysing audio recordings, the first step is to look whether it can be translated into a form of text. If it does, then you can analyse it as a text, but also you do need to listen to the audio for other signs such as:

- Can I detect the mood or the tone of the recording?
- Can I detect any emotional signs (for example, shouting, screaming, laughing, giggling, heavy breathing)?

Analysing visual recordings

Where research has been using recordings of visuals (such as artefacts, photographs, images, films, designs) the way in which data is analysed has been the subject of discussion and suggests focusing on semiotics (signs or clues), (e.g. Moss and Pini, 2016; Ledin and Machin, 2018). Based on this idea, when we try to interpret photographs or videos, we do need to look for indicators, signs and clues which emerge and then try to interpret what this meaning might indicate. Case Study 8.2 illustrates this point.

C A S E   S T U D Y   8 . 2

Boys with weapons

Figure 8.7   Boys with weapons

(Continued)

(Continued)

When you attempt to 'read' a photograph or a video you need to look at the elements that convey meaning. It is helpful to distinguish between what you see and how you interpret what you see. So it is helpful to look for indicators in a photograph and what they might show.

Table 8.1   Indicators and indications in photo example 'Boys with weapons'

Indicators	Indication
Child one (on left): holds the sword and the shield, looks straight at the camera.	Feigns aggression, he is posing for the camera.
His lips are stressed, his right hand is pointing with the sword.	Knows how to hold the shield and the sword.
Child with gun (on right): holds gun with both hands, points gun direction in front of him, his lips are relaxed, his eyes are looking at the end of the gun.	Pretends to shout, focuses on the pretend play of shouting.
Child with no toys in his hand (in the middle): his lips are sucked inside his mouth, his eyes are looking into the camera.	Poses for the camera, no interest in the weapons.
Child with bow and arrow (in the front): his left hand holds bow and arrow steady, right hand pulls the bow string back, his eyes look straight at the camera.	Feigns aggression. Poses for the camera, knows how to play with a bow and arrow.

ACTIVITY 8.3

What other indicators can you see in the photograph (Figure 8.7)? What meaning(s) might they indicate?

Try this process with a video observation.

In early childhood education these indicators can be determined by the learning outcomes of your curriculum. For example, you make video observations in an infant room that has children from the age of six months to 12 months to investigate language and communication development. Your objectives for the observation are to find out whether the children:

- recognise sounds
- respond to sounds
- associate sounds with objects
- babble

- use vowels
- use consonants
- attempt to make words.

These objectives in turn can become your signs or clues when searching for indicators that you will need to identify when you try to make meaning of your videos and explain what they indicate.

EXAMPLE: VIDEO OBSERVATION OF ALISON

Alison (eight months) is crawling towards the treasure basket and tries to grasp a wooden spoon. She starts producing the sound 'spau, 'spau' and repeats it six times. The practitioner approaches her and asks her if she wants the wooden spoon from the basket. Alison carries on repeating 'spau'. Then the practitioner offers Alison the wooden spoon. Alison grasps it, looks at it and drops it by saying 'ooo' twice while she is rounding her lips. The practitioner says:

Alison do you mean No, are you saying No to the spoon?

Alison rounds her lips again and says 'oo'. The practitioner says to her:

Do you mean No?

Then Alison smiles and repeats with rounding her lips again 'O'.

This video recording was then analysed as in Table 8.2.

Table 8.2   Analysis of video recording: Alison

Objectives of observation	Indicators	Indications	Has objective been observed?
Recognise sounds	Alison smiled when the practitioner said No and she rounded her lips	She smiled and the sound of the 'O' suggests that she recognised the No	Yes
Respond to sounds	Alison started with three 'ooo' but after the practitioner told her 'No' she moved to the use of only two 'oo' and finally in one 'o' with lips being rounded	She tried to repeat the word No	Yes
Associate sounds with objects	Not evident		Not evident

(Continued)

Table 8.2 (Continued)

Objectives of observation	Indicators	Indications	Has objective been observed?
Babble	'spau' 'spau'	She produced babbling	Yes
Use vowels	Used 'ooo'	She was able to repeat the 'o'	Yes
Use constants	Used 'sp'	She produced 'sp'	Yes
Attempt to make words	Alison was rounding her lips and from three 'os' at the end she used one	She attempted to repeat the word 'No'	Yes

Step 4: Synthesise your multimodal documentation

Once your multimodal observations have been analysed and valid interpretations have led you to conclusions, you make the assessment for each child or your pedagogy and then decide how your multimodal documentation will be synthesised to be presented as in the example in Case Study 8.3.:

CASE STUDY 8.3

How Angie is using an app for observations and documentation

Angie is an early childhood education practitioner in England. She and works with children in the Reception classroom implementing EYFS which requires her to observe daily in order to complete the EYFS Profile at the end of the year:

> I used an app called Orbit Early Years in my previous setting. At my current school, we use an online observation/tracking program called EAZMAG. This allows me to put photos to narratives, to level according to the ages and stages, note Characteristics of Effective Learning and note Next Steps. At the end of term it collates all of the observations and gives me a 'Best Fit' for all of the strands of the EYFS – this is editable, so I can alter it if it does not replicate my professional judgement. It also puts all observations into a Learning Journey which I show to parents during parent consultations and they receive a paper copy of their child's learning journey at the end of their time with me – a nice keepsake. It produces reports and tracking as do many of these electronic observation tools . . . such as Tapestry and 2Simple.

When you synthesise your multimodal documentation alongside the reflected questions presented in Chapter 7, you need to consider the following:

- *Have I used indicative examples of how learning outcomes have been met without overwhelming the documentation?*

- *Is my documentation easily accessible to be navigated by children and parents?*
- *Is my documentation safely saved and safely shared?*
- *How am I going to share my documentation (e.g. CD, paper-based copy, email, USB?). What are the preferences of the parents? What are the preferences of the children?*
- *Have I clearly tagged/indicated how the learning outcomes are met?*
- *Have I included any summative or formative assessment requirements for my curriculum?*
- *Have I clearly documented my pedagogy?*

SUMMARY

In the twenty-first century, with the increasing availability of technology, early childhood education has embraced many aspects of the digital era, such as cameras and tablets in the observation process. The use of videos and photographs for observation practices are routine in most early childhood settings. The digitalisation has brought new practices where paper-based observations are blended with the digitally based recordings to create multimodal observation recordings and documentation. Thus it is important to understand observation in multimodality terms where text, visual, audio and forms of art work are combined to offer a wealth of information for the children and the pedagogy. However, it is important to make sure that such practices are handled with careful consideration of the systems in place to ensure that the collected information is ethically and safely protected as will be discussed in the next chapter.

In the next chapter, the ethical implications of observation will be explored and how children can participate in both the planning process and in the observation itself will be discussed.

Further Reading

The following report is based on research and explores the role of the digital media in observation and documentation in early childhood education:

Flewitt, R and Cowan, K (2019) *Valuing Young Children's Signs of Learning: Observation and Digital Documentation of Play in Early Years Classrooms*. UCL Institute for Education, UK.

If you want to further your understanding on how we do visual analysis for research purposes read:

Ledin, P and Machin, D (2018) *Doing Visual Analysis: From Theory to Practice*. London: Sage.

Websites

You might want to explore some of the applications that are available on the market:

2Build a profile: **https://2simple.com/2buildaprofile/**

Tapestry: **https://www.tapestry.info/about.html**

CHAPTER 9

ETHICAL IMPLICATIONS

Chapter objectives

After reading this chapter, you should be able to understand:

- the ethical implications of observing young children;
- the importance of team involvement;
- the importance of child involvement;
- the importance of parental involvement;
- the role of the adult as a guardian of young children.

Ethical practices need to be considered throughout the observation process in the early childhood setting. It will be argued that although consent is really important, ethical practice observing young children is limited not only to consent, but also involves a number of other issues. It is strongly recommended that an ethical framework should be established for the setting when developing observation schedules.

Introduction

This chapter aims to discuss the ethical implications of observing young children and will explain the role of the adult as a guardian of young children while data are being collected for assessment purposes. It will emphasise the fact that, before setting the task of observing children, careful consideration of their right to participate (or not) should be made, along with the ethics involved in the process (Palaiologou, 2012a). It will also discuss the importance of reporting data about a child to other practitioners and parents in an ethical manner.

Ethics of the observation process: towards an ethical framework

As emphasised in previous chapters, observations should maintain an integral role within early childhood education. This role is to promote the quality of care and education that children receive and to enhance practice. Observations help the early childhood education team to extend their understanding about their programme, in addition to their understanding of the children themselves. In order to consider the ethical implications involved in observations it is essential to consider their purpose.

At the policy level, there are legislation and regulations on data protection rules. In early childhood education, practitioners are keeping much statutory information (such as dates of birth, addresses, family names and phone numbers, health records and educational psychologist reports), as well as observation recordings and assessment records of young children and a number of images of children. This information needs to be protected, safely secured and shared with those who need to be involved.

On the European stage, since 25 May 2018 all countries that belong to the European Union are now regulated by the General Data Protection Regulation (GDPR). Consequently all countries have had to either change their regulations in relation to data protection or amend them to meet the GDPR requirements. In the UK the relevant pieces of legislation are the Data Protection Act (DPA), introduced in 1998 and revised in 2018 in line with the GDPR, and the Freedom of Information Act 2000. Currently the revised Data Protection Act 2018 covers all the provisions of the GDPR and will not be affected by the outcome of the UK's potential withdrawal from the EU, commonly known as BREXIT. Subsequently all early childhood education settings that keep children's data (including observation recordings) are regulated by this act.

Although these regulations exist to protect personal data and they should underpin early childhood education practice, in this book it is proposed that in the light of the United Nations Convention on the Rights of the Child (1989) the observation process should embrace legislation and the code to create an ethical framework or protocol that is localised and meets the demands of the individual context. In that sense, as it will be emphasised later as well, an ethical framework or an ethical protocol is defined here as follows:

> Ethical protocol is a synthesis of legislation respecting and implementing children's rights under the UNCRC (survival, developmental, protection and participation) and ethical reflections based on an ethics of care promoting *ethics as creative practice, requiring the making of contextualised ethical decisions, rather than following [only] universal rules or codes* (Dahlberg and Moss, 2005: 73).

Practitioners should create an ethical framework or an ethical protocol around any observation process which is going to inform the planning of education programmes and assessments for each child. This framework will be the product of a shared agreement among all involved: the whole team, children and their families. It needs to have clear aims regarding why observation is used in the setting, what they mean in the setting, how it will be used for assessment purposes and how it will be documented. It should also include consent from all involved in the process – children, parents, the professional team – and the extent to which any observation is needed (along with how records are kept and who will have access to them). The following paragraphs will discuss what is required to construct an ethical framework for the observation process.

Team involvement

Team involvement is the starting point. As explained in Chapter 3, the early childhood education team meets and discusses both the observation design and the aims and objectives of the process. It is at this initial meeting that the creation of the ethical framework should occur. As part of this, the members of the team need to agree to a code of practice which will reflect the aims and the purposes of the observation. Mutual respect and the creation of a good working environment where all opinions are valued and everyone's expertise, interests and skills are encouraged and taken into consideration are elements in the creation of an ethical code between members of the team. Everyone is motivated and feels safe, free and confident to be involved, reflecting the aims of the observation within the curriculum with which the team is working.

In your ethical considerations the starting point is what information will be collected. This is important. Unnecessary collection of information on children or the educational programme should be avoided and/or limited. It is crucial for the observation process that the aims and objectives are well defined and explained. The aims and objectives of observations should not only be clarified, but also understood by all members of the early childhood team and agreed by all. All the team members should be able to express their views. The final result of the meeting is a decision on the observation processes, techniques and methods and the observation design should be a collaborative product. The needs of the setting, as well as the needs of the children and the team members, should be met. These needs include:

- an agreement on the accessibility of the information;
- the filing and sharing of observation recordings among team members;
- how and who will share the information with the participants involved.

ACTIVITY 9.1

Team involvement

Consider in your setting whether or not there is a team meeting in place where observation processes are discussed and designed.

Parental engagement

One of the key procedures in establishing an ethical code is to gain parental involvement and engagement. This requires active collaboration and should be *proactive rather than reactive, sensitive to the circumstances of all families, recognise the contributions parents can make and aim to empower parents* (Goodall and Vorhaus, 2011: 10). The early childhood education team has a challenging task seeking not only parental consent, but also their involvement and engagement as well. Working in early childhood education can be overwhelming as practitioners are busy implementing the curriculum, complying with legislation and delivering the learning goals of the curriculum. It is important that, despite the demands of the daily routine, the involvement of parents in the observation process is prioritised. So, parental involvement should not be limited to merely signing a consent form. Parents should be involved and participate when observations are designed as an integral part of an ethical approach to observations.

The gathering of observational evidence is crucial for early childhood education and practice so that links can be made between the individual developmental needs, learning achievements, the planning of appropriate activities and the promotion of partnership. In such a context, parental involvement should be encouraged and parents should be invited to an in-depth discussion with the practitioners. When this happens, parents can provide collaboration throughout the process. Parents can become helpful cooperators in the observation process.

The aims and objectives of the process should be explained to the parents in a transparent and understandable manner. Emphasis should be placed on why observation is important in the daily practice of the children's daily life, how it is going to benefit the education programme and furthermore how it will inform the activities designed for the children. It is also central to explain to the parents that they can have access to the records at all times throughout the process. For example, as was shown in Chapter 8, when multimodal observations and documentation are used parents can have immediate direct access and this might be a good way of keeping parents informed.

Parental involvement ought to be a choice for the parents and they should retain the right to withdraw their participation at any time.

A number of questions can help us to investigate the degree of parental involvement:

- Have the purposes of the observation process been explained to the parents?
- Have parents expressed their opinions and been allowed to make any suggestions or alterations?
- Have parents been reassured that they will be able to access the observation recordings as and when they wish?
- Are parents aware that they will be involved regularly and that they will remain informed about the observation process?

The following points highlight the steps practitioners should undertake to fulfil their responsibility for maintaining parental involvement. These are to ensure that:

- parents are kept fully informed throughout the process;
- parents are involved while the child's assessment profile is being created;
- regular meetings with the parents are taking place to keep them informed and to gain their trust and commitment and to maintain their participation.

ACTIVITY 9.2

Parental engagement

Reflecting on your own setting, consider how parental engagement is obtained and what ethical procedures you have in place to involve parents.

There is a necessity for a constant flow of information from the team and not only during parents' evenings or in parents' meetings. A small note or a photograph explaining what the child has done during a day can be a good starting point for a short discussion, but at the same time it is a valid tool for continuous communication with the parents. By making use of digital technologies the team can create a noticeboard where they can display digital photos, PowerPoint slides and videos of activities. Settings can make use of the Internet to communicate information (such as the use of a safe website or email communication).

ACTIVITY 9.3

How can parents stay interested?

Reflect on the practices of the setting you are working in or where you are carrying out your placement and discuss how you can maintain parental involvement within your own setting.

Children's participation

The UN Convention on the Rights of the Child (United Nations, 1989) sets the standards for listening to children's voices and promoting children's involvement in any decision-making that involves them. Since the UN Convention, there has been an emphasis on children having an increased control over the policies, services and curricula that concern them. As has already been explained, the ethics on observing children should apply throughout to all participants in the process. Consequently, children need to be informed and have explained to them the purposes of any observation.

The question for practitioners is at what age are children able to get involved in the process and how can they be informed about the observation effectively. When babies and young children are observed, especially below the age of two years, it is more difficult and challenging due to the children's limited understanding and their involvement will be different. Practitioners are not going to expect the babies and toddlers to voice their opinions through expressive language. Practitioners can involve babies and toddlers, however, by acknowledging that their emotions can be an indicator of their participation. For example, smiling or eye contact might be interpreted as babies and toddlers being comfortable with the observation taking place. Practitioners should treat babies and toddlers with sensitivity, being aware of and responsive to behaviours that might indicate that they do not wish to participate. However, as children grow older and start using expressive language (say, at around the age of three) the practitioner can seek to involve the children in the observation process. Play can become the best context for this and can be a tool to seek consent and involvement from very young children. Role play, children's drawing and story time can provide a helpful context for a child's involvement. For example, children can create a story about their feelings with regard to a certain activity and can illustrate this story with their own drawings.

When observation methods were discussed (Chapters 4, 5 and 6) it was demonstrated that some methods can be used by children if they are designed in ways that are understood by them (see examples of rating scales and checklists in Chapter 5). Several innovative approaches (see Clark and Moss, 2001, pedagogical documentation in Chapter 7, or the case study of how children choose which video observation they wanted in Chapter 8) have shown us ways in which children can actively participate in the observation process. However, central to ethical practice in the observation process should be the questions: *How do we know that we act with children?* and *How do we respect children's wishes to participate but equally not to participate?* (Palaiologou, 2012a, pp.5, 7).

There are further advantages to child involvement, aside from its ethical value alone. When children have been made aware that observations take place it helps the practitioner to step back and become a systematic observer. When children are aware that this will happen they are less likely to disturb this process. In addition, they know where to go when they need something. In this way your role as an observer becomes easier and more effective. Moreover, children can participate and from a very young age can start taking control of the processes that involve them.

ACTIVITY 9.4

How can you involve children?

- *Think:* how you can involve toddlers (say at around the age of 16 months) when you are trying to observe how they use their first language to interact with other children or adults?
- *Think:* how you can involve children (say at around the age of 26 months) when you try to discover why a child in a class does not take turns and does not want to share?

To summarise, ethical considerations should not be separate from the observation process, but an integral part of it. Ethical considerations should underpin the whole of the observation process. Parental involvement, as well as child involvement, should not be limited to informed consent forms. Parents and children should be invited into the process of observation and play an active role within it.

ACTIVITY 9.5

Towards creating an ethical protocol

The following list of questions can be used to check whether ethical considerations have been applied in the observation process.

- Has the whole team agreed the aims and objectives of the observation process?
- Has the whole team agreed the observation methods and techniques?
- Have the parents been informed – and has the observation process been fully explained to them?
- Have the nature of the observations (including aims, objectives and what tools will be used) been explained to the children (where applicable)?
- Have you made clear that all members concerned in the observation will have access to the material?
- Have you confirmed that all details will remain confidential?
- Do parents have the right to withdraw at any time without explanation – and are they aware of this?
- Will parents have access to all the collected information?
- Has health and safety been considered?

The role of the adult as a guardian

As mentioned earlier, several policies at the national and international level have been set up as part of the need to protect and promote children's welfare.

The concept of 'safeguarding' children aims to protect them from bullying, adverse or unfair discrimination and accidents, and to ensure access to all services. Additionally, in many countries around the world there are now policies that are intended to protect children in a variety of contexts when there is a concern, as well as when safeguarding issues arise. So, from a legislative perspective, practitioners have frameworks to work with where observation and assessment are necessary for a child's well-being. For example, Article 3 of the UNCRC (United Nations, 1989), emphasising the best interest of the child, states that all decisions taken by public or private bodies about children must take the best interest of children as a primary consideration. Governments thus have the obligation to have policies in place to safeguard children from abuse, neglect and exploitation (including physical and sexual abuse and child labour). At an international level the work of UNICEF is to promote and protect children's rights. There are several initiatives and schemes around the world.

CASE STUDY 9.1

UNICEF UK

In the UK, for example, there is a scheme called Child Friendly Cities and Communities (see UNICEF UK: **https://www.unicef.org.uk/child-friendly-cities/?sisearchengine=284&si product=Campaign_%2A%2A-Child-Rights-Partners-Generic-Broad**) where the main aim is to collaborate with local councils *to help to create child friendly cities and communities – places where all children including the most vulnerable feel safe, heard, nurtured.* UNICEF UK promotes a child rights-based approach based on a framework of seven principles to be used by all who plan and make decisions and frontline professionals who work with and for children. The principles are illustrated in Figure 9.1.

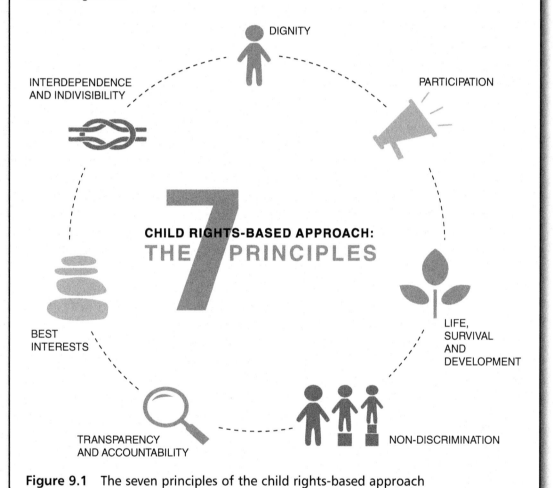

Figure 9.1   The seven principles of the child rights-based approach

Dignity

Every child and young person, like each adult, has inner dignity and worth that should be valued, respected and nurtured. Respecting children's dignity means that all children should be treated with care and respect in all circumstances – in schools, hospitals, police stations, public spaces or children's homes.

(Continued)

(Continued)

Interdependence and indivisibility

All children and young people should enjoy all of their rights all of the time because all rights are equally important. Rights cannot be 'cherry-picked' depending on circumstances. Children and young people's rights to a good standard of living or to be protected from abuse, neglect and violence are as important as the right to get together with their peers or the right to freedom of expression.

Best interests

The best interests of the child must be a top priority in all decisions and actions that affect children and young people. Decisions can relate to individual children, for example about adoption, or groups of children and young people, for instance when designing play spaces. In all cases, children and young people should be involved in deciding what is best for them.

Participation

All children and young people have the right to have a say in matters that affect them and to have their views taken seriously. In order to participate meaningfully in the lives of their family, community and the wider society, children and young people need support and opportunities for involvement. They need information, a space to express their views and feelings and opportunities to ask questions.

Non-discrimination

Every child and young person should be treated fairly and protected from discrimination, whatever their age, gender, ethnicity, religion, language, family background or any other status. Having access to equal opportunities and best possible outcomes doesn't mean being treated identically; some children and young people need more support than others to overcome barriers and difficulties.

Transparency and accountability

Open dialogue and strong relationships between children and young people, professionals and local politicians are key to making rights a reality. For this to happen, everyone needs to be supported to learn about and understand rights. Knowledge of rights also allows children and young people to hold to account the people responsible for ensuring their rights are protected and realised.

Life, survival and development

Every child has a right to life and each child and young person should enjoy the same opportunities to flourish as to be safe, healthy, grow and develop. From birth to adulthood, children and young people develop in many different ways – physically, emotionally, socially, spiritually and educationally – and different professionals should work together to help make this happen.

(https://www.unicef.org.uk/child-friendly-cities/child-rights-based-approach/)

The role of the adult as a guardian is to consider whether the observations:

- are in the best interests of the child;
- respect children's privacy, dignity and possible emotional reactions;
- will help the education programme;
- will help to understand the child's development;
- will inform practice and promote children's learning;
- ensure the safety and protection of children.

Managing the observation recordings and documentation in an ethical way

As discussed in earlier chapters, practitioners have been using observations to gain both an understanding of children's development and learning and to inform the planning of activities. For example, following the introduction of the EYFS in England (or the Foundation Phase in Wales – with its pre-set learning outcomes and learning goals) the early childhood education workforce must use formal and structured guidelines, working within a common framework of assessment scales. The curricula normally detail what information for each child will be gathered through observations for children's assessment. They also explain the documentation process of observation recordings and offer clear guidelines on how children's profiles should be created. For example, in the EYFS it is stated that records must be kept for the safe and efficient management of the setting and to meet the needs of the children (DfE, 2017, see pp.31–6). The data collected are regulated under the Data Protection Act of 2018 and the Freedom of Information Act of 2000. The EYFS offers guidance on how long records should be kept, stating that *records relating to individual children must be retained for a reasonable period of time after they have left the provision* (p.32) and makes reference to the Data Protection Act.

Moreover, with the increasing use and evolving nature of digital technologies to collect and store information there is a need to be proactive and ensure that children's observation recordings are safe. For example, in Professor Sonia Livingstone's research focusing on examining children's rights to protection, provision and participation are enhanced in the digital age, but she also cautions that Internet-enabled technologies can carry risks for children (see **http://www.lse.ac.uk/media-and-communications/research/research-projects/past-projects/researching-childrens-rights**). Advising the UK Information Commissioner's Office (ICO), Livingstone et al., (2018) consider growing up in a digital age where so much private data can be collected:

> It is significant and should be commended that the Data Protection Act explicitly mentions the UNCRC, especially the importance of ensuring the best interests of all children under 18 years old. The best interests of the child should be the key question to answer in any systematic design of services.
>
> The principle of data minimalisation is crucial. Data must be service critical, and that does not include sharing with third parties.
>
> (p.13)

It is not suggested here that digital media should not be used, but for it to be used in a cautious way to protect the observation recordings of children as well as having systems in place to ensure this. For example, the Global Privacy Enforcement Network (GPEN, 2015) suggests safety tools such as parental dashboards, pre-set avatars and/or usernames to prevent children inadvertently sharing their own personal information, chat functions which only allow children to choose words and phrases from pre-approved lists, and the use of just-in-time warnings to deter children from unnecessarily accessing inappropriate websites.

Managing observation recordings also requires a very good understanding of the law in relation to data protection. It is imperative that you have studied and understood data protection laws. In the UK, for example, the Data Protection Act guides early childhood education on children's observation data, regarding the settings as *data controllers*. This means that settings are responsible for complying with data protection laws for personal information held for children. The Data Protection Act 2018, as shown in Chapter 2, sets out clearly the six principles of how data can be protected and places the obligation for children's personal data on schools.

Similarly the GDPR (2018) states:

> *Children require specific protection with regard to their personal data as they may be less aware of the risks, consequences and safeguards concerned and their rights in relation to the processing of personal data. Such specific protection should, in particular, apply to the use of personal data of children for the purposes of marketing or creating personality or user profiles and the collection of personal data with regard to children when using services offered directly to a child. The consent of the holder of parental responsibility should not be necessary in the context of preventive or counselling services offered directly to a child.*

The ICO (2018) offer guidance on how to handle children's data:

> * *Children need particular protection when you are collecting and processing their personal data because they may be less aware of the risks involved.*
> * *If you process children's personal data then you should think about the need to protect them from the outset, and design your systems and processes with this in mind.*
> * *Compliance with the data protection principles and in particular fairness should be central to all your processing of children's personal data.*
> * *You need to have a lawful basis for processing a child's personal data. Consent is one possible lawful basis for processing, but it is not the only option. Sometimes using an alternative basis is more appropriate and provides better protection for the child.*
> * *If you are relying on consent as your lawful basis for processing, when offering an online service directly to a child, in the UK only children aged 13 or over are able provide their own consent.*
> * *For children under this age you need to get consent from whoever holds parental responsibility for the child – unless the online service you offer is a preventive or counselling service.*

- *Children merit specific protection when you use their personal data for marketing purposes or creating personality or user profiles.*
- *You should not usually make decisions based solely on automated processing about children if this will have a legal or similarly significant effect on them.*
- *You should write clear privacy notices for children so that they are able to understand what will happen to their personal data and what rights they have.*
- *Children have the same rights as adults over their personal data. These include the rights to access their personal data, request rectification, object to processing and have their personal data erased.*
- *An individual's right to erasure is particularly relevant if they gave their consent to processing when they were a child.*

(p.1)

Activity 9.6

How can children be safely protected?

Study your curriculum and and discuss how children's personal information and recordings are protected. What is suggested? What actions can you take to ensure that your data about children is protected?

Study the relevant policy or guidelines in the curriculum you are working with for children's well-being, safeguarding and protection and try to list the ethical implications addressed in them.

It is important working in early childhood education, where we tend to collect numerous pieces of information about the children, that we have systems in place to protect children's data. These systems are central not only to our legal duty to protect the children, but also to UNCRC as well as to the rights to survival and protection. Our reflection on the ethical care towards children should be integral when constructing the ethical framework/protocol of our observation planning process, especially when we consider how recordings are kept/documented. Documentation is part of these ethical concerns. The remaining question for the practitioner thus is: how are the observation recordings documented and shared in an ethical way?

Where shall the practitioner start? In the following sections it is suggested that four key questions can be asked to guide this.

1 What is the purpose of record-keeping?

The purpose of record-keeping should be in line with the aims and objectives of the observation process itself. The purpose is to enable all participants (i.e. the early childhood education team, parents and children) to monitor children's progress and inform the educational programme. Observation recordings help to ensure continuity of practice in early childhood education settings, which is the ultimate goal of the process.

Assessing children's progress and the ability to reflect upon the education programme will help the early childhood team to cover all the developmental areas suggested by the curriculum requirements, as well as maintaining an understanding of their implementation.

2 What is the use of record-keeping?

The observation process is ongoing. The continuous collection of information about a child or a group of children and the educational programme can provide evidence to support assessment and referrals, if they are necessary. All this evidence can be used as a communication tool with the parents, as well as with professionals such as educational psychologists and inspection agencies. Sharing evidence of practice is a helpful way of exploring new pedagogies and experiences.

3 Who are the participants in the process of record-keeping?

Those that share an interest in the process are not only the early childhood education team, children and the parents, but also the authorities to whom settings are accountable.

4 Who has access to the records?

Access to records should be determined by those who have a legitimate interest in the process. Access is also determined by the settings' regulations, as well as by national legislation. Parents, carers and outside agencies are those who will have an interest, as well as the early childhood education team members.

Sharing observations

How observations and records are shared with parents and/or carers is an important consideration, as accessibility in the observation recording is part of the ethical implications. Drummond (1993, p.10) says that *paramount among [the practitioner's role and responsibilities] is the responsibility to monitor the effects of their work so as to ensure that their good intentions for children are raised.*

ACTIVITY 9.7

How do we share information with the children?

The ICO (2018) states:

What information should we give to children?

You must provide children with the same information about what you do with their personal data as you would give to adults. In order for processing to be fair, there is the same need for transparency, as this gives an individual control and choice.

A full list of the information you must provide, which varies depending upon whether the personal data has been provided by the individual themselves or a third party, is given in our Guide to the GDPR.

As one of the reasons why children require specific protection is that they may be less aware of the risks of the processing, it is also good practice, to explain the risks involved in the processing, and any safeguards you have put in place. This will help children (and their parents) understand the implications of sharing their data with you and others, so they can take informed and appropriates actions to protect themselves.

You should make your privacy notice clear and accessible and aim to educate the child about the need to protect their personal data.

What if the child is pre-literate?

Article 29 recognises that very young or pre-literate children are, in most cases, unlikely to understand even the most basic written or non-written messages concerning transparency. In this circumstance it is obviously appropriate to provide privacy information that can be understood by the parent. However, this does not mean that the requirement to provide child friendly privacy information does not apply. The Commissioner expects controllers whose services are used by very young children to develop privacy information that can be accessed by children as and when they develop the necessary level of understanding, or in conjunction with their parents. You should ensure that this is periodically brought to the child's attention throughout your ongoing processing relationship with them (for example when providing regular reminders about privacy settings).

(pp.37–8)

Reflecting on the above statement, when creating your ethical framework for observation discuss how you will involve and share information with infants and toddlers. How will you involve and share observation and information with children between the ages of three and five years? What do you need to consider?

CASE STUDY 9.2

Checklist for when you design your ethical framework

The ICO has specific guidance for education (visit: **https://ico.org.uk/your-data-matters/schools/**). Although at the time of writing their guidance has not been updated to reflect the Data Protection Act

(Continued)

(Continued)

of 2018, this information is considered useful guidance. ICO has announced that these will be updated soon. The guidance includes information about using fingerprints in schools, taking photographs, assessing official information, exam results and assessing pupils' information. So, it is worth visiting this website to study how what is proposed will be in line with legislation and the UNCRC. Similarly, the ICO has published the Data Sharing Code of Practice (currently being revised in the light of the Data Protection Act in 2018). It can be accessed at: **https://icosearch.ico.org.uk/s/search.html?query=sharing+data&collection=ico-meta&profile=_default**). The following checklists can be a good starting point, however, when you consider issues around sharing data.

Using the two checklists introduced by the ICO (see below), and after studying the data sharing code of practice, discuss what implications this will have in your own setting. Reflect on the code of practice for sharing information in your setting. Does it cover all the points that are required?

Data sharing checklist: systematic data sharing

Scenario: You want to enter into an agreement to share personal data on an ongoing basis. Is the sharing justified?

Key points to consider:

- *What is the sharing meant to achieve?*
- *Have you assessed the potential benefits and risks to individuals and/or society of sharing or not sharing?*
- *Is the sharing proportionate to the issue you are addressing?*
- *Could the objective be achieved without sharing personal data?*
- *Do you have the power to share?*

Further key points to consider:

- *The type of organisation you work for.*
- *Any relevant functions or powers of your organisation.*
- *The nature of the information you have been asked to share (for example, was it given in confidence?).*
- *Any legal obligation to share information (for example, a statutory requirement or a court order).*

If you decide to share it is good practice to have a data-sharing agreement in place. As well as considering the key points above, your data-sharing agreement should cover the following issues:

- *What information needs to be shared.*
- *The organisations that will be involved.*
- *What you need to tell people about the data sharing and how you will communicate that information.*
- *Measures to ensure adequate security is in place to protect the data.*

- *What arrangements need to be in place to provide individuals with access to their personal data if they request it.*
- *Agreed common retention periods for the data.*
- *Processes to ensure secure deletion takes place.*

Data sharing checklist: one-off requests

Scenario: You are asked to share personal data relating to an individual in 'one-off' circumstances. Is the sharing justified?

Key points to consider:

- *Do you think you should share the information?*
- *Have you assessed the potential benefits and risks to individuals and/or society of sharing or not sharing?*
- *Do you have concerns that an individual is at risk of serious harm?*
- *Do you need to consider an exemption in the Data Protection Act to share?*
- *Do you have the power to share?*

Further key points to consider:

- *The type of organisation you work for.*
- *Any relevant functions or powers of your organisation.*
- *The nature of the information you have been asked to share (for example, was it given in confidence?).*
- *Any legal obligation to share information (for example a statutory requirement or a court order).*

If you decide to share, key points to consider:

- *What information do you need to share?*
- *(Only share what is necessary. Distinguish fact from opinion.)*
- *How should the information be shared?*
- *(Information must be shared securely. Ensure you are giving information to the right person.)*
- *Consider whether it is appropriate/safe to inform the individual that you have shared their information.*
- *Record your decision.*
- *Record your data-sharing decision and your reasoning – whether or not you shared the information.*

If you share information you should record:

- *What information was shared and for what purpose.*
- *Who it was shared with.*

(Continued)

(Continued)

- *When it was shared.*
- *Your justification for sharing.*
- *Whether the information was shared with or without consent.*

Adapted from ICO: **https://icosearch.ico.org.uk/s/search.html?query=sharing+**
data&collection=ico-meta&profile=_default

These two checklists provide a handy step-by-step guide through the process of deciding whether to share personal data. One is for systematic data sharing; the other is for one-off requests. The checklists are designed to be used alongside the full code and highlight the relevant considerations to ensure that the sharing complies with the law and meets individuals' expectations.

S U M M A R Y

This chapter has raised many issues on the ethical implications when observing young children. Within the policy initiatives, reforms, legislation and curricula, the early childhood education field has several reference points regarding ethical practices. However, it is argued in this chapter that in early childhood education when observation planning and processes (as well as documentation) are designed there is a need for an ethical framework to be in place. This is a combination of keeping up with legislation, respecting and implementing the UNCRC (all rights: survival, developmental, protection and participation) and reflection on the ethics of care. It is important in the observation process that all be involved (staff, parents, children), feel confident and valuable and know their voices will be heard. Finally, when documentation is concerned this needs to be again a shared product accessible to all.

Further Reading

For more on ethical considerations when working with and researching in a participatory ideology

Palaiologou, I (ed.) (2012) *Ethical Practice in Early Childhood*. London: Sage.

To further your understanding about the ethical implications of working with and researching infants and toddlers read:

Palaiologou, I (2019) Going beyond participatory ideology when doing research with young children: the case of ethical permeability and relatability. In Brown, Z and Perkins, H (eds), *Using Innovative Methods in Early Years Research*. London: Routledge.

Salamon, A and Palaiologou, I (in press) Infants' and toddlers' rights in early childhood settings: research perspectives informing pedagogical practice. In Press, F and Cheeseman, S (eds)

(Re)conceptualising Children's Rights in Infant-Toddler Early Childhood Care and Education: Transnational Conversations. [Sydney]: Springer.

Salamon, A, Sumsion, J and Harrison, L (2017) Infants draw on 'emotional capital' in early childhood contexts: a new paradigm. *Contemporary Issues in Early Childhood,* 18 (4), pp.361–74.

To explore effective partnerships in early childhood education read:

Whalley, M (2017) *Involving Parents in Their Children's Learning* (3rd edn). London: Sage.

Websites

For full access to the United Nations Convention on Children's Rights:

United Nations (1989) The Convention on the Rights of the Child Defense International and the United Nations Children's Fund. Geneva: United Nations

www.unicef.org/crc/

For more on children's voices and examples of children's participation in all aspects of daily life:

www.unicef.org.uk/UNICEFs-Work/Our-mission/Childrens-rights/Voice/

For more on a research project that takes place in Scotland on children's voices led by Professor Kate Wall in Strathclyde University visit:

http://www.voicebirthtoseven.co.uk/

The 'Look Who's Talking: Eliciting the Voices of Children from Birth to Seven' project aims to explore ways that all children's voices are heard and it has developed posters that can be easily understood by children. You can also read more on this project in the following article:

Blaisdell, C, Arnott, L, Wall, K and Robinson, C (2018) Look who's talking: using creative, playful arts-based methods in research with young children. *Journal of Early Childhood Research.* Online at: **https://doi.org/10.1177/1476718X18808816**

See also:

https://masterclass.sagepub.com/

CHAPTER 10

OBSERVING FOR DEVELOPMENT AND LEARNING

Chapter objectives

After reading this chapter, you should be able to consider:

- how we observe children's development;
- how we observe children's learning and play;
- the role of the adult in early childhood education.

Observation of young children provides rich information for understanding and extending our knowledge of children's development and learning.

Introduction: What do we know about children's development?

Development can be seen as the way in which individuals grow and change over the course of their lifespan and this can take place in different domains: biological [. . .] cognitive [. . .], emotional [. . .] and social (Crowley, 2017, p.2). As was shown in Chapter 2, development has been traditionally the subject of study in psychological theories; however, our perceptions about development are influenced also by how children are viewed in the social and cultural context. Earlier studies have shown us that child development is rooted in moral, social and political choices and problems (Hartley, 1993), with children not being seen as what they will become, but valued for what they are now (beings) (Olsson, 2009). In that sense development cannot be seen in isolation of societal views about children, but as a *dynamic interplay between biological and environmental facts* (Fernald et al., 2017) as well as cultural, political and economic facts where children play a crucial role *in influencing their own development* (Estep, 2002, p.143). Thus some curricula and early childhood practices have moved away from setting learning outcomes that relate directly to development and have adopted learning outcomes that mirror a child who is not only developing within his or her cultural context, but at the same time impacting actively in that environment by promoting *democratic and ethical ideas and ways of working together with children* (Jones, 2009, p.32).

For example, as was discussed in the Introduction and Chapter 3, in Australia the Early Years Learning Framework (EYLF) promotes a vision of children's learning based on developing their identity (being) to be able to form social relationships (belonging), communicate

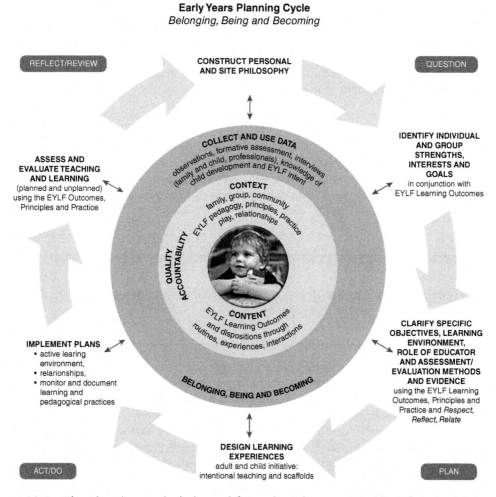

Figure 10.1 The Planning Cycle (adopted from the Educators' Guide Belonging, Being and Becoming, 2010, p. 11).

effectively and be confident learners by developing cognitive skills such as problem-solving, social skills and thinking so they can be active and informed citizens (becoming) (Australian Government Department of Education and Training, 2019). The EYLF outlines a planning cycle for practitioners as illustrated in Figure 10.1 and allows them to use their own system of planning as long as they follow the principles of the EYLF and meet good practice to promote its learning goals.

In the EYFL, where observation is central to the gathering of information to assess children, assessments are defined as: *the process of gathering and analysing information as evidence about what children know, can do and understand. It is part of an ongoing cycle that includes planning, documenting and evaluating children's learning* (EYFL, 2019, p.17) as well making judgments about the practitioner's pedagogy. It promotes the view that assessment should be based on observation of learning experiences of all those involved (children and practitioners).

Similarly, the New Zealand curriculum, Te Whāriki (see Introduction), for early childhood education was introduced in 1996 and aimed through a socio-cultural early childhood environment to provide *tamariki (children's)* early learning and development. *It emphasises the learning partnership between kaiako (teachers), parents, and whānau/families. Kaiako (teachers) weave an holistic curriculum in response to tamariki (children's) learning and development in the early childhood setting and the wider context of the child's world* (Ministry of Education, 1996, p.1). In the revised version in 2017 this view is extended and children are seen as confident learners from birth:

> *[In Te Whāriki] children are valued as active learners who choose, plan, and challenge. This stimulates a climate of reciprocity, 'listening' to children (even if they cannot speak), observing how their feelings, curiosity, interest, and knowledge are engaged in their early childhood environments, and encouraging them to make a contribution to their own learning. (Ministry of Education, 2017, p.17)*
>
> Smith, 2007)

This view reflects on the strands, goals, learning outcomes and assessment. For Te Whāriki, children have an active role in their assessment:

> *Assessment will be a mana-enhancing process for children, parents and whānau, conducted in ways that uphold the empowerment/whakamana principle. Children have increasing capacity to assess their own progress, dictate their own learning stories, and set goals for themselves (for example, learn to climb something, write their name, pursue or expand an interest or project or lead a waiata). As they learn to assess their own achievements they also become increasingly able to plan new challenges, for example, transferring their learning to a new context, taking on a new responsibility, strengthening a disposition, extending their knowledge or skills, or refining an outcome.*
>
> (p. 64)

Consequently, observation is not only limited to children's development, but around the key principles of the key strands of the curriculum: empowerment, the holistic development, family and community and relationships.

Another example comes from Reggio Emilia where pedagogical documentation is rooted. For the Reggio ideology, the core philosophy derives from the idea that children are *rich in potential and any child is endowed at birth with 'a potential for growth', a set of personal resources that can be developed into competences through meaningful interactions with a stimulating environment* (Caruso, 2013, p.33). Thus it is concerned with the creation of a learning environment where children can meet their potential and develop their cognitive skills through arts such as painting, dancing and music. Reggio Emilia views social interactions as essential for children's development and creates a learning environment based on promoting social activities. In the Reggio Emilia approach, the ideal is that *the teachers follow the child, not the plans* (Malaguzzi, 1998, p.88), with the teachers using observations to note children's interests, activities and progress in daily journals and documentation not as an assessment of children, but as a way of communicating with children and their parents.

In the UK, as mentioned in Chapter 1, each country is implementing their own curriculum. However, although they promote the idea that children should be active learners, in all four curricula emphasis is placed on developmental domains such as physical, social, emotional and cognitive development with these being related to the learning outcomes of each curriculum. In all four curricula (EYFS in England, Foundation Phase in Wales, Curriculum for Excellence in Scotland, Learning to Learn in Northern Ireland) the holistic view of child development is promoted by placing emphasis on developmental domains and this mirrors the assessment process. This is especially true in England where the EYFS is based strongly on the developmental domains and the assessment processes, as discussed in Chapter 1, are rooted in rating children's development on fixed standardised developmental scales. Although EYFS states that children should be active learners, the assessment processes reflect a view of a child that development is related with biological, emotional, social and cognitive domains.

To conclude as it can be seen from the above examples, the views we hold about children impact on how child development is referred to, especially when it comes to curricula. Consequently, the ways in which observations are designed are shaped by how we think about children's development. However, it will be discussed here, that no matter what views we hold about children and childhood, it is important to study and understand child development.

ACTIVITY 10.1

What do you think about development?

After studying Chapter 2 and in the light of the above discussion, reflect on your views of what you think a child is, examining the curriculum you are working with and try to see what views of childhood are being promoted. What are your views about child development? How important are they for your practice and why?

Why do we need to understand development?

Understanding why and how children develop in their early years is crucial to practitioners as it influences their approaches to them. As Martin (2019) advises we cannot take child development for granted as *it is an extremely complicated process that has been studied for centuries* (p.87). When working with young children it is important to understand their development as we cannot just assume that it simply happens to all young children as there are many factors impacting positively and negatively. Understanding the developmental achievements of children should be central to early childhood education as they are important for children's progression in order to acquire the skills and abilities which they will use for the rest of their lives. It is also important to be able to understand development so you will not 'miss opportunities' to support and extend children's development as well as identify factors early that might disturb that development.

Early childhood education cannot ignore the importance of children's development in their learning goals or outcomes. Development in early childhood education is a core element that shapes and guides pedagogical approaches and observation is the most valid tool with which to collect information about children's development. Although the developmental child as the dominant lens to view children and design curriculum for them has been debated in the literature (e.g. Moss, 2014; Sellers, 2013), it is important when working with young children to understand their development so we can observe their patterns of growth, play, learning and experiences as *without observing the children's development it would be impossible to create appropriate interactions, effective engagement and responsive programming* (Martin, 2019, p.87).

Key theories of development and implications for learning

In the study of development, as discussed in Chapter 2, there are psychological theories that have proposed key ideas about child development and how these impact on learning. These can be seen in the Theory box below.

THEORY FOCUS

Table 10.1 Summary of key developmental theories and implications for learning (for a detailed account of these theories see Chapter 2)

Theories	Key principles	Key theorists	Implications for learning
Psychoanalytic theory	Proposed psychosexual stages of development (Freud) Proposed psychosocial stages of development (Erikson)	Sigmund Freud Ana Freud Melanie Klein Eric Erikson	Contributed to our understanding of personality development and how later stages of development are influenced by earlier stages.

Theories	Key principles	Key theorists	Implications for learning
Behaviourism	Focused on observable behaviours based on classical and operant conditioning	John Watson Ivan Pavlov Frank Skinner	Reward behaviours we want to increase; punish behaviours we want to eliminate.
Social cognitive theory	Based on principles of modelling and imitation. Humans learn though observing others	Albert Bandura	Self-efficacy (the core belief that one has the power to influence one's own functioning and life circumstances) (Bandura et al., 2001, p. 125) Children with self-efficacy will be motivated and work hard towards their learning. Role modelling.
Cognitive theory	Focused on the process of how mental functions develop (memory, perception, attention, thinking, language)	Jean Piaget	Took the focus away from rote learning and emphasised active learning as it is based on learning as direct interactions with the environment.
Sociocultural theory	Emphasis on the importance of the social world and culture in cognitive growth. Emphasis on instruction from a more experienced peer to achieve the next step of development. (Zone of Proximal Development: the distance between the actual development as determined though problem-solving and the level of potential development (Vygotsky, 1978, p.89).)	Lev Vygotsky	Scaffolding: the teacher supports the children with the right instruction to achieve the next steps in their learning.

(Continued)

Table 10.1 (Continued)

Theories	Key principles	Key theorists	Implications for learning
Information processing	Focuses on the function of the mind and draws parallels to the structure of a computer. Memory stores information (hardware) and processes this information (software). Broke down the understanding of how we use information	Donald Broadbent	Based on the idea that we process information in small steps, teachers can develop techniques that break down into small components what they aim to teach. For example, reading is broken down into sounds, letters, sentences.
Ethology	Focuses on human development in the natural environment and how this impacts on development. Focuses on attachment (the bond children are forming with their parents)	Konrad Lorenz John Bowlby	What children do is specific to their own stage of development, their own specific life circumstances and environment. Personalised learning
Ecology	Development as part of nested environments that impact on each other	Urie Bronfenbrenner	Learning cannot be seen as an isolated activity that happens in school only. The social cultural environment of children needs to be considered.

10.2: CRITICALLY EVALUATE DEVELOPMENTAL THEORIES

After studying developmental theories (see Chapter 2) and with the guidance of the above Theory Focus what are your views of each theory? Which one do you think will help you to get a better understanding of child development and why?

While there is an emphasis on a holistic approach to development as each domain impacts on each other, traditionally development is studied in the following separate areas:

- physical and biological development;
- personal, social and emotional development;

- moral and spiritual development;
- cognitive development (attention, perception, memory, thinking, language development);
- creativity.

This helps practitioners to understand, in a deeper and more effective way, how children develop. However, even though we study development in these separate areas they often interlink and impact upon each other.

There is a wealth of literature and research on child development that the practitioner can use to seek guidance and advice (see Further Reading at the end of the chapter). Observation is always the starting point of all developmental theories that seek to expand knowledge and understanding of how children develop, as was shown in Chapter 2. Observation recordings and information are valuable resources and are key to the study of child development. The information collected by different observation techniques provides insights into many aspects of child development.

However, because of the limitations of each information-gathering technique many are used in combination to study children and to understand their behaviour. For example, when you look at a child's emotional development you might want to combine observation techniques such as a checklist, time sampling and narratives. Even in this case, the information collected might not be complete. As a result, it is very important to discuss your findings and concerns with parents in order to get a better understanding of when and why a certain type of behaviour occurs. You can then draw conclusions about a child's progress in a certain developmental area.

THEORY FOCUS

Developmental areas and key characteristics

Table 10.2   Developmental areas and key characteristics

Developmental areas	Key characteristics
Physical development	*Large motor development:*
	Balancing
	Walking
	Running
	Jumping
	Climbing
	Small motor development:
	Hand preference
	Turns with hand (pages, lids)
	Holds (pens, pencils, scissors)

(Continued)

Table 10.2   (Continued)

Developmental areas	Key characteristics
	Dresses and undresses
	Makes puzzles
	Builds with small blocks
Emotional development	Shows interest
	Shows happiness
	Shows affection
	Shows enjoyment
	Shows sympathy
	Shows empathy
	Shows distress
	Shows fear
	Shows anger
	Shows sadness
Personal development	Stays in the setting without difficulty
	Makes eye contact
	Develops relationships with practitioners
	Makes relationships with other children
	Participates in role play
	Participates in social play
	Participates in symbolic play
	Gets involved in the daily routine of the setting
Social development	*Engaged in:*
	Watching others during play or activities
	Playing by him/herself
	Parallel play
	Play with others
	Making friends
	Having friends
	Following rules
	Taking turns
	Sharing with others
	Seeing things from another point of view
	Helping others during play or activities

Developmental areas	Key characteristics
Cognitive development	*Attention:*
	Concentration span during activities or play
	Distraction
	Memory:
	Recognises familiar objects and people
	Can name familiar objects and people
	Searches for hidden, favourite objects
	Recalls and narrates stories
	Perception (how sensory information is organised and interpreted):
	Identifying objects, colours
	Locating – is able to know distances, sizes, directions
	Categorising of information into meaningful patterns
	Reasoning
	Problem-solving:
	Sorting objects by colour, size, weight
	Classification of objects (big/small, more/less)
	Language:
	Spoken language (uses single words, uses sentences, singing, takes part in conversations, asks questions, narrates a story)
	Literacy:
	<u>Writing</u>
	Holds a pen/pencil
	Pretends to write
	Pretends to read
	Attempts scribbles
	<u>Reading</u>:
	Letter-like writing
	'Reads' pictures
	Holds books
	Turns pages
	Points at text
	Narrates stories from the pictures in the book
	Understands that print conveys messages

(Continued)

Table 10.2   (Continued)

Developmental areas	Key characteristics
	Numeracy:
	Understands meaning of numbers, understands use of numbers, counting and ordering
Creativity	Makes marks on paper
	Makes shapes
	Shows interest in drawing
	Shows interest in singing
	Shows interest in dramatic play
	Shows interest in telling stories/making stories
	Combines materials and objects together to create e.g. a drawing, story

ACTIVITY 10.2

What to observe of the child's development

Choosing one of the developmental areas, focus on a target child and try to create an observation plan in order to carry out observations to assess this child's development.

- First step: find out the age of the child.
- Second step: identify what characteristics children have at this age.
- Third step: design an observation plan that will help you gain rich evidence of this child's development.

CASE STUDY 10.1

Ben is 2 years and 16 days old. He has just moved to a village with his mother, father and his older sister. His sister attends the same nursery. Ben's mother provided the nursery with his portfolio from his previous nursery, which Ben attended from the age of nine months. The checklists in his portfolio highlighted Ben's development, with a particular focus on his physical and language development. The nursery staff have already identified that Ben enjoys building, which he will do in the construction area, or the sand or water areas, and whenever he gets the opportunity to build things up high, he will. However, the staff have noticed that he prefers to do this on his own and that he stops when other children join him.

After a team meeting the staff in the nursery decide to observe Ben to collect further information about him, in order to identify what stage he is at developmentally, and to focus on his social skills to encourage him to interact more with other children. They decide to observe him every day for a week. The main focus was social development and the objectives were to observe Ben's interactions with other children during play and activities. They decided to carry out time and event samplings, tracking and narratives. The narratives were in two formats: as participant observations if something occurred and as non-participant observations. The staff in Ben's group shared roles, in order to know when they would observe him. They felt that in this way they could collect the information they needed to effectively assess his social skills. Before beginning, they undertook some further reading on social and emotional development.

Some notes on what we know about social and emotional development are as follows:

The early years in a child's life are important for his/her personal, social and emotional development. An environment that is safe, affectionate and encouraging promotes positive feelings in children and develops their social skills. From the moment children are born, they are engaged in interacting with adults in an attempt to become independent and social beings. The early stages of their lives are important for the acquisition of the social and emotional skills that will enhance their personal development.

We tend to study social and emotional development together as they are interlinked and reinforce each other. Social development has two important aspects. Firstly, children attempt to form an identity and a personality through differentiating themselves as distinctive individuals. Secondly, they try to find a place in the immediate social community and in society at large. From the beginning of life, children try to develop their 'self-concept', or an image of themselves: *It is a cognitive construction [. . .] a system of describing and evaluating representations about the self* (Harter, 1996, p.207). The attainment of the concept of self involves the development of a self-image, which is an attempt to understand ourselves and to gain an inner picture of who we are. This acquisition of self-esteem is a process whereby we come to an understanding of our self-worth and value. In the complex process of developing a concept of the self we are required to achieve appropriate socialisation skills that enable us to interact with our environment. By understanding shared values, beliefs and rules we make attempts to get to know our social environment and try to fit into our community.

Emotional development is concerned with our feelings and how we control them in order to respond appropriately on different occasions. Emotions are internal or external reactions to certain situations and will differ from child to child. For example, when children become angry in class they might express their anger by crying, whereas other children might express anger by becoming sad and withdrawn.

(Continued)

(Continued)

One of the most influential theories about children's emotional development, and one which is very relevant to the early years, is Attachment Theory, initially developed by Bowlby. Attachment is the bond between the mother or carer and the baby. Secure relationships with the family help children to form positive relationships with others. It is important to understand attachment theory, as children who come to the early childhood setting at a very young age are asked to separate from their parents or carers and spend time in the setting instead. For some children, this experience can be particularly distressing.

It is also important to understand that children's emotional responses have not yet matured and, consequently, they are not able to maintain control over their feelings of distress, anger, sadness, interest, affection or joy. Thus the early childhood environment is important in helping children to express their emotions appropriately and, at the same time, in providing opportunities for them to move towards controlling their feelings and expressing them through words.

Table 10.3 presents these narratives (snapshots) from a participant observation of Ben.

Table 10.3   Narratives from a participant observation

Time	Activity	Social group	Comments
12:00–12:02 p.m.	Ben sits at the table with two other boys and two girls. The nursery nurse is pouring them all a drink. The children are encouraged to say 'thank you'. Ben says this but sits quietly at the table corner as the other children talk.	2 boys 2 girls	When Ben is encouraged to speak he does. However, he does not feel confident enough to speak to the other children.
12:30–12:32 p.m.	Ben is washing his hands because they are covered in yogurt. He returns to the table and sits quietly next to a girl.	2 boys 1 girl	Ben shows that he is capable of washing his own hands without help from the staff, but he does not interact with the other children in the bathroom or at the table.
1:00–1:02 p.m.	The children are singing nursery rhymes and songs. They are sitting on the carpet during the last few minutes of the session. Ben is joining in with singing and arm actions. The nursery nurse has asked		

Time	Activity	Social group	Comments
	the children to pair up so they can sing 'row, row, row your boat' and rock backwards and forwards holding each other's hands. Ben remains sat still on the carpet. The nursery nurse moves Jack over to Ben and partners them up. The two boys hold hands. The singing begins. Ben is not singing but is carrying out the actions. The children are laughing when the nursery rhymes have finished. They sing the nursery rhyme again; Ben joins in and is smiling and laughing at the end.	All children 1 nursery nurse	Ben seems to enjoy the activity. However, he also seems to become uncomfortable when partnered up. When given another opportunity to participate in the nursery rhyme, Ben relaxes more and joins in with the other children.
1:30–1:32 p.m.	There are different playstations set up around the room and staff members are helping children to make a winter picture on the arts table. Ben is playing in the sandpit on his own. He is building a sandcastle.	Solitary play	Ben is choosing to play alone. Other children are playing alongside each other and together on the carpet with cars and trains, but Ben does not join them.
2:00–2:02 p.m.	Ben is on the carpet in the corner with a box of Duplo bricks and he is building with the yellow pieces. Jack has come over and has also started taking Duplo bricks out of the box. Ben stops playing after 30 seconds. Jack hands Ben a yellow piece that he has pulled out of the box. *Oh look, yellow*, he says. *Thanks*, Ben replies, taking the piece. He looks at Jack and he picks up two more pieces.	Solitary play, and then parallel play with Jack	Ben still seems wary of what other children are doing, but perhaps this is because it is only his second week in this group. It is positive to see that Ben is able to play alongside Jack with the same toys.

(Continued)

Table 10.3 (Continued)

Time	Activity	Social group	Comments
2:30–2:32 p.m.	The nursery nurse calls Ben and Jack over to make their Christmas pictures. Ben is talking to the nursery nurses quite confidently and, when asked which colours he wants on his picture, he keeps saying the same colours as Jack wants to use.	Jack Nursery nurse	Ben appears to listen to what Jack says and he repeats the same colours. It might be an attempt to 'share' with Jack.
3:00–3:02 p.m.	Ben is playing in the sand area on his own again. Jack is also present. A girl has begun to play at the opposite side of the sand tray. Jack continues to play with his bucket and spade. *Where have all the spades gone?* she asks. Jack bends underneath the tray and passes a spade to the girl.	Sand area Ben and Jack	Ben plays alongside with Jack, yet he does not seem to be interacting or sharing with him, but he stays there even when another child arrives to play.
3:30–3:32 p.m.	The children are sat all together on the carpet listening to the nursery nurse reading from a 'big book'. Ben is sat next to Jack and he pays attention to the story.	All children in the room with the nursery nurse	Although Ben is listening to the story, he has chosen to sit next to Jack.
4:00–4:02 p.m.	Ben is asleep on large beanbags.		Ben is usually picked up at 3:30, but his mother said she would be late, so the nursery staff have let him sleep.
4:30–4:32 p.m.	Ben is woken up by his mother and he smiles when he sees her. His mother puts his jacket on, collects his bag and carries him out of the room. Ben turns his head and says, *Bye, Jack*. He raises his left hand to wave 'goodbye' to Jack.	Mother Nursery nurse Jack	Ben has shown a positive sign by waving to Jack. It seems that he is starting to like Jack and is showing an interest in socialising with him.

Ben's behaviour is analysed during a half-day when he is in class.

Table 10.4   Example of event sampling technique

Behaviours	Carpet area	Construction area	Water tray	Role play area	Sand tray
Ben talks to another child	**	****	**	******	*
Ben does not talk to another child	********	********	*******	*******	*******
Ben plays alongside another child	*******	********	********	********	********
	******	********	***	****	********
					**
Ben leaves when another child arrives	**	*******	*******	******	****
		***	***		

After collecting a number of observation recordings (above are only two of a variety of examples carried out within the space of a week) staff analysed the information. They concluded that Ben is making progress in interacting with others and that he has started settling into the new setting and making positive progress in his social development. It appears from the observation recordings that it may take a while longer before he becomes completely relaxed and confident with his new situation, but he will eventually become more familiar with the new routine. The staff looked at the developmental stages and they concluded that Ben plays in parallel with other children, but that he has not yet moved to play cooperatively. They decided to discuss all the observation findings with his parents and to ask them their opinion.

What do we know about children's learning?

The early childhood learning environment is dominated by a play-orientated or play-based pedagogy. A number of studies (Moyles et al., 2001; Sylva et al., 2001; Siraj-Blatchford and Sylva, 2002; Taylor with Aubrey, 2002) found that children's learning is enhanced in settings where there is a balance between both adult- and child-initiated activities. Learning is also enhanced where practice is planned within a framework of observation and assessment, with parental involvement and by liaising with other services.

In Chapter 2 it was discussed that, in order to create a learning environment for children, some conditions of learning need to be taken into consideration. These are the emphasis on:

* children's development;
* play;
* children's needs and emotions;

- children's freedom to choose materials and activities;
- children's ownership of their own learning.

However, these conditions are not directly linked to children's learning alone. The role of the adult is also important as learning will not occur in an environment where these conditions exist without the support of adults. As discussed in Chapter 2, under cognitive psychology theory, the interactions with the environment (the Piagetian approach) and the role of the adult as a more experienced peer (the Vygotskian idea of ZPD) are central in educational settings where children develop their physical, emotional, social and cognitive skills such as linguistic concepts, lexis, language, problem-solving and mathematical concepts. Children's early experiences can be enhanced by interaction with adults during their play.

Play underpins early childhood education. It is suggested that adults hold a key role in assisting children's play both indoors and outdoors. As was shown in Chapter 2, since Froebel (1887), Pestalozzi (1894) and Montessori (1912), the role of play was emphasised as an important element in the creation of learning environments for young children. Pestalozzi, for example, viewed play as a way for children to explore the world, and in their role as observers teachers reflect upon how children play and try to support them in that way. Froebel and Montessori were among the first to see the value of play and designed learning environments that promoted play by providing materials and activities appropriate for children.

Through play, children acquire skills within a given context. From earlier on, a number of studies on play and learning (e.g. Athey, 1990; Nutbrown, 1999) have suggested that children are able to develop planned and purposeful play, and the role of the adult is to base the planning for the educational programme on this. These studies point out that learning through play can be put at risk in a framework where learning outcomes are target driven. As mentioned in Chapter 2, play for a young child is spontaneous and lacks organisation. Consequently, learning through play can become unpredictable as children's interests or needs may take unplanned and unforeseen directions. These, however, are valid learning opportunities for children as they build upon their own interests and needs and as they take ownership of their own play and learning. The role of the adult is crucial in an environment that values play as enabling children to be creative. Practitioners' support, intervention, interaction and planning can assist children's play and can enable them to benefit from that play.

In a play-based learning environment observations are equally important and integral in constantly monitoring children's progress. Observations can become a valuable tool to collect information in context and to ensure that the assessment of children will be meaningful. Such assessments will demonstrate not only what children can do and what different skills they have acquired, but also how they use those skills.

Working within a curriculum that is statutory at policy level, as in the case of EYFS in England, has some constraints as intended learning outcomes are not always realistically observable and measurable, nor are they easily achieved by children. Observing children's learning for assessment purposes in an environment with set learning goals requires:

- communication with parents in order to set appropriate expectations from both sides and to involve parents in the observation process;
- space and resources applicable to the adult/child ratio;
- built-in time for effective team meetings and the preparation of the observations' design;
- the development of effective observation systems and record-keeping;
- training.

CASE STUDY 10.2

Louise is two years and eight months. She attends nursery three times per week. In the following observation, the tracking technique has been used. It not only demonstrates Louise's preferences during play, but also how she uses her social skills during it.

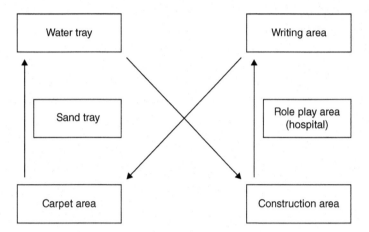

Figure 10.2   Louise's preferences of play areas

Start: 2:10 p.m. (15 minutes in carpet area)

Sat on the carpet with a friend. Louise is showing her friend photographs and narrates what she was doing when these photographs were taken (from her summer holidays).

2:25 p.m. (8 minutes, water tray area)

Louise and her friend move to the water area and they are sorting different shells into groups. Louise's friend leaves her and goes to the sand tray. After two minutes, Louise also leaves but she does not follow her friend.

2:33 p.m. (13 minutes in the construction area)

Louise plays on her own and creates a strong, well-built model using magnetic blocks.

2:46 p.m. (14 minutes in the writing area)

Louise sits at a table with two other children. She has chosen to colour in a picture of a 'Gruffalo'. She is doing this with care, and at the same time she talks to other children.

Finish: 3:00 p.m.

Children are called to the carpet area and Louise goes there with her picture.

SUMMARY

This chapter discussed observations in relation to children's development and learning. Observations offer us information and evidence for understanding and extending our knowledge of their development and learning. Observing for development and learning through play has some constraints as it requires time and a high level of skill from the practitioner. However, it is a valid tool as it informs everyday practice with children and offers in-depth information for each child and also your practice.

Working within a curriculum where there is a clear emphasis on observation of children for formative and summative purposes, practitioners should invest time to build effective ways of documenting children's learning and development so they can demonstrate the continuity of children's progress. Within this framework practitioners should be able to demonstrate skills and effective practice in observation and to lead and support the development of observation skills in others.

Further Reading

To further your understanding on development:

Conkbayir, M (2017) *Early Childhood and Neuroscience: Theory, Research and Implications for Practice*. London: Bloomsbury.

(In particular this book will help you understand the importance of brain development in all aspects of development.)

Crowley, K (2017) *Child Development: A Practical Introduction* (2nd edn). London: Sage.
Neaum, S (2016) *Child Development for Early Years Students and Practitioners* (3rd edn). London: Sage.

(In particular in this book read Chapter 8: Observing and assessing children's learning and development.)

To further your understanding on learning theories:

Bates, B (2019) *Learning Theories Simplified . . . and How to Apply Them to Teaching* (2nd edn). London: Sage.

For more information on observing development:

Beaty, J (2014) *Observing for Development in Young Children* (8th edn). Upper Saddle River, NJ: Pearson Merrill Prentice Hall.

For more on theories of play in early childhood education:

Brooker, L, Blaise, M and Edwards, S (eds) (2014) *The Sage Handbook of Play and Learning in Early Childhood*. London: Sage.

CHAPTER 11

OBSERVING FOR THE CURRICULUM

> **Chapter objectives**
>
> Reading this chapter will further your understanding of:
>
> - contemporary approaches to pedagogy;
> - approaches to the curriculum;
> - the differences between pedagogy and curriculum;
> - keys ideas on a curriculum for early childhood education;
> - the role of observation in the curriculum.
>
> Observation planning is an essential activity as it enhances practice and offers meaningful links between children's learning and development and the curriculum.

Introduction: towards an understanding of pedagogy and curriculum

In Chapter 2 we explored the social constructions of childhood and the philosophical and psychological thinking that influences pedagogy. We return to the discussion here to address the differences between pedagogy and curriculum, and identify key issues in observing for the curriculum.

In Chapter 2, pedagogy is defined as a term that aims to describe a body of knowledge which is concerned with teaching and practice in learning environments. The discussion about the nature of pedagogy is ongoing and the more we examine the concept of pedagogy, the further our understanding. Views of pedagogy have been influenced by the views of Bruner who introduced the idea of *meta-cognitive pedagogy* (Bruner, 1996) and is concerned with the extent the child is aware of her/his own thought processes when learning and thinking.

The discussion about pedagogy is a lengthy one and sometimes abstract and theoretical. Barad (2007, p.54) draws our attention to the fact that:

> to theorise is not to leave the material world behind and enter the domain of pure ideas where the lofty space of the mind makes objective reflections possible. Theorising, like experimenting, is a materials process [. . . They are] dynamic practices of material engagements with the world.

Creating learning environments is about developing an in-depth understanding of pedagogy to formulate a curriculum that underpins and reflects our views of pedagogy. Consequently, a key distinction is that pedagogy is the theoretical approach that will be implemented via the curriculum. Before we discuss the differences it is important to try to define 'curriculum'.

What is a curriculum?

Like the discussion about pedagogy, many theorists have expressed different views and approaches to the curriculum. Schiro (2008) examined ideological approaches and proposed four dominant ideologies:

- scholar-academic;
- social efficiency;
- learner-centred;
- socio-reconstruction.

The *scholar-academic ideology* approach is based on the view that knowledge is organised into academic disciplines. Thus the curriculum is organised around academic disciplines and the learners are direct subjects who reflect these.

The *social efficiency approach* views the curriculum as part of the training required to meet the needs of society. It is heavily influenced by behaviourist psychology which promotes the view that learning is a change in a human's behaviour. The focus is the concept of learning and the organisation of learning environments and experiences to lead to the desired responses.

Learner-centred ideology extends this view: it promotes the idea that learning contains the needs of the society and the academic disciplines but is based on the needs of individual learners. This ideology views the curriculum as an enjoyable experience for the learner where cognitive, social, emotional and physical attributes are helped to develop. Learner-centred curricula place an emphasis on the organisation of the environments where learners are seeking meaning through constant interactions with others and materials.

Finally, the *socio-reconstruction ideology* approach is concerned with the problems of society. Within this approach, curriculum is a social process and should be organised in a way that helps learners to understand their society and contribute to its improvement.

In an earlier study, Marsh (2004) examined a number of curricular approaches in education. He categorised these according to the emphasis of their organisation and their aims and objectives. Curriculum is:

- *such permanent subjects as grammar, reading, logic, rhetoric, mathematics and the greatest books of the western world that best embody essential knowledge;*
- *those subjects that are most useful for living in contemporary society;*
- *all planned learnings for which the school is responsible;*
- *the totality of learning experiences provided to students so that they can attain general skills and knowledge at a variety of learning sites;*
- *what the students construct from working with a computer and its various networks, such as the Internet;*
- *the questioning of authority and the searching for complex views of human situations.*

(pp.4–7)

A curriculum includes, suggests Walker (1990), the fundamental concepts of content, purpose and organisation that are underpinned by pedagogy. Pedagogy is about the values, beliefs, principles and ethics of how knowledge should be constructed and shared among the communities of learners that drive curriculum content, organisation and purpose.

Developing synergy between pedagogy and curriculum

As can be seen there are clear differences between pedagogy and curriculum. Pedagogy is the theoretical and conceptual ideas of how to organise teaching and learning, whereas curriculum is the actual organisation of the educational programme. In that sense pedagogy is the philosophical ideology of the educational setting and this might include teachers, learners and the community, whereas curriculum is the way that the learning is organised in that setting. In Chapter 2, the definition in UNESCO (2016) was discussed which views pedagogy as a holistic approach to the act of teaching to include values and beliefs, as well as praxis (= actions and practice derived from theory) so people's lives are transformed. The actions and practice in pedagogy is the curriculum.

In Chapter 2, it was also argued that what we think as society about children (socio-constructions of childhood) determine the ways societies provide education and other services such as health to children. Consequently, these ideas are reflected in the curriculum. The examples below try to demonstrate the synergy between pedagogy and curriculum – highlighting the role of observation – and the ideas each society has about children.

EXAMPLE 11.1

The curriculum in Sweden

The introduction of a UNESCO report in 2010 about the Swedish early childhood education system states:

> *The Swedish pre-school model has historically been based on the theory that a child's preconditions for development and learning are largely influenced by the social environment and the pedagogical stimulation that a child encounters during his or her childhood years. One important step for the pre-school's incorporation into the education system was the introduction of the first curriculum for pre-school (Lpfö 98, 1998). The curriculum strengthens the view of a child continuously developing and learning in all contexts and not just in specially selected situations. The curriculum states that the pre-school assignment is comprehensive and wide. The pre-school is founded on a holistic view of the child where different aspects of the child's development and learning are closely integrated to each other. This means that pre-schooling should be organized so that learning, care and upbringing should be interwoven into daily pedagogical practice and form an entirety. In this report we will use the concept 'educare' when we refer to the holistic view of a child in the Swedish pre-school tradition.*

(p.4)

As can be seen the main ideology that underpins Swedish EDUCARE is the view that children are full human beings. At the heart of this is equality as a fundamental right and high quality of care and education for every child. This view is reflected in the ECEC curriculum of Sweden: The Curriculum for the Preschool Lpfö 98, which was revised in 2010 and then again in 2016 to focus on:

- *a child's rights perspective*
- *a disability perspective*
- *the rights of national minorities*
- *the rights of the Sami as indigenous peoples.*

(Karlsson Lohmander, 2017)

The Curriculum for the Preschool Lpfö 18 is divided in two main parts: the fundamental values and the goals and guidelines.

Based on democratic ideals and on the UNCRC, the curriculum sets out the mission of the pre-school as laying the foundations for lifelong learning and is promoting values such as the view that care, socialisation and learning form a coherent whole for children's enjoyment, security and safety. Stimulating learning environments, emphasis on play and partnerships with the home characterise the pedagogical approach. As a result of such an approach the Swedish curriculum sets goals that:

specify the orientation of the education in the preschool and thus the quality development expected of the education and how it contributes to each child's development and learning.

The guidelines specify the responsibility of preschool teachers for ensuring that teaching takes place in accordance with the goals set out in the curriculum. The guidelines also specify the task of everyone in the work team, which can include preschool teachers, child minders and other staff, to provide each child with secure care and to promote development and learning in all children.

(p. 13)

Although the goals are described in the curriculum, there are no prescribed goals for children to reach by a certain age. Instead it suggests goals to strive for and sets out tasks for the team in the pre-school (who are teachers with normally three to five years of university training, supported by educated teacher assistants). These goals are set around:

- norms and values of the democratic society such as respect, responsibility and participation;
- care, development and learning;
- the influence of the child in terms of providing the foundations for children to understand what democracy is, to be able to take responsibility for their own actions and for the environment in the pre-school;
- participation and the influence of the child so children can express their opinions, take responsibility for their actions and understand the democratic principles;
- cooperation between pre-school and home;
- cooperation between pre-school class, the school and the leisure centre;
- regular and systematic documentation.

The term 'assessment of child' is not mentioned, but instead the term 'evaluation' is used as part of the goals of the pre-school curriculum. Evaluation of children is not set by the government, but teachers', parents' and children's opinions and experiences are required and valued. Observations and digital media are heavily used in order to evaluate each child's progress, as the aim is:

to acquire knowledge of how the quality of the preschool, i.e. its organisation, content and implementation can be developed so that each child is given the best possible conditions for development and learning. Ultimately this involves developing better work processes, being able to determine whether the work takes place in accordance with the goals, and investigating what measures need to be taken in order to improve the conditions for children to play, learn, develop, feel secure and have fun in the preschool. Analyses of the results of the evaluation indicate areas that are critical for development. All forms of evaluation should take the perspective of the child as the starting point. Children and parents should participate in evaluation and their views are to be given prominence.

(p.19)

(Continued)

(Continued)

Consequently, the role of observation within the Swedish curriculum is to systematically document, follow-up, evaluate and analyse *how the goals of the curriculum are integrated with each other and form a whole in the education, carrying out a critical examination to ensure that the evaluation methods used are based on the fundamental values and intentions as set out in the curriculum* (p.19) to improve the education programme and the conditions for development and learning.

The curriculum in action: visiting Swedish nurseries

In a personal visit to Swedish pre-schools in October 2018, the practitioners explained they were working on the goals set from the curriculum for each child and the goals and the observational evidence were forming the basis to evaluate each child. There were three key questions that guide their evaluation for each child in order to set sub-goals to meet the main goals of the curriculum:

Where are we?

Where are we going?

What is next?

The pre-schools have made posters with the goals. The posters are in the form of a flower to symbolise that if education and the children meet the goals of the curriculum, they will flourish. In the heart of meeting the goals of the curriculum is play as can be seen in Figure 11.1. At the centre of all these posters is play and the petals are the goals and activities that take place in the pre-school.

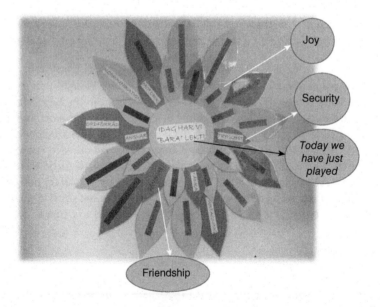

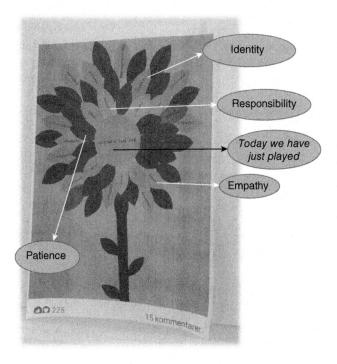

Figure 11.1 The posters with goals

In the visit in one rural pre-school that was hosting children from the age of five months up to five years, the practitioner had driven the children into the forest with a small tractor in the morning to collect mushrooms which, when they came back, they cleaned to cook as part of their lunch. When he was asked what the aim of this activity was, he indicated it is part of the goal that children can take responsibility for their own actions and also to develop an understanding of the environment.

Figure 11.2 With the little tractor children went to the forest and collected mushrooms to prepare their lunch

(Continued)

(Continued)

In both pre-schools, during the visit it was observed that they were using posters with signs and pictures with the rules to support children (especially those from migrant families in which Swedish was their second language, or children that were deaf, for example, and in need of sign language).

Figure 11.3 The use of sign language

It became obvious that the idea of *education in the preschool is to ensure that children acquire and develop knowledge and values. It should promote all children's development and learning, and a life-long desire to learn. Education should also convey and establish respect for human rights and the fundamental democratic values on which Swedish society is based* (p. 5) set by the curriculum and reflected in the daily activities and the classroom environment with the use of a variety of materials.

Figure 11.4 We use natural materials to make things

What was interesting was that they have moved away from using small chairs and tables for children for two reasons: firstly for the health of the educators as sitting in small chairs might lead to physical problems from them (such as back pains) and secondly to support the fundamental values of the curriculum:

We view children as being able to participate in all aspects of their lives according to UNCRC and we want to empower children. It feels that we 'undermine' them if we use small furniture rather than normal ones [. . .]. Children use normal furniture at home so why not at school?

Figure 11.5   The dining rooms for children in pre-schools

For more information visit: **https://www.skolverket.se/publikationsserier/styrdokument/2019/ curriculum-for-the-preschool-lpfo-18?id=4049www.skolverket.se/om-skolverket/publikationer/ visa-enskild-publikation?_xurl_=http%3A%2F%2Fwww5.skolverket.se%2Fwtpub%2Fws% 2Fskolbok%2Fwpubext%2Ftrycksak%2FRecord%3Fk%3D2704EXAMPLE 2**

EXAMPLE 11.2

Early Years Foundation Stage in England

When we discuss the development of a pedagogy for early childhood education, the starting point is a search for quality within it. In the EYFS there is an attempt to set the standards for practice and the aim is to improve quality. Early childhood education is viewed as a partnership between the settings and the parents. The ultimate aim of the EYFS is a standardised practice among settings, with parents being assured *that EYFS sets the standards that all early years providers must meet to ensure that children learn and develop well and are kept healthy and safe* (DfE, 2017, p.5).

The EYFS emphasises four key aspects of provision:

- **quality and consistency** in all settings, so that every child makes good progress and no child gets left behind;
- **a secure foundation** through learning and development opportunities which are planned around the needs and interests of each individual child and are assessed and reviewed regularly;
- **partnership working** between practitioners and with parents and/or carers;
- **equality of opportunity** and anti-discriminatory practice, ensuring that every child is included and supported.

(p.5)

To provide quality it is important for practitioners to understand children's development. To achieve this, four overarching guiding principles are recommended in the EYFS:

(Continued)

(Continued)

- *Every child is a unique child, who is constantly learning and can be resilient, capable, confident and self-assured.*
- *Children learn to be strong and independent through positive relationships.*
- *Children learn and develop well in enabling environments, in which their experiences respond to their individual needs and there is a strong partnership between practitioners and parents and/or carers.*
- *Children develop and learn in different ways (see 'the characteristics of effective teaching and learning' at paragraph 1.9) and at different rates. The framework covers the education and care of all children in early years provision, including children with special educational needs and disabilities.*

(p.6)

The EYFS opened to public debate the issues of what constitutes effective practice, what should be done in the sector and how the optimum programme should be delivered in order to reach the learning goals. There are two main concerns emerging from examining the standardised principled approach of the EYFS.

Firstly, the standards are linked to the classic developmental approach outcomes in children (the learning and development goals). The priority of the EYFS is to *provide the foundation children need to make the most of their abilities and talents as they grow up* (DfE, 2017, p.5). It thus sets a number of learning and developmental goals that children should have acquired by the end of the academic year in which they reach the age of five. The developmental approach outcomes in the EYFS leave no space for the child as 'a knower'. Instead, the environment creates the *performer child* where the child needs to perform to outcomes and outputs which are observable and measurable. It follows that practitioners are rated according to these outcomes as criteria for quality.

Secondly, the EYFS promotes teaching and learning to ensure children's 'school readiness' and gives children the broad range of knowledge and skills that provide the right foundation for good future progress through school and life (DfE, 2017, p.5). This approach to the child in the EYFS places value on children in terms of them meeting future goals, standards and learning outcomes. It assumes that children need to progress to the next stage of development, from maybe 'lesser child' to 'better child'. The terms 'development', 'developmental goals' or 'learning goals' invoke a sense that children are not yet developed (whole/holistic) and thus need developing ('improving'), or that there is an existing, pre-determined place at which a child may arrive (presumably school).

Within these views, it is important that the workforce is able to implement the EYFS, but also form a voice and a theoretical argument regarding their own practice and pedagogical values. The role of the workforce should be to:

- lead practice based on a theoretical background;
- stimulate pedagogical discussion among the team, requiring an understanding of current pedagogical practices;
- disseminate and implement current policies within the team.

ACTIVITY 11.1

The role of observation in your curriculum

Critically reflect on your curriculum and discuss what is the role of observation. Discuss:

- How observations are used?
- What do you normally observe?
- How do you link observation to your curriculum outcomes?

EXAMPLE 11.3

Reggio Emilia in Italy

Reggio Emilia is a community-supported system of early childhood education situated in a small town in northern Italy. Loris Malaguzzi introduced an early childhood system to the Reggio Emilia province, based on his vision of the child as an active, strong and powerful human being. Both Malaguzzi (1995) and his co-worker Rinaldi (1995) based their pedagogy on cognitive ideas of child development. They placed particular emphasis on Vygotsky's ideas – that knowledge is not adopted by the child, but is constructed by the child through interaction with a more mature or experienced peer or adult (Miller et al., 2003).

The originality of Reggio Emilia is that there is no written curriculum. Instead it takes a localised approach to the education of its young children. This approach is free from external and formalised pressures and standards. There are no government objectives or goals to be achieved and the starting point is the child. Consequently, the curriculum *emerges* from children's own interests and needs (Rinaldi, 1995). The Reggio Emilia approach to pedagogy is developed via a constant dialogue with the team, the children and the parents. In this approach, the child is viewed *as rich in potential, strong, powerful, competent and, most of all, connected to adults and other children* (Malaguzzi, 1993, p.10).

The view of the child as *rich* in potential, strong, powerful, competent and, most of all, connected to adults and other children's potential underpins the main principles of this pedagogical approach. Learning is viewed as a social activity that involves all participants: parents, children and the local community. Consequently, all participants are engaging in constant discussion about the activities in the classes.

Fundamental principles in the Reggio Emilia approach to pedagogy are:

- the partnerships with parents and communication with them;
- listening to the *hundred languages* that children use to communicate;
- informal assessment and documentation of children's work as the starting point for discussion among staff, children and parents;
- the physical environment, important in the Reggio Emilia for the emotional stability of the children.

(Continued)

(Continued)

In the Reggio Emilia approach the workforce collects evidence though observations and their art works about what the children are involved in (see examples in Chapter 7). This evidence is documented either in the form of individual portfolios for each child or by photographs, and these become starting points for discussions at weekly team meetings. From these discussions the planning of activities emerges. Ongoing dialogue among the staff, parents, children and the wider community forms the educational programme and its activities, this being a key aspect in the pedagogy.

Fillipini illustrates how Reggio Emilia works. The *pedagogista* (early years practitioner) works with the parents and teachers towards educational aims and goals and has a coordinating role with many facets, including administration and training (Fillipini, 1995, in Miller et al., 2003). Citing Vecchi, the *artelier* (or 'artist in residence') is closely involved in project work and in the visual documentation of the children's work (Vecchi, 1995, in Miller et al., 2003).

ACTIVITY 11.2

Compare the curricula

Compare the curricula discussed in the examples above. What similarities and differences can you identify? Reflect on the curriculum you are working with. Are there differences and similarities? How can this influence your own practice?

Start this task by identifying how each curriculum views the child and what philosophical and developmental theories might underpin each of them.

Can you identify the key pedagogical ideas that underpin these curricular approaches?

The curriculum of early childhood education

In the field of early childhood education the dominant idea of a curriculum is to link play and pedagogy (Wood, 2009, 2010a). Researchers have studied the impact of play on educational outcomes and children's development and learning (Youell, 2008; Wood, 2010b; Sluss and Jarrett, 2007; MacNaughton, 2009; Cannella, 2005; Bergen et al., 2010; Taguchi, 2010). Play is normally associated with a pleasurable and enjoyable activity, or a pattern of actions that can be either physical, verbal or mental encounters with either materials, peers or adults or the environment. Central to a play-based pedagogy is that *these activities are imbued with children's concerns with agency, power, and self-actualisation, as well as their motivations to learn* (Wood, 2014, p.154). Thus curricula are reflecting these ideas and place emphasis on a play-based approach to children's development and learning.

A curriculum in early childhood education should be based around some key principles. To begin with, we are concerned with the experiences of children which become part of their learning processes and development, with the emphasis in curriculum being on play. There is much research emphasising play is essential in early childhood education (Moyles,

1989, 2010; Nutbrown, 2006; Wood and Attfield, 2005; Wood, 2010a, 2010b). They all conclude that children in settings need opportunities to initiate their own learning, learn from each other and adults and pursue their own interests. Play provides children with such an environment and helps them to engage in experiences and with materials that advance their development and learning. In settings the curriculum is not a formalised approach to teaching and learning as seen in a primary or secondary classroom; through play, children's experiences and interests are exercised and developed.

Secondly, the early childhood education curriculum is concerned with making decisions about the content and the process of children's learning experiences. Based on observations of and reflection on daily activities, the workforce is making decisions about a variety of issues and topics that will be explored in the setting and via which children will be able to enjoy a creative and stimulating environment. Any setting should have the freedom to plan and provide a broad-based curriculum which will allow all children to meet their particular developmental and learning needs and develop good attitudes towards their learning.

Finally, another important element of the early childhood curriculum is that it involves many groups. It is important that within the curriculum children's learning and development is viewed as work in partnership. The workforce, the children, the parents, the communities and the settings should all serve as partners and should all have a voice about how the environment and activities are organised. Through observation, planning of children's development and learning, reflection on the activities and collaboration with parents and other professionals, the curriculum should offer a stimulating environment for children. Thus what is going on in the classroom is part of a decision-making process from many perspectives.

To conclude, the early childhood curriculum should be based on a pedagogical ethos where all participants are valued (the team, children, parents, communities) and feel equal in the decision-making process. Play should be central as a way for children to interact with the environment and the materials, developing flexibility of thought, trying to solve problems, putting different elements of a situation together in various ways or looking at the world from different viewpoints.

ACTIVITY 11.3

Observations inform your planning

You have developed an observation plan in order to evaluate the areas in which children tend to play during free play time in your setting. You have used a tracking technique to identify which areas children are using most during the day.

Figure 11.6 illustrates the number of children recorded who spent time in different areas of the setting. Information has been collected over a period of three weeks during play time. Study the figure and think about how you can use this to inform your curriculum. Consider:

- How can this inform future curriculum planning?
- Which areas will you enrich?
- Which areas might you consider changing?
- Which areas might you consider replacing?

(Continued)

(Continued)

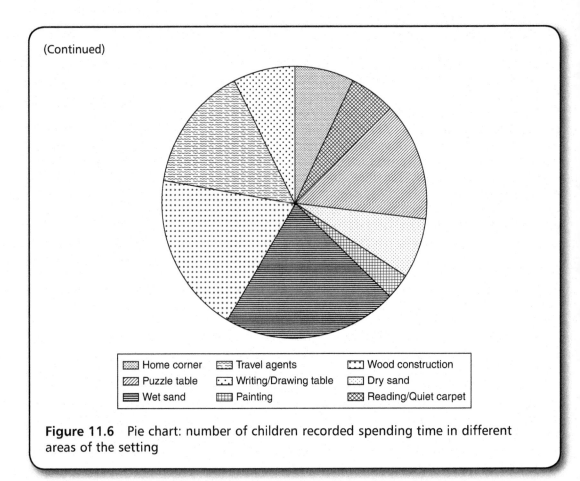

Home corner	Travel agents	Wood construction
Puzzle table	Writing/Drawing table	Dry sand
Wet sand	Painting	Reading/Quiet carpet

Figure 11.6   Pie chart: number of children recorded spending time in different areas of the setting

Observing the curriculum

Throughout this book the importance of observation in early childhood education has been explored. When observing the curriculum the workforce is attempting to inform practice and support children's learning and development. Thus rigour in observation planning is essential. It should be underpinned by a pedagogical ethos that mirrors the needs of the setting, the needs of children and the needs and expectations of parents as well as those of the community. Observation outcomes have an impact at a number of levels. To begin with, they impact on the content, organisation and purpose of the curriculum. For example, from examples of curricula throughout the book such as the Australian curriculum, Te Whāriki in New Zealand or the EYFS in England, a positive view of multiculturalism is promoted, reflecting the more diverse needs of their society. The EYFS, for example, attempts to create an ethos where all participants (staff, children and parents) are equals and respected for their own identity and to promote anti-discriminatory policies and regulations which aim to respond positively to social and cultural diversity.

Moreover, observation outcomes impact on children's learning and development by informing the development of the curriculum; they impact on parents' expectations and encourage participation. Finally, observation outcomes impact on the community as one of the fundamental aims in education is to develop children who will become active citizens. For example, it was shown that in the Te Whāriki curriculum, observation is a tool for liaising with the community and a way to invite the community into the early childhood class.

ACTIVITY 11.4

How do I use observation?

Examine the curriculum of your setting and consider how you:

- observe and assess children;
- use observation outcomes to develop your curriculum.

In this activity, consider how important the following parameters are:

- your pedagogical ethos;
- the needs of your setting;
- the needs of children;
- the needs of parents;
- the statutory requirements;
- the expertise of your team;
- your vision (what you aim to achieve in your setting);
- your outcomes in a setting.

Throughout this book it has been suggested that observation is not only an activity that describes what happens between the observer and the observed event/child, but also a process that involves clear aims and objectives, ethical considerations, planning, analysis and documentation. As illustrated in Figure 11.4 linking observation with the curriculum is about understanding the pedagogical practices that underpin your curriculum and about creating an observation plan where all participants involved understand, share and are able to implement the observation.

Analysis of observation helps the monitoring and reflection process in the setting as a way of evaluating the curriculum and extending it. When you work in a regulatory framework such as the EYFS in England or the Foundation Phase in Wales, it also helps you to meet the statutory requirements.

Linking observations to assessment

In many curricula the information collected through observations, the analysis of those observations and the recording of information have an ultimate purpose: to construct a picture of a child which has breadth and depth in terms of his/her progress, development and learning. No matter what strategies (formal, informal or statutory) are used to document, organise and interpret observations, practitioners should be able to link observations with the requirements of the curriculum for a formal reporting of this information to parents and children.

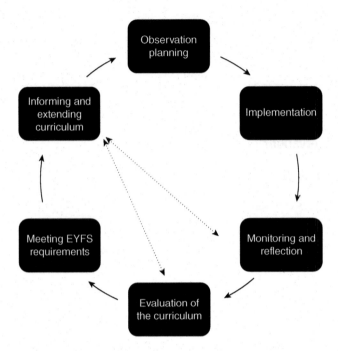

Figure 11.7 Linking observation with the curriculum

This formal reporting can be in the form of assessment or evaluation. This process of gathering information and analysing it as evidence of what children can do is called 'assessment' in many curricula. For example, in the UK, both the EYFS in England and the Foundation Phase in Wales have statutory requirements, whereas in Northern Ireland and Scotland, although there are assessment requirements, these are not statutory. Internationally, Australia, as was shown in the above case study, sets the planning cycle as a way of assessment, whereas in Sweden this process is called evaluation.

There are two types of assessment. The first – *formative assessment* – is based on daily observations and uses techniques such as photographs, video recordings, children's drawings and information from parents. Observation recordings form a picture of the everyday life of children in the setting. They provide rich information for formative evidence on which to base future planning and to extend your knowledge and understanding of how children develop and learn, as well as provide evidence of their developing competencies, persistent interests, dispositions and schemas (Athey, 1990). Therefore, it is important for observations to be an integral part of early childhood education practice. Observations are not the final process in a curriculum, but part of the actions of practitioners for constantly improving quality within the setting. Formative assessments based on observation recordings assist the practitioner to:

- offer a flexible provision for children, where activities are changed when children lack interest in them, when plans are altered to follow children's interests and needs, and where new activities take place to rekindle children's interests;
- provide evidence for starting communications with parents and to encourage parental involvement;
- provide evidence for communicating with other services and local authorities.

For effective formative assessment it is important to make observations:

- integral and a regular part of life in the setting;
- incidental, when something is happening outside planned activities;
- during activities with children.

The second type of assessment is *summative assessment*. In many curricula, such as the Foundation Phase in Wales or the EYFS in England, it can be a statutory requirement that each child will have a summative assessment at the end of the year. This is a final assessment, which includes a summary of all the formative assessments done over a long period of time and offers a more holistic picture of a child's development and learning. It is normally in the form of a folder (profile) and includes information about a child's progress/scores towards the learning outcomes and goals pre-described by the curriculum.

The summative assessment is equally as important as the formative assessment. It is not only used to communicate with authorities for inspection purposes, it is also a very helpful tool as it assists:

- transitions from one setting to another and transitions to school;
- practitioners to evaluate the activities and their implementation;
- approaches to other agencies with informed evidence, if required.

As can be seen in both types of assessment observations are vital and observational skills need to be developed from a very early stage in a practitioner's training.

Linking observation to reflect to your practice: peer observation

Throughout the book, the role of observation for gaining understanding of children's progress as well as your practice was discussed. However, observation can become a powerful tool to observe and reflect on your practice as shown in the case study below.

Observation findings can also be used in your own setting for informal training and staff development purposes. They can enhance and strengthen the links within the team (team building) and become the starting point to discuss critically and reflect on your activities and practice. Team meetings can become more effective with observation findings as you build the discussion upon evidence gathered.

CASE STUDY 11.1

Learning Walks

Observation plays a dual role in early years practice: we observe children for all of the above reasons, while we also observe our own practice in order to reflect upon and improve it. This is a continuous process informing our curriculum planning and daily practice. Although each individual tries to improve her/his own practice, this cannot happen in isolation. It requires the cooperation found in

(Continued)

(Continued)

teamwork. Throughout the literature, peer observation or collaborative observation, collegial observation and peer-to-peer reflection have been discussed as valid tools through which to share ideas about what works, what we do well in our practice and how we may enhance practice.

An interesting approach to peer-collaborative observation as a learning activity is found in Learning Walks (DCSF, 2007) which is a pre-scheduled, organised visit among the staff of a setting to each other's rooms, using specific pre-agreed criteria to focus on the teaching and learning taking place. It has been used widely in schools as a technique for peer observation, although not to assess the staff's performance. It is, rather, a way of opening a dialogue among staff about the teaching and learning that take place in the classrooms. Reciprocal learning takes place as the discussions stimulated after a Learning Walk are usually interesting, evaluative and helpful to all staff. However, for Learning Walks to be successful they need to take place in an environment of collaboration, mutual respect, trust, collegiality and security. They do not aim to be a tool for assessing the performances of individuals; instead, they are a valuable way of reflecting upon our own practice.

Example of a Learning Walk in a setting

Preparation

Prior to the Learning Walk the team meet and discuss who will participate, which rooms will be observed and who is to observe in which rooms. The manager of the setting and the 'key person' from the toddlers' room will visit all the rooms for a ten-minute period over two days. It had been agreed that this would take place during the arrival time of the children as the focus of this particular Learning Walk was on the interactions of staff with the parents and the children. The setting wanted to improve communication with parents and to investigate the level of interaction taking place during arrival time. It was discussed and agreed that:

- *Observations would be reported to the staff generally (and anonymously) on the kinds of activities that were noted.*
- *All staff would be given the opportunity to discuss these activities for consistency of practice within the setting. As these observations are merely 'snapshots' of the practice in each room, further discussion and comment from all staff would follow in order to stimulate self-evaluation.*
- *It was emphasised that the purpose of the Learning Walk was not to generate professional criticism of individuals; rather, it was to become a means of generating self-evaluation of practice in a sensitive and open atmosphere, sharing good practice and enriching a culture of learning.*

Scenario: Observation extracts from a Learning Walk in a setting

Summary of Observation 1

Room One (three years)

Before arrival time the practitioners had created a very tidy, bright room by putting the lights on. The displays were very inviting; they had children's photographs of activities done in the class, with small comments on what each activity was. The practitioners had placed wooden toys on the tables and encouraged children on their arrival to go and play with them. However, the displays looked 'too' tidy – as though the children were not allowed to touch them. There were far too many photographs for anyone to see in only two or three minutes – the time that the parents were usually in the room before they left. The children were exceptionally quiet. Two children queued at the practitioner's table as she was writing the names of the children on their drawings. The practitioner appeared to have a good, calm relationship with the children and the parents.

Summary of Observation 2

Room Two (three years)

The second room drew the parents' enthusiasm as they were walking in: in the middle of the room there was a very large lion that the children had made the previous day. Children were dragging their parents to see the big lion. The practitioners were explaining to the parents how the children had made it and what activities they planned to do that day in relation to the lion. Children were busily and independently engaged in group work while the practitioners were talking to the parents. The walls had a good variety of materials on display, incorporating 3-D work, and a couple of parents were looking at it.

Summary of Observation 3

Room Three (toddlers' room)

The room appeared to be 'empty' as there was not much material displayed on the walls (apart from a drawing of balloons by adults and some figures of Winnie the Pooh). There was no display as such, although some photographs of children were pinned on a noticeboard. However, these were not labelled and had no explanation of what was happening in the photographs. During the children's arrival time the practitioners were comforting toddlers who were crying or feeling unsettled. There was a warmth in the atmosphere of the room, yet it lacked strong visual stimulation for the parents.

Post-Learning Walks discussion

The discussion focused on the use of displays as a way of sharing the everyday life of the setting with the parents in a snapshot. It was found that in rooms where the displays were well organised, tidy and not overcrowded with information, the parents took a couple of minutes to look at them. It was also found that having something created by the children themselves as the central focus in the class during arrival time increases the parents' engagement when they bring their children into the room (lion observation). Overall, it was agreed that in the setting there was not yet enough focus on the use of displays, at least in terms of wall displays, although there was evidence from conversations that this focus was beginning to emerge. The team decided to work on displays and in a month's time to plan new Learning Walks to monitor the changes in the displays and children's active engagement in sharing their own learning.

(Palaiologou, 2012b, pp.216–18)

ACTIVITY 11.5

Peer observation

After reading the case study above, discuss what other ways you can use for peer observations. How important can they be in your context?

SUMMARY

This chapter revisited the discussion of pedagogy to identify the differences between pedagogy and curriculum. In a setting we need clear pedagogical approaches to design and implement an effective curriculum for children's learning and development. A curriculum for early childhood education should be driven by play and be appropriate to children's stages of learning and development, but at the same time provide an environment where it enriches their learning and stimulates them for further development.

There followed an attempt to reflect on different curricula by drawing examples from international curriculum practices, such as Sweden, England and Italy.

From these approaches we can see that wherever there is formally written or unwritten informal curricula, observation appears to be the main tool for practitioners. In some curricula, like EYFS and the Foundation Phase, the monitoring process of children is more formalised in terms of assessment, while in others (such as EDUCARE in Sweden, Reggio Emilia in Italy) it is less formal and less standardised. However, within each curriculum approach, in order to monitor/assess/evaluate children's progress, as well as to monitor/assess/evaluate the educational programme itself, there is a need for rigorous and systematic observation planning.

Further Reading

For more on the early childhood curriculum:

Kelly, AV (2009) *The Curriculum: Theory and Practice* (6th edn). London: Sage.
Palaiologou, I (ed.) (2020) *Early Years Foundation Stage: Theory and Practice* (4th edn). London: Sage.
Rodger, R (2012) *Planning an Appropriate Curriculum in the Early Years: A Guide for Early Years Practitioners and Leaders, Students and Parents*. London: Routledge.

CHAPTER 12

OBSERVING FOR RESEARCH

Chapter objectives

After reading this chapter, you will:

- consider observation as a research method;
- consider the differences between observation as a research method and observation as part of your practice;
- be aware that observation is a method that produces qualitative as well as quantitative data;
- understand how to record and analyse observation for research purposes.

There is a difference between when you use observations for practice and when you use observations for research. Observing for research or practice purposes should provide valid and rigorous data.

Introduction: origins of observation

As has been explored throughout this book, observations in the field of education are now widely used and form part of the everyday routine of the classroom as a way of gaining an in-depth understanding of children's development and learning in order to reflect on the educational activities of the classroom. However, observation has been used in research in many fields of study as an in-depth investigation into a single person, group, event or community. In the field of early childhood studies, pioneers such as Montessori and Isaacs introduced observations from their own fields. As was discussed in the introduction, for example, Montessori had studied medicine and she was involved in early childhood education, originally as a doctor for children with disabilities, and it was then when she developed an interest in the education of young children. Her method of systematic observation was heavily influenced by her disciplined training in medicine. Another example is Susan Isaacs, who brought psycho-analytical ideas to the education of young children. Influenced by the psycho-analytical work of Anna Freud and Melanie Klein, she was the first to bring these ideas and to modify them to the needs of an educational setting. Under Melanie Klein's influence and through systematic observations, Isaacs demonstrated that play was not only about children's mastery of the world and learning, but also an equally important means of expression and emotional relief.

Observation is widely used in the social sciences as a research method for collecting data. As discussed in Chapter 2, observation in an early childhood setting is an activity that involves systematic watching of others in their natural environment such as customs, beliefs and way of life.

In Chapter 2, where the different psychological theories were considered, the pioneering work of Erick Bick (1964) in the field of psycho-analytical infant observation was cited as a useful research tool to understand the interactions between mothers and their babies. This work was extended by the work of Bowlby. The field of cognitive psychology took observation of young children to another level with the Piagetian tests and the systematic measurements of certain behaviours that occurred when the tests were carried out. Of course observation is not only used by the social sciences, but by other sciences such as medicine, astronomy, the physical sciences and biology.

There are several chapters in books on various research methods that discuss observation for research in early childhood education (see Further Reading at the end of the chapter). The purpose of this chapter is to explain how we use observation for research and point out the differences and similarities when observation is used for research and when observation is used for practice. The most dominant observation methods used as research tools are summarised in the following Theory Focus box.

Observation and research

Planning a research project can be an adventurous process. Sometimes it is fascinating and at other times difficulties must be overcome. Maykut and Morehouse (1994, p.26) point out the significant role planning plays in a research project:

The questions we ask will always to some degree determine the answers we find. This point is important in designing a qualitative study. The research questions that guide a qualitative study reflect the researcher's goal of discovering what is important to know about some topic of interest. A qualitative study has a focus, but that focus is initially broad and open-ended, allowing for important meanings to be discovered.

THEORY FOCUS

Observation as a research tool

Table 12.1 Observation as a research tool

Method	Description	Nature	Tools	Strengths	Limitations	Examples
Naturalistic observation	Observation of behaviour in its natural context. The researcher pretends that he/she is part of the group being observed.	Natural Unstructured Participant	Written observations (narratives). Digital media to record mainly field notes (narrative, qualitative data) searching for meaning in the text.	Observation reflects participants' everyday lives, habits, customs, values.	Conditions under which participants are observed cannot be controlled.	Psycho-analytical infant observation. Bowlby's observations on attachment.
Structured observation	Observation of a behaviour in a laboratory or in a controlled context. Observer has no contact with the participants.	Controlled Structured Non-participant	Brief written observations. Rating scales. Checklists. Diagrammatic (mainly quantitative data, searching for meaning through a numerical approach).	Conditions of observation are the same for all participants so a certain behaviour can be measured/recorded.	Observation may not be typical of the participants' behaviour in everyday life.	Bandura's experiments on observational learning: Bobodoll. Behaviourists' experiments of conditioning. Piagetian tests of children's cognitive development.
Self-observation	Observation of self-behaviour in a variety of contexts as a way of investigating these behaviours.	Purpose-specific	Digital media, diaries, journals (mainly narrative, qualitative data, searching for meaning through text).	Self-observation offers an in-depth understanding of internal or external behaviours which caused certain actions/reactions.	Observations are subjective and can be skewed by the researcher's personal beliefs and values.	Self-observation is used widely in treatments for recovery (alcohol, drugs). As a student, you use self-observation when doing reflective portfolios. Early years practitioners use self-observation for reflection.

Experienced researchers agree that undertaking a research project can have unknown elements. Even though there are numerous papers and books in the literature to help a researcher, the field can nevertheless be *messy, frustrating and unpredictable* (Wellington, 1996, p.7). Even so, a review of existing literature on research is helpful in order to design the appropriate methodology on which to build the theoretical background for any study you wish to undertake.

In order to decide on appropriate observation methods to investigate your research questions, it is necessary to establish the kind of data required and to explore your research objectives. Two important issues must be taken into account when observation methods are used with children. In the first place, it is important to decide how to measure the progress they make throughout the observation process. Secondly, there is a need to choose observation methods that will enable data to be collected in order to gain an in-depth understanding of what you are investigating. Depending on the nature of the research project, observation can be used to collect either qualitative data or quantitative data. Before it is discussed how observation is used in these two methodological approaches it is important to clarify some key terms in research (see Theory Focus box below).

THEORY FOCUS

Research

Research is:

- The systematic, controlled, empirical and critical investigation of hypothetical propositions about behaviours, phenomena, relationships and their interactions in a natural or controlled environment (Kerlinger, 1970).
- *Seeking through methodological processes to add to one's body of knowledge and, hopefully to that of others, by discovering non-trivial facts and insights* (Howard and Sharp, 1983, p.6).
- A search or investigation directed to the discovery of some facts by careful consideration or study of a subject; a course of critical or scientific inquiry (OED, 2011).
- A systematic enquiry made public (Stenhouse, 1975).
- *A systematic, critical and self-critical inquiry which aims to contribute to the advancement of knowledge* (Bassey, 1990, p.35).

Research requires:

- the collection of quite large amounts of data;
- results which can be generalised;
- a hypothesis to be tested or a research question;
- the undertaking of experiments or the use of statistics;
- objectivity rather than subjectivity or subjective reality;
- that something is proved or strongly indicated;
- specific expertise.

Key terms in research:

Axiology: The researcher's values base.

Ontology: The nature of reality.

Epistemology: The relationship between the researcher and the known world.

Rhetoric: The language of research.

Methodology: The process of research.

Paradigm: The way of understanding the world and the human behaviour within it.

Key actions in research:

- establishing the research question(s);
- exploring research options and designing a research project;
- identifying the limits of your study;
- delimiting appropriately;
- recognising the potential for bias;
- determining a realistic timeline for data collection, analysis, reporting, interpretation and reporting.

The observation techniques that were discussed in Chapters 4, 5 and 6 are used in the same way in research in order to collect data. However, the significant difference is that choosing observation techniques for research is determined by the positioning of the researcher's values. When observation is used in practice the main concern is to gain in-depth information of children in order to be able to evaluate our practice and children's development and learning, and our personal beliefs and values should not be interfering with any analysis of the information we have collected via observations. For example, if we think that a child's achievements in arts are not equally important as this child's achievements in mathematics then this might impact our evaluation, and this child's achievements in arts consequently might not be noticed. In an educational context this should not been happening as all of a child's achievements should be recorded and valued.

In research, the researcher approaches the research project with lenses that derive from their ideological views, values and beliefs (axiology), and they try to make sense of the enquires of the investigation by asking questions about the nature and the rationale of the phenomenon/questions that are under investigation (ontology).

For example, in the photograph below we observe a rainbow, but how each of us attempts to explain the phenomenon depends on what we believe about the existence of a rainbow (our axiology) and what we say about the existence of the rainbow: whether it is operating under the laws of nature or whether we make different interpretation based on our feelings or views towards the phenomenon (ontology) depends on our ways of trying to understand this phenomenon (paradigm). The ultimate purpose of the research is to *assist […] the construction of knowledge by the recognition that there are different ways of viewing the world in terms of what is to be known* (Ma, 2016, p.22).

To make sense of these philosophical concepts, look at the photograph. Then ask why this phenomenon exists. Then you can have different answers. For example, if someone is embracing a religion where there is a creator (this person's axiology) the answer might be that this is a meteorological phenomenon that is caused when light and water droplets exist in the sky, and to the question of why it exists (ontology), then the answer might be because it is the creation of God (explanation based on axiology = there is a creator).

Figure 12.1   Harbour rainbow

If someone does not believe in a religion and explains the world through the laws of physics (this person's axiology) then the answer to the question about what a rainbow is will be the same: that it is a meteorological phenomenon. But as to why it exists (ontology), then the answer might be that it is caused because of reflection, refraction and dispersion of light (explanation based on axiology = physics laws).

As it can be seen, our values and beliefs (axiology) determine how we see and explain phenomena and behaviours that exist – the reality (ontology) – which differs for each of us as we do not share the same values and beliefs (axiology). Consequently, there are a number of different ways to understand the world and human behaviours (paradigms). The ultimate purpose of research is the creation/construction/advancement of knowledge and researchers, depending on their views, values, beliefs (axiology), their way of understanding reality (ontology) and how they try to explain phenomena and human behaviours (paradigms), try to question the knowledge that is to be acquired (epistemology). Epistemology, thus, is concerned with the line of questioning about what is to be known from a research project

As mentioned above, observation as a research method is ontologically determined by the axiology of the researcher. The two dominant research approaches in education (qualitative and quantitative research) are determined by two dominant paradigms as is illustrated in the Table 12.2.

Table 12.2   Two dominant paradigms

Interpretive paradigm that determines qualitative methodology	Positivist paradigm that determines quantitative methodology
Is concerned with individual institutions and people	Is outcome oriented
	Claims a stable reality
Does not attempt generalisations	Generalises from findings
Does not claim there is only one truth	Seeks one truth
Is subjective	Aims at objectivity
Validity is limited, local and contextual	Validity depends on other people's research findings

The following sections aim to discuss these two methodological traditions and how they can be combined.

Observation as a qualitative method

Maykut and Morehouse (1994) point out that a qualitative approach offers the researcher the opportunity to go in-depth and discover *important meanings* when conducting the studies. Qualitative observation helps the researcher to understand important meanings and gain insights into an under-researched field. However, this method is not as useful for measuring children's progress, but quantitative observation will provide the measurement tools in these circumstances.

Much of the discussion in the literature about these two approaches has created a somewhat exaggerated picture of their differences. These discussions tend to treat quantitative and qualitative research as though they are naturally antagonistic, ideal types of research processes. This tendency can be clearly discerned in some of the statements relating to qualitative research. However, while there are differences between the two research methods, there are also a number of points at which the differences are not as rigid as the statements often imply. Consequently, in addressing some of the features of quantitative and qualitative research, some areas of similarity will also be identified. At this point it will be helpful to broaden the discussion and investigate how combining qualitative and quantitative observation as methods can provide the full range of data required.

In order to do this we first need to investigate the role of the two research methods and then investigate the problems that may result when they are combined. It is also essential to examine how the data from these two methods can be linked in order to offer the possibility of reliable and valid conclusions.

As outlined earlier, qualitative research tends to be concerned with words rather than numbers in order to offer an *in-depth* investigation. Bryman (2012) and Silverman (2013) identify three main features of qualitative research.

First, they suggest that there is a relationship between theory and research. There are two main trends. The practitioners of grounded theory claim that the importance of qualitative research relies on the fact that it allows theoretical ideas to emerge out of the researcher's data (Strauss, 1967; Charmaz, 2000). Some qualitative researchers argue that qualitative data can perform an important role in relation to the testing of theories.

Silverman (2013) claims that more recently qualitative research has become increasingly interested in the testing of theories, a reflection of the growing maturity of the strategy. The data should offer evidence to test the theory that underpins the research in order to establish whether it can provide an alternative for future educational programmes and practice.

Second, qualitative research is informed by an epistemological position, which is described as interpretivist (Bryman, 2012). The emphasis of qualitative research is on understanding the social world through an examination of the interpretation of that world by its participants. Finally, there is an ontological view that the social phenomena researched are not separated from those involved in its construction. The epistemological and ontological views of the qualitative research reflect on its nature. Qualitative research is not a straightforward strategy (Bryman and Burgess, 1999), but rather it is complex and it is difficult to specify its nature.

Even though researchers, such as Silverman (2014), argue that it is difficult to identify the nature of qualitative research, Gubrium and Holstein (1997) suggest four traditions.

THEORY FOCUS

Four key traditions in qualitative research

Table 12.3   Traditions in qualitative research

Tradition	Characteristics
Naturalistic tradition	Seeks to understand social reality and provide a full account of descriptions of people and interactions in natural settings
Ethnomethodological tradition	Seeks to understand how social order is created through talk and interaction
Emotionalist tradition	Seeks to understand the inner reality of humans and exhibits a concern with subjectivity and gaining access to inside experience
Post-modern tradition	Seeks ways to emphasise the different ways in which social reality can be constructed

There are two reasons why it is essential to identify the nature of qualitative research and existing traditions. In the first place qualitative research includes several diverse methods that are quite different from each other. Thus, it is essential that the nature of the qualitative research you aim to apply to your study is identified in order to choose the most appropriate method for producing the required data and for investigating how theory can be tested in a social context.

The second reason for the importance of identifying the nature of qualitative research is the connection between the theory, the research forms and the collection and analysis of the data. Your study should aim to investigate how theory can be translated into activities in order to facilitate children's development and learning. The findings will feed back into the relevant theory.

Observation as a quantitative method

Quantitative research, in very broad terms, is described as entailing the collection of numerical data and investigating the relationship between these and the theory. Quantitative research uses special language – variable, control, measurements, experiment – in order to analyse the data and has a distinctive epistemology and ontology.

The epistemological and ontological views suggest that quantitative research moves beyond the mere presence of numbers and that the epistemology upon which quantitative research *is erected comprises a litany of pre-conditions for what is warrantable knowledge* (Bryman, 1992, p.12).

It often has a logical structure in which theories determine the problems which researchers address (Bryman, 2012) and is commonly used to examine patterns of interactions such as studies of teacher–child, early childhood workforce–children interaction. Surveys and experiments are the most common methodological tools of quantitative research, but structured observations and content analysis are two others (Beardsworth, 1980; Keat and Urry, 1975).

The different nature of these two research methods reflects the differences in the main features of qualitative and quantitative research. Bryman (2012) identifies some main differences between these two methods, related to the dimensions on which they diverge. These differences are related to the structure, design purposes and nature of the data of the two methods. Smith takes the argument further and claims that each of the two research strategies *sponsors different procedures and has different epistemological implications* and therefore researchers should not *accept the unfounded assumption that the methods are complementary* (1983, pp.12–13). These two research strategies are oriented by distant epistemological and ontological commitments (Hughes, 1990) and thus, qualitative inquiry should be separated from quantitative inquiry (Smith and Heshusius, 1986).

Guba (1985) and Morgan (1998) agree with the above and add the paradigm argument to this debate. They suggest that quantitative and qualitative research as paradigms differ in terms of epistemological assumptions, values and methods. Therefore, these paradigms are incommensurable (Kuhn, 1970) and there are no areas of overlap and commonality between them (Hughes, 1990; Walker, 1985; Rist, 1977). However, it is argued in the following section that, depending on the nature of the research question, there are times when these two different research methods can be combined and harmonised to facilitate the collection of appropriately rich data.

ACTIVITY 12.1

Observation for research

Study the Theory Focus boxes (Tables 12.1 and 12.3). Can you identify which observation methods are qualitative and which are quantitative and why? Once you have done this, go to the Summary box at the end to check your answers.

Combining qualitative and quantitative observation methods

In the above section, the nature of qualitative and quantitative research methods was examined and it was shown that they differ in terms of epistemology, ontology, paradigm, organisation and data analysis (see Theory Focus box above on p. 256). In combining these two different research methods, and the two kinds of argument thus stimulated, it was necessary to examine the epistemological and ontological commitments that these methods involve and also the paradigm argument that reflects the organisation of the research design and the data analysis. In addition, the issue of how the data will be linked should also be considered. In the following paragraphs therefore, an attempt is made to discuss these difficulties in order to overcome any problems which might influence the reliability, validity and generalisation of the findings.

While a great body of social researchers argue against the combination of quantitative and qualitative research due to their different natures (Hughes, 1990; Smith, 1983; Smith and Heshusius, 1986; Kuhn, 1970), a large number of others appear to be in favour of combining them or, as they claim, using multi-strategy research or mixed method studies (Bryman, 2012; Denzin and Lincoln, 2000, Cooper *et al.*, 2012; Plowright, 2010).

To begin with the paradigm argument, it is claimed that quantitative and qualitative research methods cannot be compatible. According to these theorists (Smith, 1983; Guba, 1987; Lincoln, 1990, 1994), researchers who try to combine the two methods are likely to fail due to the inherent differences in the paradigm underlying them. However, the opposing view is that the differences between the two paradigms have been *overdrawn* and the *schism* is not as wide as has been portrayed (Tashakkori and Teddlie, 1998). House (1994), in an attempt to explain this *dichotomisation*, claims that it is a result of the *misunderstanding of science*. It was believed that there was either one way or another and that there was *no guaranteed methodological path to the promised land* (House, 1994, pp.20–1).

Smith, though, has a strong argument about the incompatibility of the paradigms of these two methods:

> One approach takes a subject-object position on the relationship to the subject matter; the other takes a subject-subject position. One separates facts and values, while the other sees them as inextricably mixed. One searches for laws, and the other seeks understanding. These positions do not seem compatible.
>
> (1983, p.12)

Therefore, compatibility between qualitative and quantitative research seems impossible due to the incompatibility of paradigms that underlie the methods.

However, Datta (1994) provides arguments against Smith's idea of incompatibility and tries to justify the *coexistence* between the two methodologies and their underlying paradigms. He claims that all the paradigms have been used for many years and that many evaluators and researchers have therefore supported the use of both. A number of researchers have supported both and both paradigms have influenced policy and practice. Last, but not least, both paradigms can contribute and have contributed to knowledge.

Howe (1988) defends this orientation by calling the incompatibility of the two paradigms a *pseudo-problem* and suggests that researchers could use both of them in their research.

He argues that research philosophy should move away from the discussion of concepts and become *deconstructive* (p.15). Brewer and Hunter, in an attempt to justify the compatibility of the two paradigms, made a similar point and claimed that *rather than being wed to a particular theoretical style [...] and its most compatible method, one might instead combine methods that would encourage or even require integration of different theoretical perspectives to interpret data* (1989, p.74).

Thus, it can be argued that combining two different paradigms can actually work in favour of the research because the use of mixed methods helps the researcher gain a range of information that would not be provided by the restrictive use of one or other of the methods. Moreover, the data can be interpreted and explained under many theories in order to provide significant results, and thus the importance of *communicating results* from different paradigms helps the researchers to overcome the fact that the *world is complex and stratified and often difficult to understand* (Reichart and Rallis, 1994, p.84).

However, while combining quantitative and qualitative research might offer a rich data source the actual methods of collecting these data have certain epistemological and ontological limitations that should be acknowledged. Platt (1996) claims that the notion that research methods reflect or reveal certain assumptions about knowledge and social reality has to be questioned. When the use of research methods in practice is examined the connections are not absolute. The results of using a method associated with one research strategy should be cross-checked against the results of using the research method of another (Fielding and Fielding, 1986). The traditional quantitative approach to data collection involves relatively detailed and planned tools (Tashakkori and Teddlie, 1998). On the other hand, the most traditional qualitative research has been conducted without such preplanned methods of data collection.

Miles and Huberman (1994, p.35) illustrate this problem thus:

> *Knowing what you want to find out, at least initially, leads inexorably to the question of how you will gather information [...] some technical choices must be made. Will notes be taken? Of what sort? Will the transaction be tape recorded? Listened to afterwards? Transcribed? How will notes be written up?*

In essence, there is a data collection problem when quantitative and qualitative methods are combined which can influence the way the data will be linked when analysed. Even though a mixed method data collection approach offers an advantage for using both strategies, it can be a limitation at the same time. Armstrong *et al.* (1997) support this limitation and suggest that *reliability* and *validity* are fundamental concerns when combining quantitative and qualitative research. Thus it is important to define these two terms.

Reliability refers to the consistency or repeatability of measures of behaviour. Reliable observations of people's actions are not unique to a single observer (Tedlock, 2000). Instead, observers must agree on what they see and, in this study, the aim is for all the outcomes of observations to be discussed with the teachers who will be directly involved and also with the parents who will be indirectly involved.

Validity is the extent to which measures in a research study accurately reflect what the investigator intends to measure, so reliability is essential for valid research. Due to the difficulties associated with validity, Denzin (1970) describes two types of validity in observationally based studies:

1. External validity considers factors that ensure that the results are applicable to other situations, and;
2. Internal validity considers factors that ensure that the results are the genuine product.

When mixed methods are used researchers should check and cross-check data from combining methodologies.

Generalisation

A problem arising from the combination of quantitative and qualitative methods is generalisation. Qualitative research often relies on illustrative anecdotal methods of presenting data and thus *the critical reader is forced to ponder whether the researcher has selected only those fragments of data which support his argument* (Silverman, 1985, p.40). Quantitative research also cannot generalise its findings beyond the confines of the particular context in which the research was conducted (Bryman, 2012). However, one question on which a great deal of discussion has centred concerns external validity. It is essential to appreciate that there is a certain limitation to generalisation and that this applies to the present research.

A problem arising from the combination of quantitative and qualitative methods is generalisation. So far, there has been an attempt to discuss some of the issues that arise when quantitative and qualitative research are combined, as in this study. There have been references to the limitations that occur through the incompatibility of quantitative and qualitative research in respect of the reliability, validity and generalisation of the findings. Thus it is essential to develop a research design that will allow the gathering of data and, at the same time, minimise the acknowledged limitations. The following section presents the research design and the methodological tools for data collection and discusses the above limitations.

SUMMARY THEORY BOX

Observations techniques c.ommonly used in research:

Table 12.4   Observations techniques compared

Qualitative Research	Quantitative Research
Narratives (written, anecdotal, and running records)	Sampling
	Rating scales
	Checklists
	Diagrammatic

Observation as a research method versus observation as practice

It is important to distinguish between observation as a tool for informing practice and collecting evidence to understand children's development and learning in your early childhood setting and observation as a research tool. Throughout this book we are dealing with observation in relation to early childhood education practice. The key difference in using observation as a research tool is the generation of an intensive, detailed examination of the phenomenon or behaviour under study. The observations used as a research method are a reflection of the research inquiry in order to provide a complete collection of data that will enable the researcher to answer the research questions. The findings can be generalised.

Observation as a tool to gain evidence of your practice or children's development and learning is a systematic way of collecting a wealth of information about individual children, a group of children or activities in your early childhood setting over a period of time. However, the findings are indicative and they cannot necessarily be generalised and applied in another setting.

The Theory Focus box below presents the key differences and similarities of observation as a research tool and observation as a tool for practice:

THEORY FOCUS

Table 12.5   Observation for practice versus observation for research

Observation for practice	Observation for research
Practitioners are using observation to collect information to inform practice in a systematic way	Researchers are using observation as a method of data collection to answer research questions
Practitioners are using observation to collect information on a child's progress, development and learning in order to inform further planning to support the child	Researchers are using observation to collect data to help them answer their research questions
Practitioners can rely on other information beyond observation to acquire information for a child (i.e. parents, health visitor, educational psychologist)	Researchers rely on the research design of the research to collect data. Researchers tend to use more than one method to collect data (triangulation)
Practitioners observe what happens on the setting and employ discussions with parents to find out what happens outside of the setting (i.e. at home)	Researchers use observation in the relevant contexts of their research (i.e. observe a child in the classroom and then at home)
Practitioners can use, alongside their observation, anecdotal information for a child (i.e. views from parents to cross-reference information)	Researchers rely on what they have collected through observation and employ other research methods (i.e. interviews) to collect additional data if necessary

(Continued)

Table 12.5   (Continued)

Observation for practice	Observation for research
Practitioners want to understand children's development and learning	Researchers want to understand a phenomenon or behaviours
Practitioners want to explain children's behaviours	Researchers want to explain phenomenon or behaviours
Practitioners focus on areas of development in order to assess and evaluate them	Researchers want to examine effects of a phenomenon or behaviours
Practitioners can gain an understanding of children's development even with babies or toddlers whose language has not developed yet and meet their particular interests	Researchers can gain an understanding of human behaviour when there is lack of language or communication skills
Practitioners want to understand children's interactions and relationships in order to provide activities that will help them develop these further	Researchers want to examine human interactions and relationships
Practitioners want to understand why certain behaviours are occurring in the setting	Researchers want to examine cause and effect of a phenomenon or a behaviour
Practitioners use observation as a valid tool for the collecting of information about each child and their practice	Researchers use observation as a method to collect data
Observations can be qualitative or quantitative depending on the aims and objectives of what the practitioners want to investigate	Observations can be qualitative, quantitative or a combination depending on the positioning (axiology) of the researcher
Ethics are carefully considered and consent is acquired	Ethics are carefully considered and consent is acquired
Observation data relies on what happens when it happens and the practitioners are using multiple observations to analyse a child's behaviour relying on parents' views	Observation data relies on what has been recorded when it happens and the researcher relies on other research methods to cross-reference his/her analysis
Data is analysed and conclusions are drawn to inform planning	Data is analysed and conclusions can be generalised so implications can be suggested and furthering knowledge can be achieved
Information from observation is analysed and is used to be shared by the stakeholders (i.e. children and parents)	Findings from observations become available to a wider audience

CASE STUDY 12.1

Observation as a research tool (an example of physical development)

Although there is a plethora of literature and research about children's physical development, you want to investigate the physical development of young babies.

You are interested in investigating what physical attributes babies of the age 6–12 months have.

Research design

As part of this research project, and in order to collect in-depth evidence, you have developed a research design that involves the combination of qualitative and quantitative observation methods. Your observation schedule contains:

1. Naturalistic observations of young babies in their families and settings using digital media. To complete these, you will analyse the videos in order to categorise what physical skills you have observed in the babies.
2. Structured observation: use of rating scales.

You aim to apply some specific observations in order to identify certain physical attributes. Babies 6–7 months: give babies blocks of Lego and record and rate their reactions. Babies 7–9 months: give blocks of Lego and record and rate their reactions.

Repeat the same observation five to six times on each of these babies. Findings from each observation will be correlated in one rating scale for each child. The two rating scales will be concluded, one for the group of 6–7-month-old babies and one for the group 7–9-month-old babies. The two rating scales will enable comparisons to be made between the children's performances.

As can be seen, tools from two different methods are employed to provide data for this study. Qualitative observations will be made in order to provide data on children's physical attributes and quantitative methods will facilitate the comparison between the two age groups as a way of measuring progress in their physical development. The findings may offer insights into infants' physical development and with what objects they are interacting physically.

Observation as part of your practice (an example of physical development)

You work with babies (6–12 months) in a day nursery. You want to collect evidence to assess children's physical development. In order to collect evidence you have developed the following checklist:

Physical development	Attempting yes/no
Has little or no lag when pulled up to sit	
Can lift head and shoulders when lying on front	
Sits with back straight when supported	
Can hold head steady when upright	

(Continued)

(Continued)

Physical development	Attempting yes/no
When helped standing, takes weight on feet and bounces up and down	
Can roll from front to back	
Can roll from back to front	
Can sit without support	
While sitting can reach forward for a toy without falling over	
Moves around slowly by crawling or bottom shuffling	
Can pull self to standing position	
Can get from a lying to a sitting position	
Walks around a room holding onto furniture	
Stands alone	
Walks with adult help	
Crawls up stairs	
Walks a few steps alone	
Walks across the room when held by one hand	
Walks pushing large wheeled toys	
Can climb onto a low chair and sit down	

ACTIVITY 12.2

How observation is used in research and practice

For the above examples, try to list the similarities and differences when observation is used for research and when observation is used in practice.

SUMMARY

This chapter aimed to discuss observation as a research method highlighting the difference between observation for research and observation for practice. There are differences between these two types. Although when using observation either for research or practice there needs to be a systematic collection of information which needs to be valid and reliable, researchers should be able to demonstrate how their data is generalised and share it in the research community as part of the research process and furthering knowledge. However, practitioners should create a profile for the child where it is valid, but only share it with the stakeholders of the process (such as parents and children). In that sense observation for research differs from observation for practice in terms of how data is collected and what it is used for.

Further Reading

For more on observation as a method for research:

Plowright, D (2011) Chapter 6: Observation, in *Using Mixed Methods: Frameworks for an Integrated Methodology*. London: SAGE.

For more on interpreting observation data, read Chapter 5 of:

Silverman, D (2015) *Interpreting Qualitative Data* (5th edition). London: SAGE.

For more on the difference between observation as a research method and observation as part of practice, read Chapter 12 of:

Papatheodorou, T, Luff, P and Gill, J (2011) *Child Observation for Learning and Research*. Harlow: Pearson.

If you are doing a research project in early childhood education this book will be an excellent guide:

Robert-Holmes, G (2018) *Doing Your Research Project: A Step-by-Step Guide* (4th edition). London: SAGE.
Flewitt, R., and Ang, L. (2020). *Research Methods for Early Childhood Education*. London: Bloomsbury Academic.

CONCLUSION: OBSERVATION AND THE ROLE OF THE ADULT

Working with children in early childhood education requires a number of skills, such as a good understanding and theoretical knowledge of child development, a good understanding of children's abilities and how they learn from play, and an understanding of effective pedagogy and administrative skills. Among these skills the practitioners need very good observation, as the recordings offer insights into children's development and learning and enable the practitioner to create appropriate learning environments within the curriculum.

It is vital for practitioners to understand the theoretical underpinnings of their own practice. The view of the child as a confident learner, able to choose his or her materials and activities, will determine the observation process. Children's development and what they are able to do at a given stage of their lives then needs to be looked at. This knowledge may result from literature on general aspects of development, but also from direct observations of children themselves. Knowing the individual children in your group, and their abilities, interests and needs, is the starting point for planning new activities and experiences. The main tools of validation are observations of children, taking into account both parental and child involvement. The observation recording will then be interpreted and becomes important information for assessing early childhood education practice. These findings are an important tool to share with parents and children in order to encourage and enable the children's participation in classroom life.

It is important when working in early childhood education to acquire skills and through these skills you will be able to face the changing nature of qualifications and retain:

- an in-depth understanding of children's development at a theoretical level and an ability to implement this in your practice;
- the ability to make links between theory and practice;
- the ability to communicate with, and engage with sensitivity, young children and their families;
- to be able to reflect 'in action' and 'on action';
- the ability to be ethical;
- the means to seek continuous development;
- the ability to develop criteria and procedures for self-assessment and evaluation;
- the ability to strive for improving quality in your context.

The responsible and accountable practitioner should:

- implement the curriculum (the statutory duties and the pedagogy);
- develop play-based learning;
- promote the holistic development of children;
- ensure that all children and their families are treated equally and that diversity is promoted;
- prepare all the documentation for inspections;
- ensure the safety of children;
- promote the well-being and health of children;
- promote effective staff interactions;
- be able to achieve inter-agency or multi-agency work;
- establish partnerships with families and other services;
- meet quality standards.

Working with young children is a rewarding, but at the same time highly responsible role. You should provide an environment that enables children to have enjoyable meaningful experiences to support their development and learning, but at the same time make provision to collect evidence from playful contexts, outdoors as well as indoors. It is always worthwhile to step back and evaluate your observation records and the evidence you are collecting to see whether they cover the following areas:

- development;
- health and well-being:
- family and social relationships;
- self-care skills, independence and learning;
- safety and protection;
- emotional warmth and stability.

All these areas are regarded as equally important for a child's well-being and the practitioner has a critical role to play. In everyday practice the practitioner needs to make sure that all children under his or her supervision are meeting the above areas and to decide whether or not any additional needs have arisen that need to be addressed.

   This now becomes more and more important with the introduction at the statutory level of summative assessments in the form of the profile as in the EYFS and the Foundation

Phase frameworks. It is important to continuously reflect on the information you are continuously collecting for each child as:

> *Assessment of children should be perceived as a continuous process based on monitoring, evaluation and collaboration of all involved: practitioners, other relevant specialists, parents and children, rather than at a fixed age-related point in their development.*
>
> (Nicholson and Palaiologou, 2016)

As pointed out in Chapter 3, observations are a useful tool in identifying any needs by collecting pertinent evidence on children's progress. However, as Bromley (2009, p.2) cautions, *if there are some areas of provision that are valued less by practitioners, it may be that some children's achievements are going unnoticed.*

For the effective implementation of any curriculum, observations are central. Although in some curricula there are pre-assessment checklists, as well as standardised forms (see EYFS and the Foundation Phase), these alone cannot become independent tools for collecting evidence. As discussed in Chapter 3, when we observe children, we try to collect accurate information and specific evidence of what has been seen happening. Consequently, collecting evidence to understand each child's development and learning, and to inform practice and curriculum decisions, requires the use of a variety of observation techniques in order to collect information which, after analysis, will lead us to review what is required next.

Systematic observation can provide the practitioner with valid information in order to effectively use it to engage families in children's life in the early childhood education setting. Moreover, observations can function as a useful communication tool with other practitioners and agencies. Having collected a wealth of evidence, the required forms can be completed and additional information can also be provided if it is required.

The practitioner should master certain observation skills that can be used in other contexts. Observation skills that developed originally to observe children and the educational programme and its activities can be transferred to situations where the early childhood workforce will be asked to work either in an inter-agency or a multi-agency environment. Observing the way others work, and listening to the language they use, may benefit your own work in terms of reflecting on your own practice. Being able to wait and collect evidence will help you to communicate better, and observing and analysing how others work might become a helpful tool for furthering your understanding. Your observation skills can become your tool as you will use them to gain an insight into how other sectors operate.

The role of observation in the context of policy is dualistic. On the one hand, as previously stated, it can facilitate the early childhood workforce to implement policies. On the other hand, systematic observation (which includes the analysis of findings to inform your own practice) can help to develop a critical approach to policies and can influence practice, policy and legislation.

One of the main responsibilities of the early childhood workforce is the delivery of the curriculum in an effective way. For example, in England and Wales it is a statutory duty for practitioners to collect evidence in order to complete children's profiles. These will be used to assess children's progress, to share information, to promote partnership and for inspection purposes. Central to this statutory process is observation as a valid tool in order to collect all the evidence that you need for the effective completion of these assessments. Through observations you can develop a critical approach and voice your opinion to communicate with either other practitioners or services:

> *Clear, positive communication to staff is particularly essential when they are busy with the 'day job' and when change has not impacted on them yet. The two-way communication, through for instance regular learning labs, is crucial to gain staff trust and create and maintain motivation.*
>
> (Bachmann et al., 2006, p.9)

To sum up, early childhood education should provide a context which children can enjoy, being occupied in activities which stimulate them and which help them to develop skills. In such environments the practitioners perform the role of facilitators of children's learning and development. Practitioners should provide an environment where children make progress, taking into consideration children's equality, diversity and inclusion, so enabling children from different cultural backgrounds to interact with one another and share different experiences.

In such an environment, the practitioners should demonstrate the different facets of the role of educator, use appropriate language, respect values and practices, and praise and encourage all children. As facilitators, the early childhood workforce has a good understanding of children's development and pedagogy and of how these are both linked to their everyday practice with children. As mentioned in Chapter 2, working in early childhood requires an understanding of the different views of children that form and underpin practice, a good understanding of how children develop and the different theoretical approaches to this development. This specialised knowledge is not isolated from the development of pedagogy through reflection and evaluation of current theories alone.

One of the common findings of different research projects on pedagogy in early childhood stresses the fact that in settings where children's learning is most enhanced the practitioner's focus on child-initiated activities and planning, resourcing and assessment are integrated into daily practice (Moyles et al., 2001; Sylva et al., 2001; Siraj-Blatchford and Sylva, 2002; Taylor Nelson Sofres with Aubrey, 2002; Pugh, 2010; Brooker et al., 2010). The important tool for planning and assessment is observation. As mentioned in Chapter 3, observations should be part of the daily routine of the setting. Everyday observations of children's interactions, their progress within the activities and the analysis of the observation recordings all help the early childhood workforce to make links between theory and practice and, inevitably, to modify their pedagogical principles.

Moreover, nearly all the examples discussed in this book stress the holistic approach to children's development. To develop a pedagogy that meets the requirements of a holistic approach to children, observations become the means to understand children and parents' diversity, values and beliefs, and the wider cultural context that children and parents live in and are influenced by. This wider context is not isolated from life in an early childhood setting. Children's experiences in the family context are interlinked with their experiences in the setting. In this respect, the role of the workforce as educators has great value. The workforce needs to develop a portfolio of skills and attitudes to be able to use these skills to develop practice and to be able to understand the wider context in which children are raised. The workforce needs to listen to children attentively. Powerful tools for this are observations as they further our understanding and deepen our knowledge of children.

In Chapter 2, conditions for learning were discussed, emphasising children's development, play, their needs, their freedom to choose materials and activities and their ownership of learning. As explained in Chapter 3, observations offer rich information about children's learning which enables the workforce to inform future planning and pedagogy. Observations are starting points for sharing information among the team, but in their role as educators practitioners can use observations as evidence for and to inform pedagogy, the educational programme and its activities.

In this book, it was demonstrated that observations can be used to:

- find out about children as individuals;
- monitor their progress;
- inform curriculum planning;
- enable staff to evaluate the provisions they make;
- provide a focus for discussion and improvement;
- understand practice better;
- ensure their conclusions are 'woven' into daily practice.

All these are important aspects for the everyday practice of the early childhood workforce as they help to:

- assess children's development and learning (which is statutory in some curricula);
- assess and evaluate the programme and activities in order to inform practice;
- share this information with children in an appropriate manner for their age;
- share this information with parents;
- share this information with local authorities;
- retain this information for the purposes of inspection;
- share this information with other practitioners, to exchange ideas and to learn from each other.

The observation process as a tool assists practitioners in developing their specialised knowledge, to gain a deeper understanding of pedagogy and to expand upon pedagogical practices. The role of the workforce as educators is not isolated or distinct from their role in the context of policy. These are interlinked roles and observation skills can become a method for embracing the policy of the educational programme in order to effectively provide for children.

REFERENCES

Ainsworth, MDS (1969) Object relations, dependency, and attachment: a theoretical review of the infant–mother relationship. *Child Development*, 40: 969–1025.

Ainsworth, MDS (1973) The development of infant–mother attachment. In **Cardwell, B and Ricciuti, H** (eds), *Review of Child Development Research*, vol. 3. Chicago: University of Chicago Press.

Ainsworth, MDS (1979) Attachment as related to mother–infant interaction. *Advances in the Study of Behaviour*, 9: 2–52.

Ainsworth, MDS (1985) Attachments across the life span. *Bulletin of the New York Academy of Medicine*, 61: 792–812.

Ainsworth, MDS (1989) Attachment beyond infancy. *American Psychologist*, 44: 709–16.

Alexander, RJ (2004a) Still no pedagogy? Principle, pragmatism and compliance in primary education. *Cambridge Journal of Education*, 34(1): 7–34.

Anderson, J (1983) *The Architecture of Cognition*. Cambridge, MA: Harvard University.

Armstrong, D, Gosling, JW and Marteau, T (1997) The place of inter-rater reliability in qualitative research: an empirical study. *Sociology*, 31(3): 597–606.

Arnott, L, Palaiologou, I and Gray, C (2018) An ecological exploration of the Internet of toys in early childhood everyday life. In **Mascheroni, G and Holloway, D** (eds), *The Internet of Toys: Practices, Affordances and the Political Economy of Children's Play*. London: Palgrave Macmillan, pp.135–58.

Athey, C (1990) *Extending Thought in Young Children*. London: Paul Chapman.

Australian Government Department of Education and Training (2019) *Belonging, Being & Becoming: The Early Years Learning Framework for Australia*. Australian Government Department of Education and Training for the Council of Australian Governments.

Australian Government Department of Education, Employment and Workplace Relations (2010) *Educators Belonging, Being & Becoming, Educators' Guide to the Early Years Learning Framework for Australia*. Australian Government Department of Education, Employment and Workplace Relations for the Council of Australian Governments.

Bachmann, M, Husbands, C and O'Brian, M (2006) *National Evaluation of Children's Trust: Managing Change for Children through Children's Trust*. Norwich: University of East Anglia/National Children's Bureau.

Bandura, A (1971) *Psychological Modeling*. New York: Lieber-Atherton.

Bandura, A (1977) *Social Learning Theory*. Englewood Cliffs, NJ: Prentice Hill.

Bandura, A (1986) *Social Foundations of Thought and Action: A Social Cognitive Theory*. Englewood Cliffs, NJ: Prentice Hall.

Bandura, A (1989) Social cognitive theory. In **Vasta, R** (ed.) *Annals of Child Development: Theories of Child Development: Revised Foundations and Current Issues*, vol. 6. Greenwich, CT: JAI Press.

Bandura, A (2001) Social cognitive theory: an agentic perspective. *Annual Review of Psychology*, 52: 1–26.

Barad, KK (2007) *Meeting the Universe Halfway: Quantum Physics and the Entanglement of Matter and Meaning*. Durham, NC: Duke University Press.

Bassey, A (1990) On the nature of research in education (part 1). *Research Intelligence*, BERA newsletter, 36: 35–8.

Beardsworth, A (1980) Analysing press content: some technical and methodological issues. *Sociology Review Monograph*, 29: 371–95.

Benjamin, AC (1994) Observations in early childhood classrooms: advice from the field. *Young Children*, 49(6): 14–20.

Bentzen, WR (2009) *Seeing Young Children: A Guide to Observing and Recording Behaviour* (6th edition). Clifton Park, NY: Thomson Delmar Learning.

Bergen, D, Hutchinson, K, Nolan, JT and Webber, D (2010) Effects of infant–parent play with a technology enhanced toy: affordance-related actions and communicative interactions. *Journal of Research in Childhood Education*, 24(1): 1–17.

Bick, E (1964) Notes on infant observation in psycho-analytical training. *Psychoanalytical Study of Child*, 45: 558–66.

Bird, J and Edwards, S (2015) Children learning to use technologies through play: a digital play framework. *British Journal of Educational Technology*, 46(6): 1149–60.

Bowlby, J (1958) The nature of the child's tie to his mother. *International Journal of Psychoanalysis*, 39: 350–71.

Bowlby, J (1969a) *Attachment and Loss*, Vol. I. London: Hogarth.

Bowlby, J (1969b) *Attachment and Loss*, Vol II, *Separation, Anxiety, Anger*. New York: Basic Books.

Bradbury, A (2019) Datafied at four: the role of data in the 'schoolification' of early childhood education in England. *Learning, Media and Technology*, 44(1): 7–21. **DOI:10.1080/17439884.2018.1511577**.

Brewer, J and Hunter, A (1989) *Multimethod Research: A Synthesis of Styles*. Newbury Park, CA: Sage.

Brock, A (2012) Building a model of early years professionalism from practitioners' perspectives. *Journal of Early Childhood Research*, 11(1): 27–44. Available at **http://ecr.sagepub.com/content/11/1/27.short** (accessed 13 February 2015).

Bromley, H (2009) Observation, assessment and planning in the EYFS. Part 8: Reporting and describing progress. *Nursery World*, August.

Bronfenbrenner, U (1977) Towards experimental ecology of human development. *American Psychologist*, 32: 513–31.

Bronfenbrenner, U (1979) *The Ecology of Human Development*. Cambridge, MA: Harvard University Press.

Bronfenbrenner, U (1989) Ecological systems theory. In **Vasta, R** (ed.), *Annals of Child Development: Theories of Child Development: Revised Foundations and Current Issues*, Vol. 6. Greenwich, CT: JAI Press.

Bronfenbrenner, U (1995) The bioecological model from life course perspective: reflections of a participant observer. In **Moen, P, Elder, GH and Jr and Luscher, K** (eds) *Examining Lives in Context*. Washington, DC: American Psychological Association.

Bronfenbrenner, U (2005) *Making Human Beings Human*. Thousand Oaks, CA: Sage.

Brooker, L, Blaise, M and Edwards, S (2014) *The Sage Handbook of Play and Learning in Early Childhood*. London: Sage.

Brooker, L, Rogers, S, Ellis, D, Hallett, E and Roberts-Holmes, G (2010) *Practitioner's Experiences of the Early Years Foundation Stage* (DfE Research Report 029). London: DfE. Available at **www.gov.uk/government/uploads/system/uploads/attachment_data/file/181479/DFERR029.pdf** (accessed 9 October 2013).

Bruner, JS (1972) *Early Childhood Education*. London: Hodder & Stoughton.

Bruner, JS (1996) *The Culture of Education*. Cambridge, MA: Harvard University Press.

Bryman, A (1992) *Quantity and Quality in Social Research*. London: Routledge.

Bryman, A (2012) *Social Research Methods* (4th edn). Oxford: Oxford University Press.

Bryman, A and Burgess, RG (1999) Introduction: qualitative research methodology: a review. In **Bryman, A and Burgess, RG** (eds) *Qualitative Research*. London: Sage.

Cannella, GS (2005) Reconceptualizing the field (of early care and education): if 'western' child development is a problem, then what do we do? In **Yelland, N** (ed.) *Critical Issues in Early Childhood*. Maidenhead: Open University Press.

Carr, M (1998) Assessing Children's Learning in Early Childhood Settings: A Development Programme for Discussion and Reflection. Wellington: New Zealand Council for Educational Research.

Carr, M (2001) *Assessment in Early Childhood Settings*. London: Paul Chapman.

Carr, M and Lee, W (2012) *Learning Stories: Constructing Learner Identities in Early Education*. London: Sage.

Caruso, J (2013) *Supervision in Early Childhood Education: A Developmental Perspective* (3rd edn). London: Teacher College Press.

Chalke, J (2013) Will the early years professional please stand up? Professionalism in the early childhood workforce in England. *Contemporary Issues in Early Childhood*, 14(3): 212–22.

Charmaz, K (2000) Grounded theory: objectivist and constructivist methods. In **Denzin, NK and Lincoln, YS** (eds) *Handbook of Qualitative Research* (2nd edn). Thousand Oaks, CA: Sage.

Cheeseman, S and Robertson, J (2006) Unsure – private conversations publicly recorded. In *Insights: Behind Early Childhood Pedagogical Documentation*. Castle Hill, NSW: Pademelon Press, pp.191–204.

Clark, A and Moss, P (2001) *Listening to Young Children: The Mosaic Approach* (1st edn). London: National Children's Bureau.

Clark, A and Moss, P (2011) *Listening to Young Children: The Mosaic Approach* (2nd edn). London: National Children's Bureau.

Clark, A, Kjorholt, AT and Moss, P (2005) *Beyond Listening: Children's Perspectives on Early Childhood Services*. Bristol: Policy Press.

Cohen, L, Manian, L, and Morrison, K (2004) *Research Methods in Education* (5th edn). London: RoutledgeFalmer.

Cole, DR (2011) *Educational Life-forms: Deleuzian Teaching and Practice*. Rotrterdam: Sense Publishers.

Cooper, B, Glasser, J, Gomm, R and Hammersley, M (2012) *Challenging the Quantitative–Qualitative Device*. London: Continuum.

Cowley, S (2019) Battling baseline again. *Early Years Educator*, 22(1). Online at: **https://doi. org/10.12968/eyed.2019.21.1.14**.

Crowley, K (2017) *Child Development: A Practical Introduction* (2nd edn). London: Sage.

CWDC (Children's Workforce Development Council) (2011) *Early Years Workforce – The Way Forward*. Leeds: CWDC.

Dahlberg, G and Moss, P (2005) *Ethics and Politics in Early Childhood Education*. London: Routledge Falmer.

Dahlberg, G and Moss, P (2010) Introduction. In **Taguchi, HL** (ed.) *Going Beyond the Theory/ Practice Divide in Early Childlhood Education: Introducing Intra-active Pedagogy*. London: Routledge.

Dahlberg, G, Moss, P and Pence, A (1999) *Beyond Quality in Early Childhood Education and Care: Postmodern Perspectives* (1st edn). London: Falmer Press.

Dahlberg, G, Moss, P and Pence, A (2007) *Beyond Quality in Early Childhood Education and Care: Postmodern Perspectives* (2nd edn). London: Routledge.

Datta, L (1994) Paradigm wars: a basis for peaceful coexistence and beyond. In **Reichart, CS and Rallis, SF** (eds) *The Qualitative-Quantitative Debate: New Perspectives*. San Francisco: Jossey-Bass.

DCSF (Department for Children, Schools and Families) (2007) *Primary National Strategy: Learning Walks: Tools and Templates for Getting Started*. Nottingham: DCSF. Available at **http:// webarchive.nationalarchives.gov.uk/20110202093118/ http://nationalstrategies. standards.dcsf.gov.uk/node/88674** (accessed 15 October 2015).

DEEWR (Department of Education, Employment and Workplace Relations) (2019) *Belonging, Being and Becoming: The Early Years Learning Framework for Australia*. Canberra: Australian Government. Available at **www.deewr.gov.au/EarlyChildhood/Policy_Agenda/Quality/ Documents/A09-057%20EYLF%20 Framework%20Report%20WEB.pdf**.

DENI (Department for Education in Northern Ireland) (2013) *Learning to Learn: A Framework for Early Years Education in Northern Ireland*. Bangor: DENI.

Denzin, NK (1970) *The Research Act in Sociology: A Theoretical Introduction to Sociological Methods*. London: Butterworth Group.

Denzin, NK and Lincoln, YS (eds) (2000) *Handbook of Qualitative Research* (2nd edn). Thousand Oaks, CA: Sage.

Devereux, J (2003) Observing children. In **Devereux, J and Miller, L** (eds) *Working with Children in the Early Years*. London: David Fulton.

Dewey, J (1897/1974) My pedagogic creed. In **Archambault, RD** (ed.), *John Dewey on Education: Selected Writings*. Chicago and London: University of Chicago Press.

Dewey, J (1938) *Experience and Education*. New York: Macmillan.

DfE (Department for Education) (2013) *More Great Childcare: Raising Quality and Giving Parents More Choice*. **https://www.gov.uk/government/publications/more-great-childcare-raising-quality-and-giving-parents-more-choice**.

DfE (Department for Education) (2017) *Statutory Framework for the Early Years Foundation Stage*. DfE. Online **https://www.gov.uk/government/publications/early-years-foundation-stage-framework--2**.

DfE (Department for Education) (2019) *Reception Baseline Assessment Framework*. DfE. **https://www.gov.uk/government/publications/reception-baseline-assessment-framework**.

DfES (Department for Education and Skills) (2003) *Every Child Matters*. London: HMSO.

Dollard, J and Miller, NE (1950) *Personality and Psychotherapy*. New York: McGraw-Hill.

Drummond, MJ (1993) *Assessing Children's Learning* (1st edn). London: David Fulton.

Drummond, MJ (1998) Observing children. In **Smidt, S** (ed.), *The Early Years: A Reader*. London: Routledge.

Dunn, J. and Sweeney, T (2018) Writing and iPads in the early years: perspectives from within the classroom. *British Journal of Educational Technology*, 49(5): 859–69.

Education Scotland Curriculum for Excellence (2016) Online at: **https://education.gov.scot/scottish-education-system/policy-for-scottish-education/policy-drivers/cfe-%28building-from-the-statement-appendix-incl-btc1-5%29/What%20is%20Curriculum%20for%20Excellence?**

Education Wales (2018) *Statutory Assessment Arrangements for the Foundation Phase and End of Key Stages 2 and 3*. Cardiff: Welsh Government.

Edwards, S and Bird, J (2017) Observing and assessing young children's digital play in the early years: using the Digital Play Framework. *Journal of Early Childhood Research*, 15(2): 158–73.

Elfer, P (2005) Observation matters. In **Abbott, L and Langston, A** (eds) *Birth-to-Three Matters*. Maidenhead: Open University Press.

Erikson, EH (1963) *Childhood and Society* (2nd edn). New York: Norton.

Erikson, EH (1982) *The Life Cycle Completed: A Review*. New York: Norton.

Estep Jr, JR (2002) Spiritual formation as social: toward a Vygotskyan developmental perspective. *Religious Education*, 97(2): 141–64.

Eysenck, MW (1995) *Principles of Cognitive Psychology*. London: Royal Holloway University of London.

Faragher, J and MacNaughton, G (1998) *Working with Young Children* (2nd edn). Melbourne: RMIT Publications.

Feldman, A (1997) Varieties of wisdom in practice of teachers. *Teaching and Teacher Education*, 13(7): 757–73.

Fernald, LCH, Prado, E, Kariger, P and Raikes, A (2017) *A Toolkit for Measuring Early Childhood Development in Low- and Middle-Income Countries*. Washington, DC: World Bank.

Fielding, NG and Fielding, JL (1986) *Linking Data: Qualitative Research Methods Series*, vol. 4, London: Sage.

Fitzgerald, D and Kay, J (2016) *Understanding Early Years Policy* (4th edn). London: Sage.

Fleer, M (2017) Digital playworlds in an Australian context: supporting double subjectivity. In **Bruce, T, Hakkarainen, P and Bredikyte, M** (eds), *The Routledge International Handbook of Early Childhood Play*. Oxon: Routledge, pp.289–304.

Flewitt, R and Cowan, K (2019) *Valuing Young Children's Signs of Learning: Observation and Digital Documentation of Play in Early Years Classrooms*. London: UCL Institute for Education.

Formoshino, J and Formoshino, J (2016) The search for a holistic approach to evaluation. In **Formosinho, J and Pascal, C** (eds) *Assessment and Evaluation for Transformation in Early Childhood*. London: Routledge.

Formoshino, J and Pascal, C (eds) (2015) *Assessment and Evaluation for Transformation in Early Childhood*. London: Routledge.

Freud, S (1923) *An Outline of Psychoanalysis*. London: Hogarth.

Freud, S (1933) *New Introductory Lectures in Psychoanalysis*. New York: Norton.

Freud, S (1964) An outline of psychoanalysis. In **Stracehy, J** (ed. and trans.) *The Standard Edition of the Complete Psychological Works of Sigmund Freud*, Vol. 23. London: Hogarth Press (original work published 1940).

Froebel, F (1826/1902) *Education of Man* (trans. WN Hailmann). New York: Appleton.

Froebel, F (1887) *The Education of Man*. New York: Appleton-Century.

General Data Protection Regulations (GDPR) (2018) **https://eugdpr.org/**.

Gillham, B (2008) Observation Techniques: Structured to Unstructured. London: Continuum.

Glassman, WE (2000) *Approaches to Psychology* (3rd edn). Buckingham: Open University Press.

Goodall, J and Vorhaus, J (2011) *Review of Best Practice in Parental Engagement*. London: DfE.

GPEN (Global Privacy Enforcement Network) (2015) *Big Year for Global Privacy Enforcement Network: GPEN Releases 2014 Annual Report*. Press release. Available at: **www.privacy enforcement.net/node/513** (accessed 11 October 2015).

Guba, EG (1985) The context of emergent paradigm research. In **Lincoln, YS** (ed.), *Organisational Theory and Inquiry: The Paradigm Revolution*. Beverly Hills, CA: Sage.

Guba, EG (1987) What have we learned about naturalistic evaluation? *Evaluation Practice*, 8: 23–43.

Gubrium, JF and Holstein, JA (1997) *The New Language of Qualitative Method*. New York: Oxford University Press.

Hamilton, C, Haywood, S, Gibbins, S, McInnes, K and Williams, J (2003) *Principles and Practice in the Foundation Stage*. Exeter: Learning Matters.

Harlow, HF and Zimmermann, RR (1958) The development of affective responsiveness in infant monkeys. *Proceedings of the American Philosophical Society*, 102: 501–9.

Harter, S (1996) The development of self-representation. In **Damon, W and Eisenberg, N** (eds), *Handbook of Child Psychology: Social, Emotional and Personality Development* (5th edn). New York: Wiley.

Hartley, D (1993) *Understanding the Nursery School: A Sociological Analysis*. London: Cassell.

Hendrick, H (1997) Construction and reconstruction of British childhood: an interpretive survey, 1800 to present. In **James, A and Prout, A** (eds) *Constructing and Reconstructing Childhood: Contemporary Issues in the Sociological Study of Childhood* (2nd edn). London: Falmer Press.

Hevey, D (2017) United Kingdom – ECEC Workforce Profile. In **Oberhuemer, P and Schreyer, I** (eds), *Workforce Profiles in Systems of Early Childhood Education and Care in Europe*. On line at: **www. seepro.eu/English/Country_Reports.htm**.

HM Government (2004) *The Children Act 2004*. London: HMSO.

Hogben, J and Wasley, D (1989) *Learning in Early Childhood: What Does It Mean in Practice?* South Australia: Hyde Park Press.

House, ER (1994) Integrating the quantitative and qualitative. In **Reichardt, CS and Rallis, SF** (eds), *The Qualitative–Quantitative Debate: New Perspectives*. San Francisco: Jossey-Bass.

Howard, K and Sharp, JA (1983) *The Management of a Student Research Project*. Aldershot: Gower.

Howe, KR (1988) Against the quantitative–qualitative incompatibility thesis or dogmas die hard. *Educational Researcher*, 17: 10–16.

Hughes, JA (1990) *The Philosophy of Social Research* (2nd edn). Harlow: Longman.

Hurst, V (1991) *Planning for Early Learning*. London: Paul Chapman.

Hutt, C (1966) *Exploration and Play in Children*. Paper presented at the Symposia of the Zoological Society of London, 81, pp.61–81.

Hutt, S, Tyler, C, Hutt, C and Christopherson, H (1989) *Play, Exploration and Learning: A Natural History of the Preschool*. London: Routledge.

ICO (Information Commissioner's Office) (2018) *Guide to General Data Protection Regulations (GDPR)*. Online at: **https://ico.org.uk/for-organisations/guide-to-data-protection/guide-to-the-general-data-protection-regulation-gdpr/**.

Isaacs, S (1933) *Social Development in Young Children*. London: Routledge.

Jones, F (2009) *Rethinking Childhood: Attitudes in Contemporary Society*. London: Continuum.

Karlsson Lohmander, M (2017) Sweden – ECEC Workforce Profile. In **Oberhuemer, P and Schreyer, I** (eds), *Workforce Profiles in Systems of Early Childhood Education and Care in Europe*. Online at: **www.seepro.eu/English/Country_Reports.htm**.

Keat, R and Urry, J (1975) *Social Theory as Science*. London: Routledge & Kegan Paul.

Kerlinger, FN (1970) *Foundations of Behavioural Research*. New York: Holt, Rinehart & Winston.

Klahr, D (1992) Information processing approaches to cognitive development. In **Bornstein, MH and Lamb, ME** (eds) *Developmental Psychology: An Advanced Textbook* (3rd edn). New York: Psychology Press.

Kravtsova, E (2014) Play in the non-classial psychology of L.S. Vygotsky (trans. Anton Maximov). In **Brooker, L, Blaise, M and Edwards, S** (eds), *The Sage Handbook of Play and Learning in Early Childhood*. London: Sage, pp.21–42.

Kuhn, TS (1970) *The Structure of Scientific Revolutions* (2nd edn). Chicago: University Press of Chicago.

Kumpulainen, K (2017) Makerspaces – why they are important for digtial literacy education. In **Marsh, J, Kumpulainen, K, Nisha, B, Velicu, A, Blum-Ross, A et al.**, *Makerspaces in the Early Years: A Literature Review*. University of Sheffield: MakEY Project, pp.12–16.

Kurcikova, N (2017) *Digital Personalisation in Early Childhood: Impact on Childhood*. London: Bloomsbury.

Laevers, F (1997) Assessing quality of childcare provision: 'involvement' as criterion. *Settings in Interaction, Researching Early Childhood*, 3: 151–65.

Laevers, F (1998) Understanding the world of objects and of people: intuition as the core element of deep level learning. *International Journal of Educational Research*, 29(1): 69–85.

Laevers, F (1999) The project Experiential Education: Well-Being and Involvement – name the difference. *Early Education*, Discussion Paper No. 27.

Laevers, F (2000) Forward to basics! Deep-level learning and the experimental approach. *Early Years*, 20(2): 20–9.

Laevers, F (ed.) (2005a) *Well-Being and Involvement in Care Settings. A Process-oriented Self-evaluation Instrument Research Centre for Experiential Education*. Leuven: Leuven University.

Laevers, F (2005b) The curriculum as means to raise the quality of ECE. Implications for policy. *European Early Childhood Education Research Journal*, 13(1): 17–30.

Laevers, F (2009) *Improving Quality of Care with Well-being and Involvement as the Guide. A Large Scale Study in a Flemish Setting. Final Report*. Leuven: Kind & Gezin, CEGO Leuven University.

Laevers, F and Moons, J (1997) *Enhancing Well-being and Involvement in Children. An Introduction in the Ten Action Points* [video]. Leuven: Centre for Experiential Education.

Laevers, F, Bogaerts, M and Moons, J (1997) *Experiential Education at Work. A Setting with 5-year-olds* [manual and video]. Leuven: Centre for Experiential Education.

Lally, M and Hurst, V (1992) Assessment in nursery education: a preview of approaches. In **Blenkin, GM and Kelly, AV** (eds), *Assessment in Early Childhood Education*. London: Paul Chapman.

Ledin, P and Machin, D (2018) *Doing Visual Analysis : From Theory to Practice*. London: Sage.

Lincoln, YS (1990) The making of a constructivist. In **Cuba, E** (ed.), *The Paradigm Dialog*. Newbury Park, CA: Sage.

Lincoln, YS (1994) The fifth moment. In **Denzin, NK and Lincoln, YS** (eds), *Handbook of Qualitative Research*. Thousand Oaks, CA: Sage.

Livingstone, S, Stoilova, M and Nandagiri, R (2018) *Consultation Response to the Information Commissioner's Office Call for Evidence on Age Appropriate Design Code*. Online at: **www.lse.ac.uk/media-and-communications/research/researchprojects/childprivacyonline**.

Lofland, J and Lofland, L (1996) *Analysing Social Settings: A Guide to Qualitative Observation and Analysis*. Belmont, CA: Wadsworth Thomson.

Lofland, J, Snow, D, Anderson, L and Lofland, LH (2006) *Analysing Social Settings: A Guide to Qualitative Observation and Analysis* (4th edn). Belmont, CA: Wadsworth Thomson.

Lorenz, K (1935) Der Kumpan in der Umwelt des Vogels. Der Artgenosse als auslösendes Moment sozialer Verhaltensweisen. *Journal für Ornithologie*, 83: 137–215, 289–413.

Lpfö 98 (1998) *Läroplan för förskolan. Curriculum for Pre-school*. Stockholm: Fritzes förlag.

Lpfö 98 (2010 revised) *Läroplan för förskolan. Curriculum for Pre-school*. Stockholm: Fritzes förlag.

Luff, P (2007) Written observations or walks in the park: documenting children's experiences. In **Moyles, J** (ed.) *Early Years Foundations: Meeting the Challenge*. Maidenhead: Open University Press.

Ma, J (2016) Making sense of research methodology. In **Palaiologou, I, Needham, D and Male, T** (eds), *Doing Research in Education: Theory and Practice*. London: Sage.

MacNaughton, G (2009) Exploring critical constructivist perspectives on children's learnin. In **Anning, A, Cullen, J and Fleer, M** (eds), *Early Childhood Education, Society and Culture*. London: Sage.

Malaguzzi, L (1993) For an education based on relationships. *Young Children*, November: 9–13.

Malaguzzi, L (1995) History, ideas, and basic philosophy: an interview with Lella Gandini. In **Edwards, C, Gandini, L and Froman, G** (eds), *The Hundred Languages of Children: The Reggio Emilia Approach to Early Childhood Education*. New York: Ablex.

Malaguzzi, L (1996) *The Hundred Languages of Children: A Narrative of the Possible* (catalogue of the exhibit). Reggio Emilia: Reggio Children.

Malaguzzi, L (1998) History, ideas, and basic philosophy: an interview with Lella Gandini. In **Edwards, C, Gandini, L and Forman, G** (eds), *The Hundred Languages of Children: The Reggio Emilia Approach – Advanced Reflections* (2nd edn). Norwood, NJ: Ablex.

Male, T and Palaiologou, I (2012) Learning-centred leadership or pedagogical leadership? An alternative approach to leadership in education contexts. *International Journal of Leadership in Education*, 15(1): 107–18.

Marsh, CJ (2004) *Key Concepts for Understanding Curriculum*. London: Routledge.

Marsh, J, Plowman, L, Yamada-Rice, D, Bishop, J and Scott, F (2016) Digital play: a new classification. *Early Years: An International Research Journal*, 306: 242–53.

Marsh, J, Kumpulainen, K, Nisha, B, Velicu, A, Blum-Ross, A et al. (2017) *Makerspaces in the Early Years: A Literature Review*. University of Sheffield: MakEY Project.

Martin, S (2019) *Take a Look: Observation and Portfolio Assessment in Early Childhood* (7th edn). Canada: Pearson.

Marton, F and Booth, S (1997) *Learning and Awareness*. Mahwah, NJ: Lawrence Erlbaum.

Maykut, P and Morehouse, R (1994) *Beginning Qualitative Research: A Philosophic and Practical Guide*. London: Falmer Press.

Miles, M and Huberman, M (1994) *Qualitative Data Analysis: An Expanded Sourcebook* (2nd edn). Thousand Oaks, CA: Sage.

Miller, L and Hevey, D (2012) *Policy Issues in the Early Years*. London: Sage.

Miller, L, Hughes, J, Roberts, A, Paterson, L and Staggs, L (2003) Curricular guidance and frameworks for the Early Years: UK perspectives. In **Devereux, J and Miller, L** (eds), *Working with Children in the Early Years*. London: David Fulton.

Mills, J and Mills, R (2000) *Childhood Studies: A Reader in Perspectives of Childhood*. London: RoutledgeFalmer.

Ministry of Education (1996) *Te Whāriki. He Whāriki Matauranga mo nga Mokopuna o Aotearoa: Early Childhood Curriculum*. Wellington: Learning Media.

Ministry of Education (1998) *Quality in Action. Implementing the Revised Statement of. Desirable Objectives and Practices in New Zealand. Early Childhood Services*. Wellington: Learning Media.

Ministry of Education (2004) *Assessment for Infants and Toddlers*. New Zealand: Ministry of Education.

Ministry of Education (2017) *Te Whāriki He whāriki mātauranga mō ngā mokopuna o Aotearoa. Early Childhood Curriculum*. Ministry of Education, New Zealand, Te Tāhuhu o te Mātauranga.

Montessori, M (1912) *The Montessori Method* (trans. AE George). New York: Frederick A. Stokes. Available at **http://web.archive.org/web/20050207205651/www.moteaco.com/method/method.html** (accessed 4 April 2012).

More Than a Score (2019) 'Four-year-olds don't need exams. *Action Network*. Available at: **https://actionnetwork.org/petitions/four-year-olds-dont-need-exams**.

Morgan, DL (1998) Practical strategies for combining qualitative and quantitative methods: applications for health research. *Qualitative Health Research*, 8: 362–76.

Moss, J, and Pini, B (2016) *Visual Research Methods in Educational Research*. Basingstoke: Palgrave Macmillan.

Moss, P (2010) Forward, in **Clark, A**, *Transforming Children's Spaces: Children's and Adults' Participation in Designing Learning Environments*. London: Routledge, pp.xi–xiii.

Moss, P (2014) *Transformative Change and Real Utopias in Early Childhood Education*. London: Routledge.

Moss, P and Urban, M (2017) The Organisation for Economic Co-operation and Development's International Early Learning Study: what happened next. *Contemporary Issues in Early Childhood*, 18(2): 250–8.

Moyles, J (1989) *Just Playing? The Role and Status of Play in Early Childhood Education*. Milton Keynes: Open University.

Moyles, J (2001) Passion, paradox and professionalism in early years education. *Early Years: Journal of International Research and Development*, 21(2): 81–95.

Moyles, J (ed.) (2010) *Thinking About Play: Developing a Reflective Approach*. Maidenhead: Open University Press.

Moyles, J, Adams, S and Musgrove, A (2001) *The Study of Pedagogical Effectiveness: A Confidential Report to the DfES*. Chelmsford: Anglia Polytechnic University.

Nicholson, N and Palaiologou, I (2016) Early Years Foundation Stage progress check at the age of two in relation to speech and language difficulties in England: the voices of the team around the child. *Early Child Development and Care* (DOI 10.1080/03004430.2016.1146716).

Nutbrown, C (1999) *Threads of Thinking: Young Children Learning and the Role of Early Education*. London: Sage.

Nutbrown, C (2001) Wide eyes and open minds: observing, assessing and respecting children's early achievements. In **Collins, J and Cook, D** (eds), *Understanding Learning: Influences and Outcomes*. London: Sage, pp.134–46.

Nutbrown, C (2006) *Key Concepts in Early Childhood Education and Care*. London: Sage.

Nutbrown, C and Carter, C (2010) The tools of assessment: watching and learning. In **Pugh, G and Duffy, D** (eds), *Contemporary Issues in the Early Years* (5th edn). London: Sage.

Oberhumer, P and Schreyer, I (2018) *Early Childhood Workforce Profiles in 30 Countries with Key Contextual Data*. Munich. Online at: **www.seepro.eu/English/Home.htm**.

OECD (2001) Starting Strong Early Childhood Education and Care. Paris: OECD.

OECD (2010) *Education at a Glance*, OECD indicators. Paris: OECD. Available at **www.oecd.org/publishing/corrigenda** (accessed 5 October 2015).

OECD (2018) Early Learning Matters: Findings from the International Early Learning and Child Well-Being 2017 Field Trial. *OECD Early Learning Matters*, November. In Focus 1.

OED (Oxford English Dictionary) (2011) Oxford: Oxford University Press.

Olsson, LM (2009) *Movement and Experimentation in Young Children's Learning: Delouze and Guattari in Early Childhood Education*. London: Routledge.

Palaiologou, I (2011) *Transdisciplinarity in Early Years: A Case for Doxastic Pedagogy?* Paper presented at the British Early Childhood Education and Care Conference, Birmingham, February.

Palaiologou, I (2012a) Introduction: towards an understanding of ethical practice in early childhood. In **Palaiologou, I** (ed.) *Ethical Practice in Early Childhood*. London: Sage.

Palaiologou, I (2012b) Observation and Record Keeping. In **Veale, F** (ed.), *Early Years for Levels 4 & 5 and the Foundation Stage*. London: Hodder Education.

Pascal, C and Bertram, T (2013) Small voices. Powerful messages: capturing young children's perspectives in practice-led research. In **Hammersley, M, Flewett, R, Robb, M and Clark, A** (eds), *Issues in Research with Children and Young People*. London: Sage.

Pellegrini, AD (2011) Play. In **Zelazo, P** (ed.) *Oxford Handbook of Developmental Psychology*. New York: Oxford University Press.

Pence, A (2017) Baby PISA: dangers that can arise when foundations shift. *Journal of Childhood Studies*, 41(3): 54–8.

Pestalozzi, JH (1894) *How Gertrude Teaches Her Children* (trans. LE Holland and FC Turner, ed. with an introduction by Ebenezer Cooke). London: Swan Sonnenschein.

Piaget, JJ (1929) *The Child's Conception of the World*. New York: Harcourt Brace.

Piaget, JJ (1952) *The Origins of Intelligence in Children*. New York: International Universities.

Piaget, JJ (1954) *The Construction of Reality in the Child*. New York: Basic Books.

Piaget, JJ (1962) *Play, Dreams, and Imitation in Childhood*. New York: WW Norton.

Piaget, JJ (1968) *On the Development of Memory and Identity*. Barre: Clark University Press.

Piaget, JJ (1969) *The Child's Conception of Time*. London: Kegan & Paul.

Pink, S (2007) *Doing Visual Ethnography* (2nd edn). London: Sage.

Platt, J (1996) *A History of Sociological Research Methods in America 1920–1960*. Cambridge: Cambridge University Press.

Plowright, D (2010) *Mixed Methods*. London: Sage.

Pratt, D (1994) *Curriculum Planning: A Handbook for Professionals* (2nd edn). Fort Worth, TX: Harcourt Brace.

Pugh, G (2010) The Policy Agenda for Early Childhood Series. In **Pugh, G and Duffy, B** (eds), *Contemporary Issues in the Early Years: Working Collaboratively for Children* (4th edn). London: Sage.

QCA/DfEE (Qualifications and Curriculum Authority/Department for Education and Employment) (2000) *Curriculum Guidance for the Foundation Stage*. London: QCA.

Reichart, CS and Rallis, SF (eds) (1994) *The Qualitative–Quantitative Debate: New Perspectives*. San Francisco: Jossey-Bass.

Rinaldi, C (1995) The emergent curriculum and social constructivism: an interview with Lella Gandini. In **Edwards, C, Gandini, L and Froman, G** (eds), *The Hundred Languages of Children: The Reggio Emilia Approach to Early Childhood Education*. New York: Ablex.

Rinaldi, C (2005) Documentation and Assessment: What is the Relationship?, in **Clark, A, Kjørholt, A and Moss, P** (eds) *Beyond Listening: Children's Perspectives on Early Childhood Services*. Bristol: Policy Press.

Rinaldi, C (2006) *In Dialogue with Reggio Emilia*. London: Routledge.

Rist, RC (1977) On the relations among educational research paradigms: from disdain to détente. *Anthropology **and** Education Quarterly*, 8(2): 42–9.

Roberts-Holmes, GP and Bradbury, A (2017) Primary schools and network governance: a policy analysis of reception baseline. *British Educational Research Journal*, 43(4): 671–82.

Rumbold, A (1990) *The Rumbold Report: Starting with Quality*. London: HMSO.

SCAA (School Curriculum Assessment Authority) (1996) *Nursery Education: Desirable Outcomes for Children's Learning on Entering Compulsory Education* (ED 433 091). London: SCAA and Department for Education and Employment.

Schiro, MS (2008) *Curriculum Theory: Conflicting Visions and Enduring Concerns*. London: Sage.

Scottish Government (2015) *Early Years Collaborative*. Edinburgh: Scottish Government. Available at **www.gov.scot/Topics/People/Young-People/early-years/early-years-collaborative** (accessed 5 October 2015).

Sellers, M (2013) *Young Children Becoming Curriculum: Deleuze, Te Whāriki and Curricula Understandings*. London: Routledge.

Shaffer, D and **Kipp, K** (2007) *Developmental Psychology: Childhood and Adolescence* (7th edn). Belmont, CA: Thomson & Wadsworth.

Silverman, D (1985) *Qualitative Methodology and Sociology: Describing the Social World*. Aldershot: Gower.

Silverman, D (2011) *Interpreting Qualitative Data: Methods for Analysing Qualitative Data* (4th edn). London: Sage.

Silverman, D (2013) *Doing Qualitative Research*. London: Sage.

Silverman, D (2014) *Interpreting Qualitative Data*. London: Sage.

Siraj-Blatchford, I and Sylva, K (2002) *The Effective Pedagogy in the Early Years Project: A Confidential Report to the DfES*. London: London University Institute of Education.

Sluss, DJ and Jarrett, OS (2007) *Investigating play in the 21st century. Play and Culture Studies*, 7. Lanham, MD: University Press of America.

Smith, AB (1998) *Understanding Children's Development* (4th edn). Wellington: Bridget Williams Books.

Smith, AB (2007) Children and young people's participation rights in education. *International Journal of Children's Rights*, 15: 147–64.

Smith, JK (1983) Quantitative versus qualitative research: an attempt to clarify the issue. *Educational Researcher*, 12: 6–13.

Smith, JK and Heshusius, L (1986) Closing down the conversation: the end of quantitative-qualitative debate among educational inquiries. *Educational Researcher*, 15: 4–12

Stenhouse, L (1975) *An Introduction to Curriculum Research Development*. London: Heinemann Educational.

Strauss, A (1967) *Qualitative Analysis for Social Scientists*. New York: Cambridge University Press.

Swedish Ministry of Education and Science (1998) *Curriculum for the Pre-school*. Stockholm: Fritzes.

Sylva, K, Melhuish, E, Sammons, P and Siraj-Blatchford, I (2001) *The Effective Provision of Pre-school Education (EPPE) Project*. The EPPE Symposium at the BERA Annual Conference, University of Leeds, September.

Taggart, G (2011) Don't we care? The ethics and emotional labour of early years professionalism. *Early Years*, 31(1): 85–95.

Taguchi, HL (2010) *Going Beyond the Theory/Practice Divide in Early Childhood Education: Introducing Intra-active Pedagogy*. London: Routledge.

Tashakkori, A and Teddlie, C (1998) *Mixed Methods: Combining Qualitative and Quantitative Approaches*. Applied Social Research Methods Series, Vol. 46. London: Sage.

Taylor Nelson Sofres with Aubrey, C (2002) *The Implementation of the Foundation Stage in Reception Classes: Confidential Report to the DfES*. Richmond: Taylor Nelson Sofres.

Tedlock, B (2000) Ethnography and ethnographic representation. In **Denzin, NK and Lincoln, Y** (eds), *Handbook of Qualitative Research* (2nd edn). London: Sage.

Turner, T and Wilson, GD (2010) Reflections on documentation: a discussion with thought leaders from Reggio Emilia. *Theory into Practice*, 49: 5–13.

Tyson, P and Taylor, RL (1990) *Psychoanalytical Theories of Development: An Integration*. New Haven, CT: Yale University.

UNESCO (2004) *Curriculum in Early Childhood Education and Care*, UNESCO Policy Brief No. 6, September.

UNESCO (2010) *Caring and Learning Together: A Case Study of Sweden*. UNESCO Early Childhood and Family Policy Series no. 20. Paris: UNESCO.

UNESCO (2016) *Innovative Pedagogical Approaches in Early Childhood Care and Education (ECCE) in the Asia-Pacific region: A Resource Pack*. Singapore: UNESCO and ARNEC (electronic version). Online at: **https://bangkok.unesco.org/content/innovative-pedagogical-approaches-early-childhood-care-and-education-ecce-resource-pack**.

United Nations (1959) *Declaration of the Rights of the Child*. Available at **www.humanium.org/en/convention/text/** (accessed 18 September 2007).

United Nations (1989) *Convention on the Rights of the Child*. Available at **www.unicef.org.uk/UNICEFs-Work/UN-Convention/** (accessed 18 September 2007).

Urban, M (2018) (D)evaluation of early childhood education and care? A critique of the OECDs International Early Learning Study. In *Improving the Quality of Childhood in Europe*, Volume 8. Brussels: Alliance for Childhood.

Vygotsky, LS (1962) *Thought and Language*. Cambridge, MA: MIT Press.

Vygotsky, LS (1966) Play and its role in the mental development of the child. *Soviet Psychology*, 5: 6–18 (trans. (2016) *International Research in Early Childhood Education*, 7(2)).

Vygotsky, LS (1978) *Mind in Society: The Development of Higher Psychological Processes.* Cambridge, MA: Harvard University Press.

Vygotsky, LS (1986) *Thought and Language* (2nd edn). Cambridge, MA: MIT Press.

Vygotsky, LS (1997) Research method. In **Rieber, RW** (ed.) *The Collected Works of L.S. Vygotsky*, Vol. 4. New York: Plenum Press, pp.27–65.

Waksler, FC (1991) *Studying the Social Worlds of Children: Sociological Readings.* London: Falmer Press.

Walker, J (1990) *Fundamentals of Curriculum.* New York: Harcourt Brace Jovanovich.

Walker, R (1985) *Applied Qualitative Research.* Aldershot: Gower.

Walsh, G (2016) The national picture: Early Years in Northern Ireland. In **Palaiologou, I** (ed.), *Early Years Foundation Stage: Theory and Practice.* London: Sage.

Wellington, JJ (1996) *Methods and Issues in Educational Research.* Sheffield: University of Sheffield.

Welsh Government (2015). *Evaluating the Foundation Phase: Final Report.* Cardiff: Welsh Government.

Welsh Government (2017) *Foundation Phase Profile Handbook.* Cardiff: Welsh Government.

Willan, J (2007) Observing children: looking into children's lives. In **Willan, J, Parker-Rees, R and Savage, J** (eds), *Early Childhood Studies* (2nd edn). Exeter: Learning Matters.

Winnicot, DW (1986) *Holding and Interpretation: Fragment of an Analysis.* New York: Hogarth Press.

Winnicot, DW (1987) *The Child, the Family, and the Outside World.* New York: Addison-Wesley.

Winnicot, DW (1995) *Maturational Processes and the Facilitating Environment: Studies in the Theory of Emotional Development.* New York: Stylus.

Winnicot, DW (2005) *Playing and Reality.* London: Routledge.

Wood, E (2009) Developing a pedagogy of play for the 21st century. In **Anning, A, Cullen, J and Fleer, M** (eds), *Early Childhood Education: Society and Culture.* London: Sage.

Wood, E (2010a) Developing integrated pedagogical approaches to play and learning. In **Broadhead, B, Howard, J and Wood, E** (eds), *Play and Learning in the Early Years: From Research to Practice.* London: Sage.

Wood, E (2010b) Reconceptualising the play-pedagogy relationship: from control to complexity. In **Edwards, S and Brooker, E** (eds), *Rethinking Play.* Maidenhead: Open University Press.

Wood, E (2013a) The play-pedagogy interface in contemporary debates. In **Brooker, E, Edwards, S and Blaise, M** (eds), *The Sage Handbook on Play and Learning.* London: Sage.

Wood, E (2013b) Contested concepts in educational play: a comparative analysis of early childhood policy frameworks in New Zealand and England. In **Nuttall, J** (ed.), *Weaving Te Whāriki: Ten Years On.* Rotterdam: Sense Publishers.

Wood, E (2014) Free play and free choice in early childhood education – troubling the discourse. *International Journal of Early Years Education*, 22(1): 4–18.

Wood, E and Attfield, J (2005) *Play, Learning and the Early Childhood Curriculum* (2nd edn). London: Sage.

Yelland, N (2016) iPlay, iLearn, iGrow: tablet technology, curriculum, pedagogies and learning in the twenty-first century. In **Gurvis, S and Lemon, N** (eds), *Understanding Digital Technology and Young Children: An International Perspective.* London: Routledge, pp.38–45.

Yelland, N (2018) A pedagogy of multiliteracies: young children and multimodal learning with tablets. *British Journal of Educational Technology*, 29(5): 847–58.

Yelland, N and Gilbert, G (2017) Re-imagining play with new technologies. In **Arnott, L** (eds), *Digital Technologies and Learning in the Early Years.* London: Sage, pp.32–44.

Youell, B (2008) The importance of play and playfulness. *European Journal of Psychotherapy and Counselling*, 10(2): 121–9.

INDEX